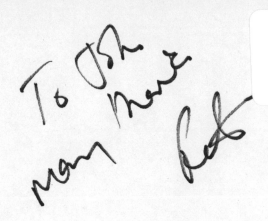

To Osh
Many thanks

THE SOCIAL PRODUCTION OF TECHNICAL WORK

SUNY Series in the Sociology of Work
Judith R. Blau, Editor

THE SOCIAL PRODUCTION OF TECHNICAL WORK

The Case of British Engineers

Peter Whalley

State University of New York Press

First published
in U.S.A. by
State University of New York Press
Albany

Printed in Hong Kong

Library of Congress Cataloging-in-Publication Data
Whalley, Peter, 1947–
The social production of technical work.
(SUNY series in the sociology of work)
Bibliography: p.
Includes index.
1. Engineers—Great Britain. 2. Engineering—
Social aspects—Great Britain. I. Title. II. Series.
TA157.W447 1986   305.5′53   85–14813
ISBN 0–88706–252–0

For my parents
Joseph and Irene Whalley
and for Nicholas

Contents

List of Tables   ix
Preface   xiii

1 ENGINEERS IN ADVANCED INDUSTRIAL
   SOCIETY   1
   Engineers in Advanced Industrial Capitalism   1
   The Sociology of Technical Workers   2
   The Problematic of Engineers   11

2 INDUSTRY: OLD AND NEW   15
   Research Design   15
   Old and New Industrial Settings   16
   Engineers at Work   26
   Technical Work   37

3 KNOWLEDGE, TRUST AND LABOUR MARKETS   39
   Professionalisation in Britain?   40
   Engineers as Technical Staff   41
   Theory and Practice   53
   From Knowledge to Trust   58

4 THE ORGANISATION OF WORK   66
   Specialisation and the Division of Labour   68
   Autonomy or Deskilling?   70
   The Organisation of work at Metalco and Computergraph   71
   Organisational Design   81
   Deskilling at Metalco?   83
   Potential Sources of Deskilling   88

5 EXPERTS AND MANAGERS   92
   Managers or Experts?   96
   Equities   112
   Labour Market Orientation   116

Contents

6 AUTHORITY, PROFIT AND PARTICIPATION   124
   Personal Authority   125
   Engineers and Business   131
   Managers and Markets   148

7 COLLECTIVE ORGANISATION   151
   Professionalism   152
   Trade Unionism   158
   Ambivalences   172
   The Growth of Technical Unionism   180

8 THE SOCIAL PRODUCTION OF TECHNICAL
   WORK   184
   The Social Production of Trusted Labour   185
   Production and Reproduction   191
   Engineers as Trusted Workers   194
   The Future of British Engineering   197

Appendix: The Interview Schedule   200

Notes   206
Bibliography   220
Index   230

List of Tables

2.1   Characteristics of the sample   20

2.2   Sample size by department   21

3.1   Qualifications of engineers   42

3.2   Qualifications of all technical workers in engineering departments at Metalco   43

3.3   Characteristics of first job held   44

3.4   Relative value of education and experience   55

3.5   Usefulness of degree for present job   56

4.1   Components of involvement and autonomy scales   72

4.2   Involvement and constraint scores by department   78

4.3   Qualifications, involvement and constraint   85

5.1   Level and locus of ambition of staff engineers   97

5.2   Disadvantages to management: Metalco staff engineers   102

5.3   Disadvantages to management: Computergraph staff engineers   104

5.4   Effect of education on career expectations of staff engineers   111

5.5   Perception of equity in career   114

5.6   Equity in career by department   117

5.7   Labour market orientation by company   119

5.8   Labour market orientation by department   119

6.1   Perceived functions of management   126

6.2   Constraints on technical work   133

6.3   Financial knowledge and technical work   136

6.4   Desire for participation   140

6.5   Attitudes towards worker directors   144

6.6   Reasons for supporting increased participation of
      manual workers   146

6.7   Reasons opposed to worker directors   147

7.1   Professional memberships   153

7.2   Professional membership by department   155

7.3   Trade union membership   162

7.4   Attitudes to trade unionism   163

7.5   Reasons for joining a trade union   164

7.6   Reasons for not joining a union   165

7.7   Reasons to consider union membership in the
      future   166

7.8   Labour market perception and attitudes to
      unionism   168

7.9   Ambition and union membership   170

7.10   Career satisfaction and union membership   170

7.11   Organisational constraint and union membership   171

7.12   Attitudes to strikes   176

7.13   Managerial expectations and willingness to strike: staff engineers only   177

7.14   Membership and union policy   179

Preface

The main disadvantage of maintaining confidentiality in research is that I cannot thank by name all of the people at 'Metalco' and 'Computergraph' who helped with this project. To the senior management and personnel staff at both companies I owe particular thanks for giving me access and for facilitating the research with all the means at their disposal. Thanks, too, to the union representatives who agreed to the research and helped facilitate access. But thanks most of all must go to the engineers themselves. Not only did they submit to my pestering with good grace, but allowed me into their homes and put up with hours of often personal questioning. They made the interviews and field research a pleasure.

I can, however, thank Allan Silver by name. It was Allan who interested me in the ideas which shaped this research. He provided ongoing guidance, encouragement and assistance, and made funds available to provide support for the research in England from a grant from the International Division of the Ford Foundation (No. 74–0594). Thanks for all of these things, but thanks most of all for being a good teacher. My colleagues and friends on this wider comparative project, Robert Zussman and Steven Crawford, provided ideas, support and good conversation at a number of crucial phases in the research.

Though it is impossible to thank all those who have contributed to one's intellectual development, I would like particularly to thank Sigmund Diamond, whose support and encouragement helped me become a sociologist in the first place.

In England, I owe a special debt of gratitude to Bob Blackburn, Sandy Stewart and Ken Prandy, and their colleagues at the Department of Applied Economics at the University of Cambridge, for giving me space, library facilities and, most importantly, intellectual stimulation and ideas during my stay there. Professor John Coales and the President and staff of Clare Hall provided pleasant and necessary collegiality. Lex Donaldson, Barry Evans, Mike Fores, Ian Glover, Jeff Henderson, Tony Hinkins, Dorothy Hobson and Stewart

Ward all helped in various ways to get the project done: my thanks to them all. I would also like to thank the officials of the trade unions and professional associations who provided me with interviews and information.

During an early phase of the project, when I was still commuting from the United States, Irene and Joe Whalley and Gwen and Derrick Thurley provided both a 'home away from home' in the full sense of that now clichéd phrase, and also put up with their homes being transformed into offices. Gwen Thurley, in particular, provided much valued secretarial assistance.

Back in the United States, Alan Barton, John Bell, Judith Blau, Herb Gans, Lilly Hoffman, Robert Karasek, James Kuhn and Judy Wittner each read all, or part, of the various drafts of this manuscript and helped remove some of the infelicities, while Ken Johnson answered my computational queries with forbearance. To each my thanks.

Columbia University and Loyola University of Chicago both provided computer time and facilities. I would like especially to thank Art Krumrey and his staff in Academic Computing Services at Loyola for their assistance and forebearance, and Lucille McGill for typing the tables.

It is conventional for authors to exonerate from responsibility for the final product all those who help them. I willingly go along with this convention. Except in one respect. Pam Whalley's contributions to this enterprise have been so enormous – reading every line, hearing every idea, not once but many times, criticising, arguing, supporting – that she cannot be fully absolved of responsibility for what remains, at least not for what virtues there are. I can only say thank you.

PETER WHALLEY

1 Engineers in Advanced Industrial Society

This is a book about the work lives of engineers in two British factories, but in another, perhaps more important, sense it is a book about how technical work is socially produced in advanced capitalist societies. Despite widespread speculation about high-tech industry's impact on the social structure of such societies, we know comparatively little about how technical work gets organised, how the technical job market is structured, and still less about technical employees' perception of themselves and their positions in society. If the systematic application of knowledge to production is indeed the characteristic project of advanced society, then we need to improve our present understanding of how that project gets carried out.

Taking a close look at 'Computergraph' and 'Metalco' – the former a small, rapidly expanding, electronic and optics company, located in north London: the latter a large, traditional metal-working company, rooted in the grimy, redbrick landscape of the industrial West Midlands – helps illustrate the social forces which are operating to structure technical work in all Western societies. The distinctive configuration of these companies, and of British engineering as a whole, may be unique, but the social processes that produce and reproduce it are not.

ENGINEERS IN ADVANCED INDUSTRIAL CAPITALISM

We live in a period of rapid industrial and technical change. The smokestack industries of the first industrial revolution are declining, their unionised blue-collar workers face the greatest threat to their economic and political power since the 1930s. In all Western societies the very regions whose prosperity was built on traditional industry are physically and socially decaying. At the same time we are bombarded with images of a high-tech future: instead of turbines, micro-electronics; instead of dirty factories, clean research labs;

1

instead of grimy overalls, white coats; computers in every school, an engineer in every family. In the place of the decaying industrial civilisation we are offered a 'post-industrial' society based on science and high-tech production.

Of course much of this rhetoric is overblown. The new industries are unlikely to absorb the surplus workers from the decaying old ones: many – oil and chemicals for example – are highly automated,[1] others use the cheapest available labour to do simple assembly work and are ready to move to the Third World at the first sign of agitation for higher wages. But one part of the high-tech rhetoric does reflect reality. The growth of high-tech industry has made technical work and the employees who carry it out central features of the social landscape of advanced capitalist societies.

New product technology, for example, is increasingly tied to the latest developments in scientific and engineering knowledge, and research has come to be the first and most basic part of many product cycles. In the extreme case of biogenetics, an industry has been set up in the *expectation* of scientific advances. Some analysts have even argued that education, training and improved technology have overtaken additional labour and capital inputs as the dominant source of increased productivity, and that knowledge has taken over from labour power as the motor for economic growth (Bell, 1973).

If these new industries of our high-tech future require large technical investments to survive, they also need the technical specialists to run them. Hence the rapid growth in numbers of so-called 'knowledge workers', and in particular of scientific and technical employees. In Britain roughly three-quarters of a million engineers and scientists were employed in 1971, compared to only 86 000 in 1921. Between 1911 and 1971 their employment expanded eleven times. In this same period (1911–71) the percentage of manual workers dropped from nearly 80 per cent of the labour force to to 50 per cent (Routh, 1980).[2] Similar changes have occurred in all advanced societies. In the United States, for example, the 1980 census reported over one and half million engineers, and the occupation was growing at two and a half times the national average, despite a slowdown during the recession of the late 1970s.

THE SOCIOLOGY OF TECHNICAL WORKERS

This growth of technical employment has raised many of the same sociological questions that the expansion of clerical labour did earlier. If such employees do not work for themselves, or employ others, should they be seen as workers, suffering perhaps from a degree of false consciousness? Or are they a 'new middle class', the corporate equivalents of the self-employed professionals and artisans of the nineteenth century? Or simply capitalist functionaries? If they do not manage, how can they be differentiated from manual workers? What, if anything, secures their allegiance to the capitalist firm?

Though these questions can be asked about clerical labour (Crompton, 1976, 1979; Lockwood, 1958; Mills, 1953), they take on an added dimension when asked about technical workers. For technical employees, engineers included, are not simply carriers of administrative decisions made at a higher level in the bureaucracy. They are not just bearers of delegated authority. Their jobs require a distinctive and important expertise, and it is the relationship of this expertise to the operation of the profit-making firm that has seemed so central and so problematic to many social analysts.

For some, this technical expertise is the source of a potential crisis since as technical managers, professionals, or even members of a highly skilled new working class, engineers are expected to challenge the authority structure of the capitalist firm. For others, these experts function only as corporate staff and their skills remain closely tied to the search for capital accumulation. Still others argue that engineers' expertise is under attack from employers who seek only to proletarianise them. But whatever the specific predictions the transformation of production, rooted in the growing importance of technical and scientific knowledge, is expected to transform the politics of the workplace and, ultimately, that of the larger society.[3] Engineers, it seems, stand on centre stage.[4]

Technical Expertise and a Crisis of Legitimacy

The most dramatic of these arguments have been those positing a growing crisis of legitimacy in the capitalist firm. Though their arguments differ radically in their implications, Bell (1973), Freidson (1973), Galbraith (1967), Gorz (1967), Mallet (1975) and Touraine (1971) have all predicted a potential conflict between the value systems of technical experts and those of private business. Engineers' commitment to the rational pursuit of public knowledge is expected to conflict with employers' pursuit of profit maximisation. Bureaucratically based claims to authority may be undermined if engineers only accept orders stemming from technical exigencies rather than positional whim. And their desire for autonomy, necessary if the company is to maximise their usefulness, may conflict with employers' requirements for control. The integration of technical staff into the capitalist firm, it is agreed, is not so easy as it has been for clerical and administrative employees.

But although there is agreement on the source of these strains, there is little agreement on the mode of their resolution, nor on the way they will be played out in different national contexts. Exponents of the technocratic, professional, and new working class theses each offer very different versions of engineers' future roles.

Engineers as Technocrats

One tradition of thought, going back through Veblen (1921) to Saint-Simon (1952), and revived more recently by Galbraith (1968), suggests that technical expertise is the basis for the development of a newly powerful *technostructure*. In Galbraith's terms, there will be 'a new shift in power in the industrial enterprise, ... from capital to organised intelligence' (Galbraith, 1968, p. 56). Effective power within the corporation shifts away from owners and non-technical managers into the hands of technically trained managers and specialists. For Galbraith, like Veblen nearly half a century earlier, it is this technostructure that alone is capable of operating technologically sophisticated corporations.

> It will no longer be practical to leave its [industry's] control in the hands of business men working at cross-purposes for private gain, or to trust its continued administration to less suitably trained experts ... the material welfare of the community is unreservedly bound up with the due working of this industrial system and therefore with its unreserved control by engineers, who alone are competent to manage it. (Veblen, 1923, p. 33)

While this quotation from Veblen should make us doubt the specifically modern quality of the technocratic argument, high-tech industries may be expected to dramatically highlight the critical role of engineers only implicit in traditional industries.

Engineers, Professionalism and Post-industrial Society

The technocratic thesis does not sharply distinguish between technical managers and specialists, and one strand of the argument feeds into the 'managerialist' tradition of sociological thought which argues for the importance of control rather than ownership in advanced industrial society (Burnham, 1941; Dahrendorf, 1959; Zeitlin, 1974). In contrast, writers in what we might call the 'professionalisation' tradition emphasise the technical expertise itself and see it as the basis for a developing occupation-based control of production.

The traditional view of engineers, at least in the United States and Britain, is to see them as professionals, albeit not very successful ones. Like all professionals they are seen as bearers of special skills with which they have secured privileges at work and in the marketplace. As Larson puts it:

Professionalisation [is] the process by which producers of special services sought to constitute *and control* a market for their expertise. Because marketable expertise is a crucial element in the structuring of modern inequality, professionalisation appears *also* as a collective assertion of special social status and as a collective process of upwards mobility.... Professionalisation is thus an attempt to translate one order of scarce resources – special knowledge and skills – into another – social and economic rewards. (Larson, 1977, pp. xvi–xvii)

Engineers are simply the professionals who apply knowledge and expertise to the production process.

Engineers have not always had an easy time with professionalisation, particularly in the United Kingdom. Most are company employees with little opportunity for setting up as self-employed consultants. They have had to sell their expertise to powerful corporate clients who reserve for themselves the right to judge an acceptable performance, and their close association with manufacture has sometimes produced status problems in societies where making things is the preserve of the working class.

None the less some American writers, most notably Daniel Bell (1973) and Eliot Freidson (1973), have seen new, science-based industry as providing the basis for greater *professional* power. Not only do engineers have a much greater presence in such companies, but the skills they use there are more theoretical. Such theoretical knowledge not only requires university training, putting it out of the control of employers, but its generality encourages greater inter-company mobility and an orientation to a wider professional audience than does the experiential knowledge used in traditional industries. As Freidson (1973, p. 51) puts it: in high-tech industry,

> the jobs or organisational positions are dependent on management for capital, supportive services, and at least some lines of communication ... the *tasks* of these workers are not. Their tasks are not created by, or dependent on management, nor are the qualifications to perform them so dependent. Finally, evaluation of the performance of the tasks does not rest solely with management.

Freidson's vision of post-industrial society is one in which the possessors of knowledge 'hire' capital. The American doctors' relationship with their facilitating hospital becomes a paradigm for the relationship between all kinds of experts and their employers.[5]

This professionalised power would be most fully institutionalised by securing a legal monopoly over access to training and jobs (Larson, 1977), something far from engineers' reach (see Chapter 3), but even short of full-fledged professionalism, the rise of expert labour may change the structure of organisations. There is an extensive literature on the 'debureaucratisation' of work organisations as the demands of professional employees for autonomy and more collegial work relations transcend the traditional emphasis on the bureaucratic control of non-professional employees. Bell's post-industrial thesis has been paralleled at the level of organisational research by predictions of an emergent collegial workplace, as employers are forced to adapt to professional demands (Bennis, 1973; Burns and Stalker, 1961; Lawrence and Lorsch, 1967; Scott, 1966 and 1981).

New Working Class

The search for occupational closure through professional (or craft) control over accreditation and job access is, however, largely an Anglo-Saxon phenomenon, and professionalism as an ideology is particularly strong in the United States. In countries where the state has played a much larger role in the development of industry – in France, for example, or Germany – engineers' positions are modelled more closely on the civil service pattern, where position in the bureaucratic hierarchy is assigned on the basis of a particular level of educational attainment (Child *et al.*, 1983; Loveridge, 1983). In such systems any expert revolt against bureaucratic authority is likely to take an organisational form. Thus when the neo-Marxist Serge Mallet (1975) argued, like many of the American professionalism school, that the commitment of technical employees to the 'higher rationality of science' posed major problems of organisation and legitimacy for their employment in the capitalist firm, he predicted not increased occupational control, but the emergence of a *new working class*, in which engineers and other technical staff would ally with the manual workers who worked alongside them in the company.

As André Gorz put it when developing a similar analysis, engineers and other technical workers pursue

> an activity which measures the scientific and technical potential of an enterprise in scientific and technical terms and which sees this 'technological capital', this 'human capital' – the cooperation of polished teamwork, the possibility of conquering new domains of knowledge, new chances for the domination of man over nature – destroyed by the barbaric command for financial profit. (Gorz, 1967, p. 104)

The new working class thesis sees this as leading to a growing identity as workers: workers not *despite* their technical skills, but *because* of them. Technical employees

> discover that they are wage earners like the others, paid for a piece of work which is 'good' only to the degree that it is profitable in the short run. They discover that long range research, creative work on original problems, and the love of workmanship are incompatible with the criteria of capitalist profitability and this is not because they lack economic profitability in the long run, but because there is less risk and more profit in manufacturing saucepans. (Gorz, 1967, p. 104)

For the French theorists, in fact, the blue-collar/white collar boundary is becoming increasingly irrelevant in the work situation of high technology industries. In the conflict between technical rationality and profit, engineers will discover the irrationality of capitalism. In demanding to use their knowledge, engineers will come face to face with their status as workers.

Corporate Staff and Capitalist Hegemony

Technological and scientific determinism is at the core of all of the preceding positions. Engineers' capacity to generate a crisis of legitimacy derives from their possession of *autonomous* knowledge, a knowledge that is, in some important sense, independent of the locus of its use.

Though immensely influential, even, as Mallet suggests, within Marxism, this view has not gone unchallenged. An equally influential tradition has treated technical knowledge as inextricably shaped by the social system in which it is produced rather than as an independent entity exogenously shaping society. In particular, a number of recent Marxist and neo-Marxist writers have seen technical knowledge as essentially subordinate to capitalist control, and a critical tool in the process of capital accumulation (Burris, 1980; Burawoy, 1978; Gouldner, 1976; Noble, 1977; Poulantzas, 1975). From this perspective, engineers' knowledge is deeply implicated in the control structure of capitalism. Though often as diverse in their predictions as those who see technical knowledge as creating a crisis of legitimacy, these writers share a common perspective that engineers' knowledge can only be understood within the context of capitalist hegemony (Gramsci, 1971).

The distinctive attribute of engineers for Poulantzas, for example, is their performance of 'mental' labour.[6] But mental labour for Poulantzas has specific political and ideological connotations which tie its participants to capital and divides them from the working class. It can be one of two kinds. Workers who supervise are separated from the working class by political relations since the managerial control of labour reproduces within the factory the political dominance of capital that exists in the larger society. But 'mental labour' is also performed by non-supervisory personnel, by 'experts' who are distinguished from the working class by ideological relations, by their monopoly of a special knowledge. The engineers'

> work of technological application of science takes place under the sign of the dominant ideology, which they materialise even in their

'scientific' work; they are thus supports of the reproduction of ideological relations actually within the process of material production. Their role in this reproduction, by way of the technological application of science, takes the particular form under capitalism of a division between mental and manual labour, which expresses the ideological conditions of the capitalist production process. (Poulantzas, 1975, pp. 236–7)

This perception of the ideological nature of this special knowledge came to be shared by Gorz in his later work.

Hierarchy in production and society overall can be preserved only if expertise is made the preserve of the privileged, the monopoly of those who are socially selected to hold both knowledge and authority. (Gorz, 1976b, p. 62)

Or, as David Noble puts it in his history of American engineering:

The technical and capitalist aspects of the engineers' work were the reverse sides of the same coin, modern technology. As such, they were rarely if ever distinguishable: technical demands defined the capitalist possibilities only insofar as capitalist demands defined the technical possibilities. (Noble, 1977, p. 34)

If engineers are experts, they are experts firmly under the control of the employer.

Science, still more technology, is capitalist science and capitalist technology, and its bearers, engineers, are inherently tied to the capitalist order. Noble argues that the process of harnessing science to production was done by engineers as the direct agents of capital in its search for capital accumulation. The maintenance of the 'secrecy' of engineers' knowledge – their monopoly over it – is essential to ensure the continued subjugation of the rest of the workforce. In particular engineers are the recipients of the knowledge of production processes won from craft workers (Braverman, 1974).

From this perspective Mallet's postulation of a 'new working class' is wishful thinking. Though engineers might, on occasion, be won over to the side of manual workers, it is more likely that any militancy they display will be in defence of their own privileged position. Any demand they make for self-management will be for themselves alone; their critiques of higher management likely to be 'meritocratic' rather than egalitarian; their militancy a resistance to proletarianisation, not a sign of proletarian status. Engineers, if not simply 'petty bourgeoisie', are certainly members of the new middle class.

Seen thus, high-tech industry will simply buttress capital's control of the labour process. As technical knowledge becomes more arcane and less susceptible to acquisition by experience, workers will be less and less able to challenge management's legitimation of their decisions on technical grounds. The growth of technical staff will provide an increased buffer between capital and labour defined in traditional terms.

Structural Ambiguities, Contradictions and Proletarianisation

Not all Marxist writers, even among those who reject the new working class thesis, have seen technical staff as so firmly tied to capital. Carchedi and Wright, for example, while recognising the role that engineers have played in the capitalist accumulation process also insist on the importance of their employee status. Engineers are, they argue, located in structurally ambiguous or contradictory class locations.

Carchedi (1977) sees engineers as performing both functions of global capital and of collective labour. Like most continental European writers, he assumes that engineers routinely engage in the supervision of manual labour, or that they did so until the recent past. Engineers, in Carchedi's vision, originated as the technically trained assistants to the entrepreneur. In supervising, or even in designing supervisory systems, engineers carry out one of the functions of capital, but in coordinating and designing they also perform labour. This dual function gives engineers their ambivalent location in the social structure.

In the United States and Britain, however, many engineers do not supervise other labour, they function solely as technical experts. Wright's American version of the argument recognises this and distinguishes between managers and staff experts (Wright, 1976, 1978). The latter he sees as occupying a 'contradictory position' between the self-employed petty bourgeoisie and working-class labour. Their autonomy is rooted in the fact that their productive knowledge has not yet been subjected to 'real' control by the employer. As employees they have one foot in the working class; but having some control over design and their own labour process, they keep one foot in the petty bourgeoisie. Since the self-employed petty bourgeoisie is itself a remnant of pre-capitalist simple commodity production, technical experts are seen as occupying a position which is also contradictory between two modes of production.

In the long term, however, both Wright and Carchedi consider these ambiguous or contradictory positions to be unstable since, despite their theoretical innovations, both accept the traditional Marxist thesis that there is a long-term tendency for labour to be proletarianised under capitalism. Thus they share the basic assumption of the deskilling school (Aronowitz, 1971; Braverman, 1974; Cooley, 1976; Crompton and Gubbay, 1978; Oppenheimer, 1973), that the increased numbers and importance of engineers in high-tech industry will lead to the fragmentation and rationalisation of their jobs, and ultimately to the devaluation of their labour power.

The deskilling thesis argues, essentially, that as long as engineers were employed in small numbers, or primarily supervised others, employers were willing to grant them a privileged position. The emergence of large numbers of staff employees, however, renders them too expensive and potentially too powerful. Unwilling to pay the increased wage-bills, and fearing the loss of control predicted by the post-industrial theorists, employers will then introduce the control mechanisms successfully used against nineteenth century craftsmen to restructure technical labour.

The deskilling theorists reject the argument that the scientific base of engineers' jobs protects them from rationalisation, and argue that engineers will soon find their jobs fragmented and simplified. The remaining complex tasks will be bundled into a smaller number of senior positions while the simpler tasks are allocated to a cheaper and more controllable labour force of technicians. The privileges which previously set engineers apart as a new middle class will be removed in a process of proletarianisation.

THE PROBLEMATIC OF ENGINEERS

These discussions, reviewed briefly here and addressed in more detail in the subsequent chapters, are important. They are about issues of long-standing sociological concern: the social location of the middle layers of the occupational structure, the impact of technology on the workplace, and the role of knowledge in structuring class and work relationships. But much of the writing often appears to be the outcome of logical analysis rather than empirical research: the elaboration of new twists in already formulated logics of industrialism or capitalism rather than attempts to come to grips with real social change.

Very few investigations have been done of how technical work is actually organised inside the plant. We know little of how engineers or other technical workers see their own positions, or how actual changes in the organisation of work might shape such perceptions. What research we do have on engineers has often been done with much narrower issues in mind than those we have been discussing here. We know something about engineers' education and socialisation, a little about their relations with management, but generally such research has been pushed into the straitjacket of occupational sociology: a focus, for example, on whether or not engineering is a profession.[7]

A prime aim of this book, therefore, is to address some of these macro-sociological issues that make the organisation of technical work so important, but to do so by closely examining technical workers in the everyday practice of their work. To look at who they are, what they do, and how they see themselves, while bearing in mind that large-scale social change has to manifest itself in concrete settings and in individual lives.

To do so, however, it is necessary to break down the complex images that we have been discussing – 'post-industrial society', 'new working class', 'proletarianisation' and the like – into a series of more discrete claims and questions. It is these issues which form the basic organisational structure of the book and it will be useful to present their broad outlines here.

What, for example, is the real nature of engineers' knowledge, and how does it shape the occupational structure? Though most social theorists take the scientific base of engineering work quite seriously, even when they see it harnessed to capitalism, labour market categories of skill can be socially constructed with little regard to any real technical base. Claims to science may serve more of a legitimation function than represent any real continuity between the work of the practising engineer and the pure scientist. In Chapter 3 I examine the occupational structure of technical work in Britain, and look at the kinds of claims British engineers make about the nature of their specialised knowledge.

To look at the structuring of the occupation, however, does not tell us what engineers actually do, nor how high-tech industry affects what they do. The professionalisation and deskilling theses make diametrically opposing claims about the likely impact of new industry on the structure of engineers' work but they are based on very little evidence of the task structure of engineers' work. These claims will be the subject of analysis in Chapter 4.

Many predictions about engineers' changing social position are based on a particular understanding of engineers' relationship to management. In some cases engineers are presented as if they were a technically trained branch of management; in others, as if they were a non-supervisory expert staff. In Chapter 5 I examine these issues in the context of engineers' careers.

In Chapter 6 I explore the relationship between engineers and managers in light of their different claims to authority: claims based on expertise and on position. It is the clash between these claims, and the clash between technical and business values, that is at the heart of the post-industrial and new working class debates. If, however, engineers do remain integrated in the firm, then we need to know how this integration is secured. Chapter 6 also discusses engineers' desire for involvement in the non-technical aspects of the management of the firm, and examines the issue of workplace democracy in light of engineers' concerns.

In the absence of detailed studies of the workplace, sociologists have often used collective organisation as a surrogate measure of structural change. If employees increasingly join professional associations then this is used as evidence of changes in the workplace fostering the professional model: if they behave like professionals they must be professionals. If employees join unions then this is used as evidence that their conditions are being proletarianised: if they behave like workers, they must be workers. Put like this, of course, the fallacy is obvious, but in the absence of studies of the workplace it is a tempting mistake. Chapter 7 explores engineers' response to professional and union forms of collective organisation in the context of the concrete work situations which they face.

In the final chapter a more adequate theoretical model of technical work and technical workers is developed. I shall argue that engineers are trusted employees, part of a wider service class in industrial capitalism, and that engineers' responses to their changing employment situation can best be understood within this framework. This final chapter also compares the British system of structuring technical work with that in place in France and the United States, and attempts to go beyond cultural explanation of these national variations, to examine how they are created and reproduced in the organisation of work and the structuring of occupations.

Before turning to a systematic discussion of these issues, however, Chapter 2 reviews the research design and provides a descriptive outline of the two companies and the kind of work that engineers carry out there.

2 Industry: Old and New

If only a few of these predictions about 'new classes' and a 'post-industrial society' are correct, we are living in the middle of a major change in the way we organise and experience work; a change as great as that produced by the growth of the large corporations which created the administrative jobs that have been the staple of middle class careers for most of this century. But are we?

To examine such claims, evidence of the growth of high-tech industry and an increase in technical employment is not enough. We need to examine the structure of work and the impact of such work on the employees who carry it out. Yet descriptions of technical work in high-tech companies have been largely anecdotal, and comparisons with work in traditional industry are rare or non-existent. We know little about how technical experts see themselves and their world, and when we do, the data is usually collected in a way that divorces it from any organisational context. The research design we shall discuss in the first part of this chapter was designed to remedy this deficit.

RESEARCH DESIGN

Nowhere is the shortage of research on technical work more acute than in Britain. Despite the upsurge in interest which led to the Finniston report (Finniston, 1980), the last two book-length studies of engineers are both products of the sixties, and neither used organisational material (Gerstl and Hutton, 1966; Prandy, 1965). Two more recent investigations have a similar weakness (Roslender, 1980; McLoughlin, 1981).

What was needed, therefore, was a research design which satisfied the need for two interlinked types of information: information on the organisation of work which could only realistically be supplied by comparative case studies, and information about engineers' ideological responses which required in-depth interviewing. It was particularly important that these two strategies be interlinked because most

15

of the arguments discussed in Chapter 1 suggest a causal relationship between organisational structure and ideological response. This required that interview material be contextually located in specific organisational settings, so that the questions were not asked in a vacuum but could be specifically interpreted in the organisational contexts to which they were responsive.

The comparative case study approach has the advantage over research at a single site of providing a bench-mark against which to compare high-tech industry. Other studies which have looked at the impact of technological and organisational change on workers' attitudes (Gallie, 1978; Goldthorpe *et al.*, 1969; Low-Beer, 1978) have found it difficult to draw inferences in the absence of a comparative reference point. It also facilitated field-work by focusing the observational research.

The major disadvantage of the case-study method is the difficulty in generalising to a wider population. Generality, however, should not be confused with typicality. In trying to understand the processes which shape the structure of technical work, I am not concerned with arguing that Computergraph and Metalco are typical members of their respective industries – though the evidence suggests that in most respects they are – but that by studying them closely, and seeing how the product and labour markets, the search for profit and the demands for career success, the education system and technological constraints, all shape the *particular* formation of work and the *particular* opinions of engineers, we can understand better how these forces operate in the society more generally.

OLD AND NEW INDUSTRIAL SETTINGS

Underlying most of the arguments discussed in Chapter 1 is an assumption that engineers in modern, high-technology industries find themselves in a different position from the one they have held in traditional, low-tech industries. To examine this assumption we need to specify which aspects of 'modernity' are most directly relevant. One reference that 'new' has had in this context is to new *production* technologies. Chemical plants and oil refineries have been seen as the archetypical workplaces of the future (Blauner, 1964; Mallet, 1975). Support for this view was provided by the influential research of Woodward and her colleagues (1958, 1965), who argued that their scale of 'technical complexity' – ranging from the simplest 'unit-batch' production to the most complex 'continuous-process auto-mated' systems, with 'small batch', 'large batch' and 'mass produc-tion' as intermediate steps – measured the historical development of production techniques. If 'Fordist' mass production has replaced small-batch craft work, so continuous-process production and the fully automated factory will soon replace the assembly line.

There are a number of problems with this view. Outside the oil and chemical industries continuous process plants remain comparatively rare, and while some progress is being made in the robotisation of the factory this seems to be occurring in relatively traditional industries such as car manufacturing, rather than in more characteristically high-tech industries. In other equally modern and science-based industries, a wide variety of production technologies are to be found. In specialised electronics plants, for example, small-batch production is very common, while traditional mass-production assembly lines turn out personal computers in their thousands.

It is true that the logic of rationalisation and large-scale production leads to the standardisation of production activities. If the market is large enough, and the product stable enough, any product is likely to move from unit to batch, to mass, to automated production; but in the innovative stage of any product's life, or where there are unstable or limited markets, it is unlikely that such a process can be carried very far.[1] Production runs would be too small to justify rationalising the production line. This, however, is a function of market structure, not of modernity *per se*. There is no necessary linkage between production technology and advanced industry.

A more critical dimension of technical modernity, and one which lies closer to the centre of the theoretical debates over the position of technical workers, is 'knowledge technology', which refers to the level of technical knowledge applied to design and production. Knowledge technology is at the heart of the argument about post-industrial society; that its 'axial principle', as Bell (1973) put it, is theoretical knowledge, and that its production processes are char-acterised by a direct relationship with science. It can be operational-ised as the proportion of engineers and technically trained staff employed in a company, or the ratio of research and development spending to value added or net sales, all publicly available data.

Although knowledge technology is the most important factor to consider, it also seems intuitively sensible to take chronological age into account. Stinchcombe (1965) has made the case that the age in which an industry is founded shapes its structure in numerous important and complex ways, and taking age into account also gives the developmental arguments the most weight possible in a cross-sectional design. Therefore it was decided to seek a new industry with a high knowledge–technology content and of recent origin, and an old industry with a relatively low knowledge–technology component and which dated to the heyday of the first industrial revolution. The electronics and metal-working industries were finally chosen as the most appropriate.

I also decided to select plants in communities typical of their industries to take into account the broader contexts of 'advanced' or 'traditional' settings, and to avoid unusual labour market features. Thus I looked for electronics plants located in the South East of England, while metal-working plants were sought in the industrial North and Midlands. Though there was a risk of confounding industrial and regional factors, addressing the *a fortiori* arguments seemed more important than controlling for particular variables.[2]

Research Procedure

It was not easy to gain access to companies willing to grant the kind of research facilities needed, but once Computergraph and Metalco had given permission, neither they nor the unions placed any restrictions on the research beyond a requirement to maintain confidentiality.

Both companies made available what records they had of salary scales, benefits, career patterns, recruitment practices, turnover rates, modes of evaluations, job evaluation practices and the like, but in many cases this was very little. Much of the data was hand-assembled to meet the needs of the project and even so was often full of gaps. It was impossible, for example, to put together a complete educational record for all the technical staff at Computergraph. Turnover statistics and promotion patterns were also difficult to establish in anything more than a sketchy way for either company. Neither company had the elaborate centralised personnel files or career development systems characteristic of many American firms.

This organisational research was followed by observation and informal interviewing. Most often this meant following engineers through their daily routines and sitting in on meetings with customers, management and other engineers. I observed the complete range of technical activities at both companies in this way, though naturally this was easier in some situations than others. In the open plan R & D department at Computergraph it was easy to observe unobtrusively, but I was much more visible accompanying production managers on their rounds on the shop floor. In general, however, the sight of someone wandering around, notebook in hand, is a common situation in the environment in which engineers work.

One difficulty of the observation phase stemmed more from my fascination with the engineers' work – and my tendency to be distracted by it – than from anything else. Much of their work is intrinsically interesting and it was sometimes a struggle not to spend time studying the machinery rather than the engineers themselves; but this may well have aided my acceptance.

A good deal of time was spent simply 'hanging around' with groups of engineers. Once the initial introductions and explanations had been made I was accepted readily. Both higher management and engineers accepted the promise of confidentiality and were free with their comments, negative and positive.

I spent three months at Metalco, while at Computergraph the field work involved about three days per week spread over five months.

The Interview Sample

Deciding on a sample for the formal interviews involved some difficult decisions about defining the population. As we shall see in Chapter 3 there is no general consensus as to what constitutes an engineer in Britain. Discussions of British technical workers as 'technicians' and 'engineers', common in national policy debates, have little meaning at the level of the firm, and there is no close match between educational qualifications and position in the division of labour.

After a period of direct observation and discussions with managers, engineers, union officials and professional associations, a dual strategy was adopted. First, although not without difficulty, a number of positions were identified for which the 'normal' qualification requirement was a Higher National Certificate or Diploma (HNC or HND). All occupants of such positions were included in the population regardless of their qualifications. In addition, from the job grades below these, employees with an HNC/D or higher qualification were included, as were all qualified engineers in production management positions. Excluded from the population were engineers holding managerial positions more than one level removed from technical practice.

These criteria included both 'engineers' identified by the most widely accepted qualifications, and 'engineers' identified by their position in the division of labour; these being the two principal ways in which engineers are usually identified. This strategy was not entirely acceptable to everyone. In particular the professional associations regard 'engineers' without a degree or a professional qualification as 'technicians' or 'technician engineers', and claim that all appropriately qualified employees, i.e. graduates and those with professional qualifications, are engineers, whatever their position in the firm. However it is the tension between such educational and organisational criteria that I wished to explore, and, as we shall see in Chapter 3, the professional institutions' claims remain a contentious issue in British industry.

Available resources permitted a one-third sample of the engineers at each site to be randomly selected. This provided 56 engineers from Metalco and 54 from Computergraph. There were only two refusals, both production engineers from Computergraph.[3] The background characteristics of the sample are given in Table 2.1 and their distribution by department is shown in Table 2.2.

TABLE 2.1   *Characteristics of the sample (per cent)*

	Metalco	Computergraph
Staff engineers	62	66
Technical managers	38	33
Age distribution*		
15–25	2	7
26–35	55	48
36–45	23	28
46–55	11	15
56–65	9	2
Social background		
Unskilled manual	20	20
Skilled manual	32	26
Lower white-collar	18	39
Professional and		
managerial	23	15
NA	7	0
Marital status		
Married	87	76
N =	56	54

* Average age in both companies = 37.
NOTE   For details of education see Chapter 4.

TABLE 2.2   *Sample size by department*

	Metalco				
	Drawing office	*Methods*	*Planning*	*Production engineers*	*Production management*
Sample	10	17	16	6	7
Population	30	50	44	25	19

	Computergraph					
	Drawing office	*Production engineers*	*Production management*	*R & D*	*Test*	*Service*
Sample	7	8	7	18	5	9
Population	25	21	19	55	16	27

The interview schedule (reproduced in the Appendix) was a structured series of open-ended inquiries that took about two or three hours to complete. All the interviews were recorded in both written and taped formats, and although resources did not permit making complete transcripts of the tapes they have been used to ensure the accuracy of the quotations and to provide additional qualitative depth to the analysis.

The engineers were extremely willing to talk. Because personal contact was always made – sometimes quite extensively so – before the formal interview, the latter developed a conversational quality conducive to an open discussion. The interviews were conducted either in the engineers' homes or in empty offices at the work site. The choice was largely a matter of convenience. An examination of the background characteristics of the engineers revealed no differences between the two, and the location of the interview seemed to have little effect on the quality.[4]

This research design combined the advantages of both observation and interviews. In particular the central importance of organisational structure in shaping engineers' responses and orientations could not have been understood in any other way.

METALCO AND COMPUTERGRAPH

In the second part of this chapter I want to describe Metalco and Computergraph in more detail, and provide a sense of the daily routines of a variety of engineers before breaking these apart to deal analytically with the structure of technical work.

Metalco

It would be difficult to imagine a company more clearly embodying the features of a traditional British manufacturing company than Metalco.[5] Headquartered in the heavily industrialised West Midlands, Metalco has been making a wide variety of metal products since the earliest days of the Industrial Revolution. Its traditional strength is in production rather than in product innovation and it does little technical development work. The company spent only half a per cent of its sales revenue on R & D in 1977, and employed less than 1.4 per cent of its workforce in technical jobs. By comparison the engineering industry as a whole has about 1.9 per cent employed in technical work, and for employers with over 5000 employees the figure rises to 3.1 per cent. Even by its own somewhat generous count the company employed only 800 engineers in the whole group.

Although a large corporation by British standards – with a worldwide employment of over a hundred thousand, and sales of more than £1.5 billion (1977) – it is decentralised into relatively autonomous operating divisions. Head office primarily functions as an in-house merchant bank overseeing major capital expenditure. Apart from this capital control, headquarters staff usually confines itself to securing corporate uniformity on senior management pay, benefits and so on. This is accompanied by a credo stressing the advantages of flexibility and adaptability to a changing market: a credo which also serves as a defence against union attempts to bargain with the corporation as a whole. It is an article of faith among central management that nothing should be done to disturb this situation.[6]

A major feature of this decentralisation strategy is an elaborate structure of divisions, companies, and profit centres within each company. Each unit is expected to treat other units as if they belonged to an external market: so, for example, a group technology centre sells its services to other divisions. The aim is to exert 'profit discipline' at the lowest levels.

The field-work was carried out in two operating divisions: the 'Massfas' division mass produces small metal fixtures on a 120-year-old site close to Head Office, while 'Pressco' makes large pressed-metal assemblies on a site about thirty miles away. The overwhelming impression given by both divisions is that these are factories *making* things. Signs of production are everywhere: noise, dirt, scrap, smells. Massfas' mass-production machines are lined up in rows in old redbrick mills separated by the canal that used to be the factory's main source of transportation. Pressco's plant is larger and more modern – a product of the 1930s – but its machinery is bigger, dirtier and much noisier, occupying huge corrugated-iron sheds. Both divisions' engineering offices are located in available space scattered around the production facilities.

Neither division does much design or development work. Massfas' products are either licensed from other more innovative companies or produced to internationally agreed 'standards'. Pressco produces most of its output under contract from the automobile industry and leaves most of the design to the customer. Of a combined employment of about seven thousand workers on the two sites at the time of the research, there were only 152 qualified technical staff, primarily engaged in some form of production engineering.

The attention of the technical staff is focused on 'getting the tonnage out of the door'. Even those primarily engaged in mechanical design generally work on special-purpose machinery or tool design; only a few staff at Pressco design new products, and even here the focus is on helping customers with designs that can be easily and cheaply produced, or acting as customer liaisons during modifications. This functional subordination is reflected in engineers' lack of visibility to higher management. They are simply a staff function for production.

This invisibility is compounded by the problems faced by all non-management employees in Metalco's pervasive bureaucratic structure, an environment in which even the most senior staff engineers need to channel requests through their managers to get things done. Both divisions' organisational structures divide up the technical function into a series of small technical offices, either attached to separate production shops or in specialised offices of their own. These various offices employ engineers engaged in five recognised functions: planning engineers, who estimate costs and plan the flow of production; production engineers, whose main function is 'firefighting' problems as they arise in the production process but who are also expected to innovate new processes; line managers, who are responsible for supervising manual workers and whose job has only recently been opened to qualified engineers; methods engineers, who design special purpose machinery and innovate new techniques of manufacturing; and the product designers, who design new products – such few as there are – and prepare the technical drawings which are the basic documentation of all production processes.

The corporation as a whole has suffered badly from the increased competition facing all of the British engineering industry. Just prior to the research, Pressco division had severely reduced recruitment and closed plants in other parts of the country, and one of the production lines had been working a three-day week because of declining demand by a major customer. Massfas division had reduced its methods development programme by 15 per cent in 1972, and made a further 20 per cent reduction in 1975. The budget of one unit of the methods programme at Massfas had been reduced from £45 000 to £10 000 between 1973 and 1977 despite galloping inflation.

These earlier cutbacks, which, paradoxically, had improved the job security of the remaining engineers, had left one permanent reminder: the unionisation of all of the non-managerial technical staff. Most are members of the Technical and Supervisory Staffs Section of the Amalgamated Union of Engineering Workers (TASS), though a few sections were in the Association of Scientific, Technical and Managerial Staffs (ASTMS).[7] The company recognises these unions for collective bargaining purposes for technical staff but not for the few managers who are members.

Computergraph

If Metalco captures the image of the traditional metals manufacturing company, then Computergraph is a classic innovative, high-tech company. It was founded by an inventor/entrepreneur in his back room in the late 1940s to apply electronic control systems to the operations of a traditional industry. This product line expanded, largely through the inventiveness of the original owner and a few close colleagues, into a highly sophisticated range of computer-based equipment. Like many such companies, however, it experienced cashflow problems, and it was finally taken over in the early 1970s by a larger company active in a number of related businesses.[8]

At the time of the research Computergraph employed approximately 900 employees on four sites. Its north London head office, where about half the employees work, houses the central administration, sales, marketing, service engineering, and most crucially, the research and development department (R & D). Located in a cramped Victorian area of residential streets, small shops and office buildings, this was the original manufacturing site. Three new sites had been added more recently: two small sites in other parts of north

London – one a small sheet-metal shop, the other a machine shop – each employing about seventy people, and a recently opened 300-employee assembly plant in an East Anglian New Town sixty miles to the north. Only the small machine and pressed-metal shops provide the kind of 'industrial' environment so pervasive at Metalco; the new assembly plant is the kind of mass-produced factory now prevalent in many suburbs, offering a clean working environment and little noise. Many of the assemblers of the smaller units are women, while the larger units are batch assembled by operators putting together a single machine at a time.

The company was growing rapidly. Sales revenue had been increasing at about 20 per cent per annum over the previous years, reaching £20 million in 1978, and its five-year plan sought to expand total manpower by 30 per cent and R & D engineers by over 50 per cent. Like many high-technology companies Computergraph is heavily dependent on a single product line, and the company was actively seeking to expand its range by both in-house R & D and acquisition. Research into new laser-based application had been underway for over four years, and the company was in the process of applying micro-processor technology to traditional applications.

Computergraph is best understood as an R & D department that grew a production arm. The development function as a whole employs nearly 17 per cent of the total workforce, spends 8 per cent of the total sales revenue, and is central to the company's survival in the market place. When anyone in the company talks about 'engineers' without a qualifier it is usually R & D staff they are referring to.

Computergraph's major product is a very complex piece of electronic and optical equipment. Before shipment, each model undergoes a six-week testing programme by test engineers working in a large room at the end of the main assembly area in the new factory. It is installed and repaired by service engineers, much of whose time is spent overseas, and who come back to the head office only for reassignment.

Not all the company's engineers are electronics specialists. The production engineering unit was expanding to deal with the longer production runs, and the design office provided the mechanical engineering expertise to design the mechanical aspects of the equipment, including the sheet-metal casings. The design office was also the source of the production drawings which guided the assemblers' work.

In contrast to Metalco's bureaucratic structure, Computergraph is a company where technical knowledge carries as much weight as hierarchical position. Particularly in the R & D department, the expertise of even junior engineers is respected and not restricted by formal hierarchies.

There was only limited union membership among technical staff. Only one R & D engineer was a member and although a number of draughtsmen and production engineers belong to TASS there was no collective bargaining agreement. Some of this was due to management attitudes which were fairly hostile to unionisation. In fact the East Anglian plant was opened to replace some of the London manufacturing sites, partly because of a history of poor labour relations with the Amalgamated Union of Engineering Workers (AUEW), the craftsmen and assemblers' union. The management installed by the new corporate owners had been recruited from American-owned electronics companies and took what it liked to call a 'strong line' with the 'militants'. As part of this they had moved production to its new factory where the union was much weaker, and at the time of the research were threatening to deal with labour unrest at the two small London plants in the same way.

ENGINEERS AT WORK

A critical feature of the theoretical accounts discussed in Chapter 1 is their emphasis on social change at the point of production. Yet we have very few accounts of what engineers actually do. In the following section I have tried, in an illustrative way, to draw on field notes to provide a sense of the daily activities of the range of engineers to be found at Computergraph and Metalco.

Planning

At the heart of the engineer's role in traditional industry is the planning of production, and it was my introduction to Metalco's engineers. I spent one of my earliest days at the factory in the company of Joe Brown, a senior planning engineer at Metalco's Pressco division who had worked for the company for 23 years. Although he was one of the most senior engineers in the planning department, he was at a stage in his career where he was unlikely to move into management.

Pressco's planning department is in an open plan office attached to the production sheds. It is divided by a half-glass dividing wall from the estimating department with which it was once integrated, and tucked away in one corner is the small methods unit which prepared special purpose machinery. Everyone in the planning department – with the exception of the departmental manager who has his own glassed-off office – works on cluttered desks in a slightly shabby room which probably hasn't changed much since the factory was built in the 1930s. Although Joe Brown is a senior planning engineer in the department, the only way I could find his desk was to have it pointed out to me; there were no signs of distinction between it and those of the newest recruits from technical college.

Planning engineers estimate costs and plan the flow of the product through the production system. They must understand the nature and availability of existing plant, consider new techniques and capital equipment if the order or project is big enough, and be able to transform drawings into flow charts to control production. The essence of the job is to transform the design drawings of the product into a set of discrete processes. These are then assigned to particular machines in stages, and organised into a time-flow chart.

Although some of the planning engineers work in small teams, at the time of the research Joe was working on his own, and on the day I spent with him he took most of the morning preparing a planning sheet for a rather routine product that was about to go into production. Since the job was small and relatively routine, it did not require any special purpose machinery, nor the ordering of new capital equipment. The basic problems involved the scheduling of machinery and raw materials, and establishing a basic set of timings for the job. Joe took the former in his stride, though not without a few grumbles at the intransigence of one particular production manager who never gave him the information he needed. It was the latter problem which brought forth the series of bitter jokes with which he greeted me.

At one level, the allocation of timings to a production process is a technical question: how fast does the machine run, how complicated is the product being made, how much handling is involved? But it is also the central political question in any factory in which production workers are paid on piece-rates, since the time negotiated for each job is the essential determinant of workers' take-home pay. If timings are 'generous' workers can complete more pieces of work during the week than if timings are 'tight'.

Joe felt he knew how long a particular job should take: 'I've been here long enough to know how to make this component. I know how long it takes. That's what they pay me for.' His complaint was that production workers wanted to stretch out times to make up for a government-inspired freeze on basic rates, and that higher management was inclined to go along to avoid production hold-ups. This upset Joe's pride in his own technical work. It also upset him because the production workers' take-home pay was outstripping his own, since staff were not eligible for production bonuses.

Joe told me most of this over tea which we had at his desk, and while talking he was continuously interrupted by George S. and Alec W., who sat at adjacent desks and were happy to join in with more tales of the 'outrageous' take-home pay on the shop-floor, and the 'ridiculous' times that management have accepted on particular jobs. After the break Joe continued to draw up the planning sheets.

Planning engineers are the direct beneficiaries of the division of labour which strips manual workers of control over their own workflow, and this antagonistic relationship is built into the job. For many engineers, production workers are the agents who carry out their plans, build their machines, service their designs, and so on; and for the engineers concerned they are *their* plans, their machines, their designs. While Joe's timings were produced in Pressco's interest, he felt they were his responsibility. He had the craftsman's pride in a product which he had planned, even if the execution was left to others.

Joe goes home for lunch so I went to one of the works' canteens with one of the junior engineers. Fred S. took great delight in showing me Pressco's elaborate gradation of dining-rooms: for works, junior staff, management and senior management, and finally for the directors – the 'local feudal system' was his phrase. Fred told me that when he first started to work at the company he tried to eat with some of his school friends who became craftsmen, but had been made to feel so uncomfortable that he had given up. He thought life would be better for everybody if all the elaborate status distinctions were abolished.

After lunch Joe switched to the troubleshooting part of his job. Water had been getting into a basic product while being shipped to the customer and the transport manager had put in a request for help. The problem had eventually landed up on Joe's desk, though he wasn't quite sure how or why. However, after giving it some thought, he had come up with a simple and cheap answer to the problem. This particular afternoon he planned to go and tell the transport and quality managers about it. On his way, he looked in his boss's open office door and told him his plans.

The quality manager, who had already received a lot of complaints about the problem, was pleased with Joe's solution and authorised him to order the necessary parts. We then went to talk to the transport manager. This involved walking through the large production sheds and through the mud around the work site on a typically cold and damp English March day. The transport manager, as Joe predicted, spent most of the time explaining why the problem was not really his fault. Back in the office, Joe reported the results to his boss who authorised him to complete the final paperwork.

Most of Joe's work during the day relied on experience, knowledge of the firm, and common sense rather than any formal technical training. He did have to know how to read an engineering drawing since these drawings are as central to production as written documents are to other administrative tasks, but most of the knowledge he had accumulated by being at the company for a long time.[9]

The day I spent with Joe is fairly typical of how he and his colleagues spent most of the time while I was there, but this was a period of relative depression in the industry and not many new projects were coming across their desks. This shortage of new work was the reason the estimating function, which had once been combined with planning, had been put into a separate department. The estimators' work is very similar to Joe's. They take customers' drawings, calculate how to make them the cheapest way using the resources available, and then submit a company estimate for the job. In the old days if the company won a contract the estimator who originally costed the job would plan it and follow it through into production. The decline in business, however, meant that only about two per cent of estimated contracts ever reached the planning stage, and the company had decided to put some of the engineers to work on preparing estimates full time.

Research and Development

The environment of Computergraph's R & D unit could not be more different from that of Metalco's planning department. Although located in an old building in a dense urban environment, inside it is a large, bright, open-plan office, with new furniture and modern acoustic dividers. Alongside is a lab with the latest in electronics and graphics equipment. When I got there at 8.30, on the day I was going to spend with him, Alan Sullivan was already at his desk, though most of the other engineers had not yet arrived. Computergraph had a flexitime system for its London staff and Alan was one of the few early risers among the engineers.

Alan, thirty at the time of the research, was senior electronics designer on one of the project teams in which the department was divided. He had in fact once been the project manager of the team but, not liking administration work, he had switched back to a purely technical position without any loss of grade or salary, something impossible to imagine at hierarchy-conscious Metalco.

When I got there he was 'thinking about the control panel', or so he claimed; but as he immediately commented, there is no way that I or anybody else would ever know. The project the team was working on was in its final stages and, since the prototype was almost ready for field testing, most of the team's work involved eliminating the final bugs. When I had left at 6.30 the previous evening, two other members of the team had still been playing with the machine in an attempt to debug it.

Perhaps because he thought he should be doing something more visible, Alan then went to the lab section to work on the machine. There were only two people employed as 'technicians' in the R & D division to which the project belonged, so most of the hands-on work with the machines was done by the engineers themselves. Alan spent about forty-five minutes, screwdriver and soldering-iron in hand, trying to solve a bug in the system. This process continued when the rest of the team arrived and for most of the morning I received a basic education in electronics.

At 11.30 there was a team meeting with the chief engineer and the project manager, Paul Byron. The discussion centred on the necessity for a new control panel for the machine under development. This was controversial, because the need for it had come up only after a design review and consultation with customers, and there was some feeling that it was illegitimate to change the specifications at this late stage. However, Ted Bryant, the chief engineer, argued that senior management had made the decision to go ahead and the question, therefore, was simply how long it would take.

Once this was announced the meeting turned into a straightforward technical discussion in which all the engineers, Alan included, participated as equals. After the meeting the project team gathered around Paul Byron's desk and continued to work out a division of labour to get the job done, which Paul guided and finally allocated. Alan went back to his desk to do some more thinking and sketching. Each of the team spent the rest of the day working on their individual problems. John Y. called up suppliers. Tom S. and Barry J. continued to work on the machine, while Paul Byron spent the afternoon consulting with the mechanical designers in the drawing office.

A point worth noticing here is that the hierarchical structure of the department is visible primarily in the range of problems for which each level is held responsible. Ted Bryant's job is to coordinate the overall budget, initiate new projects, and liaise with sales. Paul Byron's job is to monitor the budget, keep the project to schedule and allocate responsibilities among the team. Alan Sullivan, on the other hand, is there simply to solve the technical problems that arise in developing a machine that meets the initial specifications. His technical responsibility is *greater* than Ted Bryant's, but the range of his responsibilities is much *narrower*.

At each level jobs are allocated in terms of specifications that need to be met. Paul Byron was given a project to get in at a certain time, and under a certain budget to meet certain specifications. Alan Sullivan was given a technical task to solve in a certain time, and at certain cost. At each level the goals are allocated, the solutions left to the engineers. Once a goal is allocated the other questions become unproblematic. The personality trait most admired in such circumstances is the capacity to get the job done.

There is a long-term rhythm to most R & D work. A two or three year cycle is not uncommon for a large project and individual engineers have their work allocated in large chunks. The early stages of a project, for example, could require a single engineer to concentrate six months on developing a theoretical solution to a particular problem. At end of the project the same engineer could be physically building the early prototypes. It is these long cycles of work, and the large chunks of work over which they are given individual responsibility, which differentiates R & D work from most other forms of engineering.

The nearest that Metalco could come to providing working conditions like those in R & D was in Massfas' methods unit, which had once served as a development unit for both new products and new production methods. But that was in the expansionary sixties. New management in the seventies had drawn back from innovation, and with it had gone most of the development work. Many methods engineers still had the technical autonomy of the R & D engineers but their organisational freedom was being diminished, and increasingly they were being encouraged to think of careers in other departments. Enough was left of the old atmosphere to suggest, however, that it is not necessarily the age of the industry that is important, nor even its dominant knowledge technology, but rather the company's willingness to pursue innovative production or marketing strategies.

Test and Service Engineering

Another indication that function rather than industry might be the most appropriate unit of analysis is given by the case of Computergraph's test department. Steven Smith is a systems test team leader in the test unit at Computergraph's East Anglian plant. At the time of my research, the test unit had just moved to the new factory and most of the test engineers were new hires replacing London test engineers who had not wished to relocate. Steve Smith, however, was one of the old guard and while he tested machines himself he also was responsible for four junior engineers.

The test environment is very different from R & D. The unit occupies one end of the single-storey factory in an open space surrounded by closed-in dark-rooms where some of the graphic tests are analysed. The machines for testing, each about the size of two large upright pianos, stood side-by-side in the middle of the room, each the responsibility of an individual engineer. When I met Steven at 8 a.m. he was about to run some of the photographic tests. He had been working on his present machine for about four weeks and was three-quarters of the way through the six-week testing cycle. While waiting to get a free dark-room he showed me the 91-page test routine book which had been prepared by R & D, and which guided the procedure.

Most of Steve's morning was spent conducting and analysing a series of photographic tests, but he broke the routine by talking to one or other of the junior engineers. Nominally the test engineers' job is among the most individualistic of all engineers' work. Each machine is the responsibility of a single engineer who carries out all the tests, 'signs off' the machine as acceptable, and then begins the complete cycle over again on another machine. In practice, however, the unit is friendly and cohesive. The rhythm of testing is such that there are plenty of breaks for conversation, and although the test lab manager is nearly always around, it is the rhythm of the test sequence itself that provides the ultimate discipline.

At lunchtime I went with most of the unit to a local pub. This turned into a generalised gripe session about having only thirty minutes for lunch, and the absence of flexitime at the new factory. Most of the assembly workers were women, who had voted for the short lunch hour so that they could finish work earlier, and it was company policy to have uniform working hours for all personnel at the factory: a very different situation from Metalco's array of status distinctions.

After lunch, Steve had more time to talk. A production hold-up had left one of his team with no new machine to work on so Steve delegated some of his own testing. He said that testing was essentially an entry level position for engineers with any ambition: 'During the last six years, seven or eight have gone on to jobs in R & D, seventeen or eighteen to the service department and another two or three into management. I've turned down a service job once because I didn't want to travel, but this job is finally getting to me and I could use the extra money.' Jack S., the unit manager, overheard our conversation, and came over: 'If the engineer is any good they'll get bored in about two or three years once they've mastered the job, but it's good training and the company won't hire an engineer straight from college for an R & D or service job, so this is a good place to begin.'

This is the kind of work where the claims that high-tech industry is breaking the boundaries between blue- and white-collar work should seem most appropriate. The work the test engineers do is not involved in the control of manual labour, either directly or indirectly. In actual fact, it *is* manual labour. The reason that it is classified as technical work and that the company employs qualified engineers to do it, is that it is very complex, highly skilled, and requires responsibility. Yet the fact that it is classified as technical work ties it to a career ladder with routine links to much more senior positions, links which are not normally accessible to the assembly workers who build the machines the engineers are testing.

The service engineers require essentially the same skills as the test engineers, but because they have to act on their own away from managerial oversight – they have more 'responsibility' in the official argot – they are more highly graded in the company hierarchy.

Production

If test and service engineers are skilled workers, production superintendents are clearly managers. Richard Taylor is a production superintendent at Massfas: one of the three qualified engineers – Richard is a university graduate – who had recently been moved into line management with the company. Richard used to be in production control and moved into line management because 'this is where the opportunities are'. I met him in his glass-walled office up a short series of steps from the shop-floor which it overlooked. The noise on the shop-floor was deafening, and was not much better in the office, which was flanked by two similar ones each occupied by two foremen who report to Richard.

Even if I hadn't met him previously it would have been easy to pick Richard out. He was the only one wearing a suit and tie. The foremen under him wear short grey overalls, and the operatives dress in boilersuits. Another sign of his status was his clear desk. The desks of the foremen in the adjoining offices were covered with forms of one kind or another. It is foremen who deal with the routine paperwork which monitors the flow of materials and output through the shop.

When I got there, Richard told me he was sorry that it would not be a typical day: 'There's no meetings, so you won't be able to see what I really spend my time doing, sitting in meetings.' He didn't seem all that unhappy at the prospect. What he actually spent most of the morning doing was making rounds of the shop-floor, consulting with his foremen and the shop-stewards. At 11.30 he had to attend a short photographic session, along with the appropriate foremen and the plant manager, for one of the operatives who was retiring. Richard didn't seem particularly at ease with the ritual jokes and pleasantries that were passed around as the photographer took the pictures in a corner of the shop. 'This is part of the job I'm not very good at,' he commented afterwards, and in fact he seemed much less at ease than the plant manager, who had once worked on the shop-floor and had worked his way up.

The unease of college graduates in dealing with production workers was often mentioned at Metalco when the question arose of using qualified engineers in line-management positions. In fact it was one argument used against the suggestion that an engineer should start as foreman rather than move into production as superintendent after a few years in a technical office, since it is the foremen who have most of the daily interaction with operatives.

For lunch we went to the management dining-room where, after a pre-lunch gin and tonic, we were served a three-course meal by waitresses at cloth-covered tables. 'One of the perks of the job,' Richard whispered, as we sat across the table from two much more senior managers from another department. 'You have to wait years for this in a technical department.' Although he was referring to the status trappings, the comment also indicated the more general reasons why engineers increasingly sought production jobs at Metalco: the prospects are much greater. There are far more managerial level positions in the production units than in technical departments, and at bureaucratic Metalco one had to manage someone to acquire position and prospects.

After lunch Richard had a long discussion with John F., the production engineer attached to the shop, about the relocation of one of the rows of machinery to improve production flows. This was a job Richard clearly preferred, but it was the production engineer who was going to deal with all the technical details while Richard was left with the responsibility of dealing with the industrial relations problems. It was a job he didn't relish. 'They have no long-term interest in the good of the company,' he said, referring to the shopfloor workers, 'They don't have any ambition either. They are content to do the same job for life. We are overmanned in any case, but I'd never get anybody to agree to cut staffing levels, short of a crisis.' I asked him if he thought he worked harder than the manual workers. 'It depends,' he said, 'you can't really compare.'

The production superintendent's job at Metalco is largely one of continuous routine, mixed with occasional crises over industrial relations. Richard had to plan for the future, order new machinery, and deal with industrial relations as they cropped up, but even here the key decisions were made above his head. His role was largely to serve as cog in the bureaucratic chain of command. Like Joe Brown, Richard complained that high management gave way too easily to the shopfloor, and 'undermined the efficiency of the place', a common complaint among Metalco engineers of all kinds.

John F. is the production engineer in Richard's shop but his superior is not Richard but the technical manager, who also has the responsibility for engineers in other sections. Unlike Richard, John F. is a local lad who had been through a technical apprenticeship with the company. He was much more at ease with the production workers than Richard, and not simply because he was not their direct boss. Most of the day, John was monitoring the output of a new machine. Whenever he needed to make adjustments he had to ask the production worker running the machine to do it, until finally five o'clock came around when the production workers finished for the day, and then he began to adjust the machine directly. 'I'm not supposed to do this, but nobody seems to mind what I do after hours, and this is the only way to get things done.'

Design

Strictly speaking the term draughtsmen is only applicable to very junior members of Computergraph's design office, since all the other mechanical designers had official titles of design engineer, but most mechanical engineers in product design at both companies would not object to being called draughtsmen, nor to the place where they worked being called a drawing office. They worked at drawing boards, lined up in rows, and many wore white coats. Like all the other engineering units there were no visible distinctions between the junior draughtsmen doing detailing work and the senior designer preparing the preliminary sketches for a major new product. Only the department manager had a separate office of his own. The similarity of the physical arrangement between the companies reflected the similarity of their work and the interchangeability of their skills.

Ron Dwyer was my guide at Computergraph's drawing office. He was the designer in charge of mechanical design for the project that Alan Sullivan was working on in R & D. His main responsibility was to coordinate the design of the physical casing in which the electronic instruments were to be held. He was essentially working alone on the project, though he had been promised the help of one of the junior draughtsmen if he needed it. His first agenda on the morning I met him was to meet with Paul, the R & D project manager, to consult about the changes required by the new control panel. They both stood and discussed the question while looking at the drawings that Ron had prepared of the casing.

Although, strictly speaking, Paul is not Ron's boss, and much of the discussion took place as technical equals, when it came to setting priorities it was clear that Ron responded to Paul's suggestions in much the same way that Paul's own R & D team had done. When I asked Ron about this, he told me that a block of his time had been assigned to the R & D team by his own departmental manager, in coordination with Paul's boss. The only time that trouble would arise was if Paul suddenly needed extra help to get the project ready for a new deadline, and then 'they [the two managers] will have to sort it out between them.'

The designers at both Metalco and Computergraph were somewhat disillusioned with the way their talents were used. At Metalco it was because the company had cut back on new design. At Computergraph the mechanical designers felt overshadowed by the electronics designers in R & D. 'They [senior management] often forget how complicated the mechanical design is. They've all been electronics engineers, and that's all they know.' Ron was also upset by the demands made to improve production documentation: 'It's just endless paperwork. Every modification they make requires new drawings.' Most of the day Ron spent drawing the modifications that he had discussed with Paul.

As at Metalco there was no formal division of labour between creating the design and doing the actual draughting. Ron did the complete drawing from design sketch to detailing. There were some so-called detailers in the department, working under temporary contracts, but they were largely restricted to circuit-board drawing. According to Ron, detailing was only done as a specialised task on very big jobs. 'If the job's small enough it's not worth the effort. We don't have the massive flows of production drawings like they do in the aircraft industry where they employ loads of detailers. I did that once, when I was starting, but it would drive you nuts if you had to do it for long.'

The major difference between working in the drawing office and working in R & D is the much shorter job cycle with which Ron operated.

TECHNICAL WORK

Reviewing these sketches of engineers' work, there are a few things worth mentioning even at this preliminary stage. The first is that the typical British organisation of technical work consists of a department with a manager supported by a variety of grades of technical staff, all of whom report direct to the manager. This is a bureaucratic organisation of work, not a professional one.

Second, there is a good deal of variety in engineers' work which is not caught by the distinction between old and new industry. Computergraph design engineers had more in common with the draughtsmen at Metalco than they did with the R & D engineers in their own company.

Third, career structures are critically important. It was not the characteristics of the job that sharply distinguished test engineers from operatives, but the fact that they were tied to engineering career ladders with good expectations. Richard Taylor, for example, was bored with much of his daily routine as superintendent but he knew he was paying his dues in order to move on to higher things.

Fourth, although not all engineers have the autonomy of the R & D engineers, few are under close supervision; indeed a distinctive characteristic of their jobs is that they are expected to perform them responsibly without supervision.

Fifth, though engineers might complain about their poor salaries, they show little sign of worker consciousness. If they do join unions, as those at Metalco had, it is not likely that this is a sign of class solidarity with the operatives in the plant.

3 Knowledge, Trust and Labour Markets

The feature of high-tech industry most fascinating to social analysts is its close connection with modern science. If the dominant image of the first industrial revolution is that of the artisan, drawing on a combination of native genius and long experience to invent a new loom or steam engine, the image which dominates portraits of new industry is that of a white-coated scientist pushing back the frontiers of knowledge in search of new products and new technologies. Much of this imagery owes its inspiration to commercial advertising, which has drawn on the prestige of science to support all kinds of product differentiation, from toothpaste to foot deodorants. But there is a core of truth to the imagery. The emergent industries of the twentieth century – chemicals, pharmaceuticals, electronics, biogenetics, aeronautics – have been critically dependent on technical advances closely related to discoveries of basic science. The path from the science laboratory to the factory has been growing shorter and shorter.

As far as engineers are concerned, however, the critical assumption of this post-industrial imagery is that these developments have fundamentally changed the nature of their knowledge base. No longer, the argument goes, can good engineering be adequately carried out by anyone with a practical training and experience. To take advantage of the new technology engineers will need to be trained in 'engineering science'. This will mean university education, and because only appropriately trained engineers will be able to evaluate their performance, engineers will at last be able to free themselves from employers' dominance and professionalise their occupation (Bell, 1973; Freidson, 1973).

Thus the development of science-based high-tech industry is expected to have the same impact on engineering that the development of the germ theory of disease had on medicine in the nineteenth century, i.e. allow the group which possesses monopoly access to the scientific knowledge to secure a monopoly over practice. In medicine it was doctors who finally asserted their dominance by controlling access to the medical schools where scientific medicine was taught (Larson, 1977; Jamous and Peloille, 1970). In science-based industry, engineers will be the ones with the training in engineering science. Or so the story runs.

PROFESSIONALISATION IN BRITAIN?

To effect such a change would require a major transformation in the traditional manner of training British engineers. The traditional educational route for a British engineer has been to leave school at fiteen or sixteen and enter a company-based technical apprenticeship scheme. Here they attended day-release classes at a local technical college and followed a combined classroom and industrial training programme leading to the Higher National Certificate (HNC). Previous generations of engineers took such courses part-time in the evening or had similar training entirely within training schools set up by such companies as Rolls-Royce, Metropolitan Vickers and General Electric. Further part-time study could then lead to full professional certification. Such an education does not expose an engineer to very much science or theoretical knowledge, rather it emphasises the continuities between engineering and the artisan experience.

None the less a number of groups have been pressing for just the kind of changes that the post-industrial model predicts, and have used similar kinds of arguments. The professional institutions, for example, have cut off entry to full professional membership for those engineers trained by the part-time route and restricted full professional status to graduate engineers. Some of them are even considering restricting membership further.[1] The Finniston Report recommended the development of special four-year programmes for 'super-engineers' (Finniston, 1980, pp. 96–7), and pressed for the continued expansion of degree-level education.[2] The joint government/industry sponsored training boards have also encouraged employers to upgrade their engineering staff by employing only university-trained engineers in critical innovative positions,[3] and they have been actively supported by various coalitions of engineering educators and manpower specialists.[4] All of these have drawn extensively on the argument that the transformation of the engineering knowledge-base from craft to science requires the reshaping of the occupational structure.

The models for technical work that the professional associations and the training establishment would like to impose on British engineering vary slightly in their specifics – largely over whether certification should be a function of the state education system or the voluntary professional associations – but they share a common core. They envisage a tripartite division of non-manual technical work between 'chartered engineers', 'technician engineers' and 'technicians'.

At the top will be the professional, chartered engineer, university educated and (possibly) professionally certified, 'who is able to assume personal responsibility for the development and application of engineering science and knowledge' (CEI, 1975a, p. 5). More practical engineering will be the responsibility of the technician engineer who 'can apply general principles and established techniques' (Engineers' Registration Board (ERB), 1976, app. 1); these are the engineers who qualified under the part-time route.[5] Below both of these should be the technician, able to apply 'proven techniques and procedures ... under the guidance of a Technician Engineer or Chartered Engineer' (ERB, 1976, app. 1).[6] Each of these types of labour should have their own training and credentials, and employers should provide each of them with their own range of tasks and career ladders. Different educational experiences, they argue, create different types of labour.

ENGINEERS AS TECHNICAL STAFF

Although these arguments have received wide circulation in academic and administrative circles, they have not been greeted with much enthusiasm by employers. British employers do not think that only 'professional engineers' have the knowledge to function in senior technical roles, nor that formal academic training is always the most appropriate for the kind of work they require. Instead, as the United Kingdom Association of Professional Engineers argued to the Finniston Commission:

> There is an alarming tendency among employers and particularly engineering employers ... to pretend that there is no important difference between their technicians, technical engineers and Professional engineers. Many regard all their technical employees as different grades of the same kind of staff. (UKAPE, 1978, p. 30)

Instead of an occupational division of labour – professional engineers supported by technician engineers and technicians – technical managers of departments are supported by staff with a range of academic credentials, and those with the highest qualifications do not automatically have more autonomy or authority over those with lesser qualifications. Put another way, British companies employ a wide range of people with a variety of technical qualifications to do similar jobs. This was certainly the case at both Metalco and Computergraph. Less than half the sample met the 'professional' definition of an engineer by having a degree or full membership in a professional institution (Table 3.1). This table actually underrepresents the diversity of the technical departments at Metalco and Computergraph since staff without qualifications in the lower grades were not sampled. Table 3.2 therefore presents an educational picture of the

TABLE 3.1   *Qualifications of engineers (per cent)*

Highest level qualification received	*Metalco*	*Computergraph*	*Total*
Craft apprenticeship[a]	0	4	2
GCE 'O' or 'A' levels[b]	2	15	8
'Technicians' qualifications[c]	5	6	6
Higher National Certificate or equivalent[d]	29	30	29
Higher National Certificate or equivalent plus endorsements[e]	14	6	10
Professional qualifications[f]	21	7	15
BSc	25	28	27
BSc plus additional qualifications[g]	4	6	5
N =	56	54	110

[a]   Completion of engineering craftsmen's apprenticeship.
[b]   These are both high school qualifications. The Ordinary level General Certificate of Education is normally taken at 16, the Advanced level GCE at 18.
[c]   A miscellany of low level technical qualifications, including the Ordinary National Certificate (ONC).
[d]   Higher National Certificate in Engineering, or the Diploma (HND), or the Full Technological Certificate (FTC), all part-time qualifications roughly equivalent to two years of a degree programme.
[e]   As above (d), but with additional endorsements; prior to the 1970s, this was an entitlement to professional association membership.
[f]   Membership in a major professional association entitling the claim to C. Eng. or Chartered Engineer, normally based on possession of (e). Those members who also possess a degree are included under the BSc category.
[g]   A degree plus either professional membership or a postgraduate qualification.

TABLE 3.2 *Qualifications of all technical workers in engineering departments at Metalco (per cent)*

	Drawing office			Methods			Planning			Production engineers			Total		
	Managers	Engineers	Technicians[a]	Managers	Engineers	Technicians	Managers	Engineers	Technicians	Managers	Engineers	Technicians	Managers	Engineers	Technicians
Degree (or +)	0	0	0	14	8	0	0	7	25	17	0	13	9	5	12
Professional qualifications	0	0	0	57	17	0	57	27	0	42	9	0	41	14	0
HNC (+) or equivalent	50	54	26	14	58	50	43	47	25	8	27	13	25	49	25
ONC or lesser qualifications	50	46	74[b]	14	17	50[b]	0	20	50[b]	33	64	73[b]	25	32	62[b]
N =	6	13	19	7	24	6	7	15	24	12	11	15	32	63	64

[a] Those graded below grade T4 or its equivalent.
[b] These employees were excluded from the population for sampling.

total population of Metalco technical workers (it was not possible to construct a similar table for Computergraph). As can be seen, though most technical workers without qualifications are in junior grades, a number have been promoted to senior staff positions, even into management. Some of this diversity is a reflection of the wide range of qualifications and courses that exist in British higher education outside of the university system. Some of it follows from historical changes in the educational structure.[7] None the less, even when all these factors are taken into account, employers still seem willing to use these supposedly different types of labour as substitutes for each other. 'Engineers' by qualification are employed in 'technicians'' grades, and vice versa.

The education and career routes by which engineers have arrived in their present jobs are also varied (Table 3.3). Thirteen per cent

TABLE 3.3   *Characteristics of first job held (per cent)*

Type of job	Metalco	Computergraph	Total
Unskilled manual	2	6	4
Skilled manual	7	11	9
White-collar administrative	2	7	5
'Technician' unqualified	18	17	17
'Engineer' technical position qualified to HNC level or above	71	59	65
Total N	56	54	110

began in manual positions and, though these are older men, this by itself is not evidence that such opportunities are no longer available, since younger unqualified technical workers who began in manual work are still in the junior grades. Another 21 per cent started in white-collar positions, mainly technical, without any qualifications. Though this pattern is common to much of British industry,[8] from the perspective of the professional model it is obviously problematic. It implies either 'overqualified' engineers are being used to do technicians' work, or that 'underqualified' technicians are being used to do engineers' work. Not only does it undermine the professional associations' capacity to secure monopoly access to particular positions, but for the training establishment it represents a waste of national resources, and a failure by British industry to maximise its own productivity.

For the companies, however, it is positions not qualifications that are important:[9] positions with titles, ranks and physical locations. And though neither Metalco nor Computergraph had the formalised charts and documents so readily produced as symbols of organisational efficiency by French and American companies, they could, with a little help from long memories and the backs of envelopes, provide lists of organisational positions. It is into this graded system of positions that employers recruit their technical staff from a variety of educational and work backgrounds.

Metalco

Technical workers are, first of all, non-manual salaried staff employees. The major dividing line in the organisation of labour remains that distinguishing 'staff' from 'works' employees. Staff employees are paid a monthly salary rather than an hourly wage, have better fringe benefits, have different car-parks, and eat in different canteens. Under normal circumstances they would also expect to receive higher pay.

At Metalco, however, in the middle and late 1970s, things were not 'normal', and many technical staff had a lower take-home pay than the production workers. This was largely a consequence of government-imposed pay restrictions which had had a much greater impact on salaried staff than on production workers; particularly when the latter, as at Pressco, were paid piece-rates, which were much harder to control. Despite this, the technical employees' status as 'staff' clearly distinguishes them from the manual workers.

Technical jobs at Metalco are organised into departments and grades. The department locates the engineer in the functional division of labour and provides the channel through which commands flow; grades locate engineers in the hierarchical structure and provide the basic unit of collective bargaining. At Pressco, for example, TASS had the bargaining rights for grades T1 through T4. Pay levels, and other rights and privileges, such as the use of particular canteens, car-parks, and 'clocking-in' rules, were organised along grade lines. They also provide the framework for organising job responsibility and skill requirements.

The grading system at Metalco varied slightly by division but Pressco's is representative of most of the company's manufacturing plants. There are six formal grades for technical staff, T1 to T6, but most engineers are concentrated in just two grades, T3 and T4, which in turn are divided into three sub-categories. Grades T1 and T2 are preliminary training grades to which newly qualified staff are appointed and through which they pass rapidly, while T5 and T6 are generally reserved for managerial appointments. Above T6 managers have individual contracts.

At Massfas division, where a similar system is in place, the original grading was done by a joint team from management and union. They graded a series of 'bench-mark' jobs and then 'slotted in' the others. At both plants a committee establishes grades for any new positions, and evaluates claims from engineers or their managers that a particular job has 'grown' and needs to be regraded.

These grades mark differences in responsibility rather than technical expertise *per se*. It is not technical skill in its own right that is rewarded, but the company's willingness to let jobs be carried out without supervision. Thus part of the job description of a senior Metalco engineer (T4C) reads: 'decisions and recommendations are usually accepted as technically accurate and feasible, but are reviewed to ensure adherence to policies and objectives'. The equivalent section for a junior engineer (T3C) reads only that 'main decisions and recommendations are based on independent study but difficult, complex, or unusual matters are usually referred to a higher authority.' In other respects the job descriptions are identical. This is reflected in the organisation of the technical offices where T3s do similar, though less advanced, work to T4s; both are subordinate to the office manager.

Grade levels have greater import in the company status system than they do on job descriptions. At the time of the research, for example, T3s were expected to clock-in in the morning whereas T4s were not, though the unions were fighting to eliminate the distinction. Similarly, management had once claimed that T4s were a managerial grade, and hence were not entitled to overtime payments, but the union had successfully fought to have this distinction eliminated, claiming – appropriately enough given the actual organisation of the departments – that T4s rarely if ever carried any supervisory or budgetary authority. The existence of single bargaining unit for grades T3 and T4 means that there is continuous pressure to eliminate the non-monetary distinctions between them.

The situation is different with respect to the largely managerial T5 and T6 grades. At this level, position dominates over grade level. It is managerial position which determines entitlement to a company car, to eat in the managers' canteen, to have a reserved parking place, and most importantly, to enter the organisation charts as an individual, not one of a grade.

These grades also provide the framework for the organisation of career ladders at Metalco which, although they do not have the formality and structure of more bureaucratic settings, possess many elements of an internal labour market. Most engineers began their careers with the company and stayed a long time; 61 per cent had never had another job. Though the average age of the engineers was 37, they had worked, on average, for less than 2 companies. Even those between 55 and 65 had only worked for an average of 2.6 companies during their careers. The average length of service, if we include apprenticeship time, was 14.8 years.

Except when the company is engaged in rapid expansion – a rare event in recent times at Massfas, but a sporadic occurrence at Pressco when a new contract was secured – Metalco only recruits from outside when special, internally unavailable expertise is required; an electronics engineer for a special project had been a recent example. Otherwise the technical staff are recruited straight from school or college and work their way up the technical ladder.

Ronald King had a fairly typical career with the company. He joined Pressco division's technical apprenticeship scheme at 16 with six General Certificate of Education Ordinary Level subjects ('O' levels) from the local grammar school. During the apprenticeship he took an Ordinary National Diploma (OND) and then a Higher National Certificate (HNC), both through day-release at the local technical college. Upon finishing, he joined the estimating department where he had been for 12 years. Now a senior staff engineer (T4C), he needs to make the difficult move into management to go further.

At the time of the research this was still the most common training route, though the number being sponsored to university was increasing. After taking the ONC at 18, those considered academically able enough transfer to the 'student' apprenticeship scheme, where they are sponsored by the company to a 'sandwich' degree at university.[10] At the end of four years spent alternating between the university and the company, the new graduates are offered regular positions by the company. Some students are also accepted for university sponsorship at 18 having taken Advanced Level General Certificate of Education ('A levels') at school, and the divisions occasionally participate in a group-wide graduate recruitment scheme.

Of the engineers in the sample, 65 per cent had received their formal qualifications through participation in a Metalco-sponsored training scheme; 39 per cent had undergone technical apprenticeships and received HNCs; while 20 per cent had been sponsored to university by the company (79 per cent of all the company's engineering graduates).

It is still possible to enter a technical staff position with a craft apprenticeship, but this is becoming rare.[11] There are also signs that the traditional practice of recruiting production engineers off the shop-floor is declining – the last appointee had been a graduate – but there is no official policy to that effect.

The distinctive feature of this recruitment process is the strong emphasis on practical training which the company controlled. This is particularly true for education at the local technical college, over which the company has considerable influence. But it is also true for university graduates, not only because of the sandwich structure and company sponsorship, but because companies tend to develop 'working relationships' with the few universities to which they sponsor students.

Whatever their education, all new technical staff begin at the bottom of the technical grades (T3a), along with staff promoted from the shop-floor. Promotion to senior engineer (T4c) is partly a matter of proving competence and partly a matter of time. Since these are essentially personal grades, promotion does not require a senior position vacancy. No formal educational credentials are invoked, though naturally there is some correlation due to management's intimate involvement in the credentialling process. Technical management positions, however, are filled by competition and educational credentials do seem to carry some weight. Movement between departments generally takes place only at managerial level, or when an engineer moves sideways in the hope of securing a managerial position in the future.

One additional reason that managers tend to be more highly qualified is that credentialled engineers tend to rise through the ranks more quickly than those without qualifications. Not only are the latter an older group (average age 44 compared to 36 for the sample as a whole), but they are often too old by the time they reach such a position to expect further promotion into management. Though experience can be substituted for qualifications on the route to becoming an engineer, it none the less takes time.

Metalco operates, therefore, with a single pool of technical workers. Though different qualifications carry with them different career advantages – those with a degree, for example, are more visible to senior management than the more numerous engineers with an HNC – such pay-offs occur only at managerial levels.[12] Technician, engineer, technical manager are, for Metalco at least, sequential stages on the same job ladder. Although everyone does not get to climb to the top, everyone who does get there has traversed the previous stages. There is little sign of an occupationally segmented labour market; at least not within the non-manual strata.

Computergraph

The social distinction between works and staff is not as all-pervasive at Computergraph as it is at Metalco because the company is not dominated, physically or numerically, by its production activities. Most engineers work at head office, where there are relatively few production workers. The terms of employment for manual workers and non-manual staff are also similar – manual workers have extensive sickness benefits for example. None the less engineers are still salaried staff rather than hourly workers, and in one respect the difference between the groups is even greater than at Metalco, since manual workers are widely and militantly unionised while few technical staff are union members.

In contrast to Metalco's system of broad grade groupings, Computergraph's elaborate grading system makes use of thirteen distinct grades and many more job titles. This is a fully developed job evaluation system in that each position had been evaluated separately and graded according to a scheme developed by a consulting firm specialising in such programmes.[13]

In comparison with the Metalco system, which established broad similarity of grading across technical functions, Computergraph's system makes distinctions between departments as well as within them. Senior and entry-level positions can have different grades in different departments. In R & D, for example, which has the highest overall grades, an entry level electronics engineer (electronics engineer II) is grade 4, whilst the project manager is grade 9 and the chief engineer a grade 11.[14] While in the test department an entry level position of test engineer is a grade 1 and there are two more senior grades (2 and 4), a test supervisor (7) and a test manager (9). In the service department the grades run from 5, the basic grade of service engineer, to 9 for the service manager. As at Metalco, engineers do not supervise other engineers or technicians unless they possess a managerial title.

Computergraph's grade system is surrounded with much scientific rhetoric. Each job has been 'objectively' graded according to three criteria: 'know-how', 'accountability', and 'problem solving', each of which is a composite of a number of sub-criteria. 'Accountability', for example, is a total score consisting of three subtotals for 'level of autonomy', 'magnitude of financial impact of job' and 'amount of job impact on end result'. 'Problem solving' consists of two dimensions; type of problem set and the type of thought required to solve the problem.

The differences between the job grades reflect – as they did at Metalco – variations in the amount of responsibility over technical work that an engineer is granted. The more senior engineers receive their higher grades because of increased scores for 'accountability' rather than 'know-how', for which all engineers in the sample have similar scores.

Though the system obviously contains a built-in theory of organisational design and reward legitimation, personnel management admits that its primary function is to provide a defensible order to the company-wide pay structure rather than be taken seriously as scientific management. The company readily 'slots in' jobs based on common sense perceptions of their relative worth, and had 'bent' the system to take account of market factors, giving higher grades to staff in short supply such as computer programmers and designers, and lower ones to those whom the company could obtain easily, such as test engineers.[15]

As at Metalco the job grading structure provides a single scheme which crosses putative occupational divisions. The staff in the drawing office, consisting largely of unqualified draughtsmen – 'technicians' in occupational parlance – have similar grades to the R & D engineers, the majority of whom are 'professionals' by the strictest of institute standards. As at Metalco there is a visible distinction between managers and non-managers in the organisation of departments, but this is less institutionalised in the grading system since it is possible to be an engineer grade 9 in the R & D department and be paid more than the production engineering manager (grade

7). Even within R & D it is possible to be paid the same as principal engineer as project manager. None the less the very highest rewards are only available to those who become managers (see Chapter 5 for a further discussion).

Computergraph differs from Metalco in that, although there are a series of orderly job ladders with clearly marked career routes, there is not a single pool of engineers, but a series of separate pools with only limited interchange. The engineers are divided both by discipline and by function. The distinction between electronics and mechanical engineers separates the design and production engineering offices from R & D, test and service departments, while different tasks and functions distinguish the test and service departments on the one hand, from R & D on the other, and design from production.

Computergraph also places more reliance on outside recruitment than does Metalco. Only two of the engineers interviewed had had no other job, and both of these were in the test department. This was, in the large part, a consequence of recent growth and expansion, but the need for a variety of different types of engineers makes a large-scale training programme too expensive to operate.

In the case of electronics engineers the company depends on two sources of entry-level recruitment; for young R & D engineers it relies on a number of large electronics companies in the same commuting belt; for test engineers, on ex-RAF technicians. Designers and production engineers are recruited on the open market, though a number are ex-manual workers promoted from within the company.

None the less, there are also a number of internal recruitment routes. Test engineers look to service engineering for promotion. Service engineers look to R & D or sales if management positions in their own department are not available. R & D offered rewards for high level technical specialisation within the department. Lateral moves between production engineering and first line production supervision are common, and both these groups still draw heavily from the shop-floor; 38 per cent of the production engineers and 43 per cent of the production managers (counting only those with some background in technical jobs) had begun in manual occupations – two-thirds of these in skilled jobs – and had spent an average of thirteen years on the shop-floor.

The design engineers in the drawing office have the most specialised careers. The Engineering Manager argued that this is a consequence of the electronics orientation of the company: 'An electronics engineer can understand the mechanical side fairly easily, but it doesn't seem to work the other way around; most of the designers tend to think the electronics side is a bag of tricks.' Perhaps in consequence the designers came the closest of any group to belonging to a distinct occupation, that of draughtsmen. Most of the draughtsmen at Computergraph, unlike those at Metalco, are not technically qualified; 71 per cent had an ONC or less. Most of them learned their skills on the job, either as apprentice draughtsmen (43 per cent) or by promotion from craft positions (29 per cent). Their lack of formal qualifications had not restricted their external mobility, however. Draughtsmen had the widest experience of any group, having had an average of 5.7 jobs compared to the overall average of 3.7.

By comparison, none of the R & D engineers had less than an HNC and over half had a degree and yet were graded at similar levels. Higher qualifications do not automatically result in higher grades, though they do have a potential for generating greater career rewards in the long run.

Computergraph engineers have spent much less time with the company·than those at Metalco, despite a similar average age. The average stay is just over six years, while the median is less than five. By contrast only 20 per cent of Metalco's engineers had spent less than five years with the company. However some 'old-timers' had been with the company since its beginnings, and a quarter had over a decade's service.

Computergraph does not, therefore, operate a fully fledged internal labour market, if nothing else its relatively small size and rapid growth prevent it. Even more than Metalco, however, it provides promotion routes from low level technical jobs to higher grades, and from there into management. Some 41 per cent of the company had started in jobs which could not reasonably be regarded as 'engineers'' positions. It accepts experience gained in climbing those ladders, whether internally or externally, as a criterion of skill and competence for many, if not all, of its technical positions. There was no significant difference between managers and non-managers in the type of job in which they had begun their careers. It also gives similar grades to engineers with different backgrounds and experience; the R & D engineers are generally the most qualified in the company but there was considerable overlap in grades with other departments.

Qualifications and Positions

The most obvious contrast between the two companies is between Metalco's almost total reliance on 'home-grown' engineers and Computergraph's recruitment on the external market. This seems to support the argument that 'new' industry will be more reliant on 'transferable' knowledge – knowledge belonging to the engineer and saleable to a variety of customers. The usual basis for this argument, however, is that such knowledge is acquired under the independent auspices of the university, but most engineers at both companies are not university trained and received their formal certification through employer-controlled apprenticeship schemes. Indeed, Computergraph's engineers, except for those in R & D, have less formal education than Metalco's. While the two companies differ in the extent to which they use labour markets internal to their respective companies, they both rely on an industry-based training and recruitment system controlled by employers as a class.

It could be argued – and was argued by a representative of a professional association I talked to – that many of Computergraph and Metalco's 'engineers' were not engineers at all but technicians; but this is a polemical position. Differences between the various educational categories may show up over career lifetimes, but as far as present position in the division of labour is concerned – and this is one of the central theoretical concerns of the study – all of the sample are 'engineers' by any of the criteria used in the workplace. The only exceptions, in fact, erred in the other direction, since younger engineers in junior grades were included in the sample because of their superior qualifications. It is the differences between the occupational model advocated by the professional associations, which emphasises qualifications, and the organisational model operated by Computergraph and Metalco, as well as by most other British companies, which stresses positions, that requires explanation.

THEORY AND PRACTICE

This pattern of recruitment and deployment – and there is extensive evidence that it is pervasive in British industry (Mace, 1979; Mace and Taylor, 1975; Mace and Wilkinson, 1977) – raises an interesting question. If 'science' is so critical to engineering practice, and it can only be learned in the university, why do British companies resist the professional structuring of the division of labour? Surely they are being irrational, even on their own terms, if they willingly ignore the advantages that practitioners of engineering science could bring them. Put less crudely, this is in fact the charge that is often laid against them: because of cultural conservatism and resistance to scientific advance they are undercutting their own potential profitability (Finniston, 1980). A critical question remains, however. Is the knowledge that engineers use in their daily practice usefully categorised as science? The evidence of engineers' own testimony suggests not.

In much of mechanical engineering, for example, the job is surrounded by a 'cult of experience'. Reg Hawkins, a senior design engineer in Computergraph's R & D, invoked the 'art' of the mechanical designer to explain why the electronics-trained Engineering Manager did not fully understand what he did.

> I think he thinks that just because we make it look simple that there's nothing to it. But it's creative being a designer. I can't just look the solution up in some book. You have to have a 'feel' for it and a lot of experience to know what'll work and what won't.

Jim Mitchell, a production engineer, talked about the requisite instinct necessary to understand why one of the machines at Metalco's Massfas division was being troublesome.

> Some of the shop-floor workers, and a lot of the office types too I think, think all I have to do is follow some instruction manual to figure out what's wrong, but you can get a mechanic to do that. You need to have a sense of all the interactions, it gets to be a kind of instinct.

Even young R & D engineers stressed the critical importance of experience.

> When you come out of college you think you know everything, but it's a different world out here. When it comes to knowing how to get the 'biggest bang for the buck', you have to have been around for a while, what you learn in books won't help much.

In fact, only 8 per cent of the engineers felt that the knowledge they had learned at college could not have been learned on the job (Table 3.4).

TABLE 3.4   *Relative value of education and experience (per cent)*

	Qualifications				
	Less than an HNC	*HNC equivalent (including endorsement)*	*Professional qualifications*	*Degree*	*Total*
Education essential	0	0	6	23	8
Experience a substitute	71	70	94	68	73
Experience essential	29	30	0	9	19
Total N	17	43	16	34	110

NOTE χ^2, sig. = .0004.

I suppose it was useful to learn a lot of the stuff at college, it probably made it easier when we first started, but you could pick it all up on the job. A lot of the stuff, like the physics, I've never used.

This was most obviously true for positions such as production manager which had little direct technical component.

There are more and more of us [engineers] coming into production, but it can't be because of our university training. I never get to use any of the theory I learnt in university, I don't even get to use the technical experience I picked up when I was a production engineer. This is a people job. In many ways my degree gets in the way because I think the shop-floor mistrust me for it. (graduate production manager, Metalco)

But it was also true of much more technical jobs:

I use some of the theory occasionally, but what I really know about this job I learnt when I started here. Before the cutbacks we had a much bigger department and I learned all I know doing some of the detailing for [a senior designer]. Design is that kind of a job. (Metalco methods designer)

Even three-quarters of the graduate engineers feel that most of what they learned in college could be *substituted* for by appropriate experience or on the job training (see also Mace and Taylor, 1975).

> I occasionally come across something that I think my university training helps me with, but there's nothing you couldn't figure out without it. One of the senior managers who likes to recruit graduates is always going on about how we think differently, but I think he's just being a snob. It helps with career prospects, I'm sure of that, but when it comes to doing the job it's really experience what counts.

When asked if they thought that a degree was, or would be, useful in the job they were presently doing, most engineers responded negatively, including over half of the graduates (Table 3.5).

> No, except for getting ahead in management it's a waste of time. I'd know far more if I'd spent the time learning on the job. (Graduate planning engineer, Metalco)

Despite all the claims about the increased importance of 'science' to high-tech industries there is little difference in these responses between the two companies, and even in the R & D departments only 38 per cent of the engineers thought a degree was a useful attribute for doing the job.

TABLE 3.5   *Usefulness of degree for present job (per cent)*

Usefulness of degree for present job	Qualifications				
	Less than an HNC	*HNC equivalent (including endorsement)*	*Professional qualifications*	*Degree*	*Total*
Yes	29	12	6	41	23
Yes, for management	6	0	6	12	6
No, other qualifications are equivalent	0	2	19	9	6
No	65	86	69	38	65
Total N	17	43	16	34	110

NOTE χ^2, sig. = .001

No, you don't need the degree. In many ways an HNC would have been better, you get more practical training that way. In fact you could pick up all of this on the job, it would take you longer that's all. (R & D, Computergraph)

All the engineers, whatever the position or qualifications, rejected the idea that access to engineers' positions should be restricted to graduate engineers.

That's just the institutions blowing their own trumpet. Anybody who's any good should be allowed to do the job. There's a lot of people around here who could do the job. Some people don't get the chance to go to university, or even to do an HNC, but they pick it up on the job. It's ridiculous trying to keep people down because they don't have qualifications.

Engineers in R & D at Computergraph certainly use scientific advances more than do those at Metalco. One of the company's R & D teams daily awaited results from a government science laboratory which would indicate that a laser experiment was showing enough promise to be incorporated in their two-year plan. But it is the *results* of scientific advance that they use and using knowledge is not the same as creating it. Unlike pure science's orientation to the production of knowledge, engineering is about making things, what the Germans call *Technik* (Fores, 1978). It is an industrial commonplace that only so much engineering can be learned in the classroom.

However, the resistance to academic training goes beyond the mode of acquiring technical skills to a basic concern with exposure to the customs and practices of the factory. The desirable characteristics of the engineer, even the manager, are those of the 'practical man' rather than the technocrat. The language of the factory is self-consciously 'tough', in contrast to the 'soft' worlds not only of the university but also the worlds of commerce and finance. It is the world of practicalities rather than 'ivory tower theory', of 'making things' rather than 'paper pushing'. A 'real education' requires exposure to the 'real world' of the factory, to the rites and traditions of the workplace rather than the 'airy-fairy ideas' of the classroom.

The problem with a lot of the new graduates is they think they can treat the job as an intellectual exercise, but developing new methods isn't something you can do in the lab. There are real people you have to convince. You've got to be practical.

The image of the practical man is stronger the closer one goes to production. Thus many self-taught production managers at Metalco readily make rude noises about 'head in the sky' production engineers whose only class-room experience was during their HNC day-release time. These production engineers, in turn, make similar noises about development and methods engineers, particularly if they possess degrees. Similarly at Computergraph, as one moves away from production towards R & D the anti-academic rhetoric weakens, though it is never entirely absent even in the high-technology research groups. Even many experienced R & D engineers extol the virtues of practical experience and complain that 'some of the new graduates can't even use a soldering iron', and then take pride in wielding it themselves.

In a culture which takes 'theoretical' as a term of abuse, even amongst research engineers, the support for academic qualifications is bound to be weak. Paul Willis (1977) argues that the discourse of practical rather than academic reasoning is distinctly working class, and certainly when contrasted to the language of the 'educated' middle class, this is so. But this simply reflects the ideological role of formal education for many sectors of the middle class, and such status uses of discourse can equally be used within classes. A preference for the language of practical reasoning (Oakeshott, 1962) serves to distance 'practical' managers and engineers from their academically trained colleagues while, at the same time, linking them to the production workers. Even when comparing themselves to manual workers, these British engineers claim superiority only in skill – 'I can do their job, they can't do mine' – almost never in terms of qualifications.

In some ways this cult of practicality probably encourages engineers to downplay the value of their technical training, especially in departments such as R & D. But its pervasiveness does suggest one reason why employers have failed to impose the professional division of labour, and why the institutions have received relatively little support from practising engineers.

FROM KNOWLEDGE TO TRUST

What, then, does divide senior engineers from junior technical staff, and technical staff from craftworkers if, as we have seen, engineers themselves insist on the continuities in the knowledge between themselves and manual workers? Instead of looking at the nature of the skills engineers possess, we need to look at the nature of the jobs that engineers do. If there is one common denominator underlying the range of activities performed by the engineers I described in the last chapter, it is not a coherent body of intellectual knowledge, but the degree of discretion that is built into their jobs. This varies, of course. There is more discretion in R & D than in the drawing office, and I shall document these differences further in the next chapter, but in comparison with manual workers, engineers have considerable autonomy on the job. Engineers have the freedom of the factory, as Joe Brown did. They are responsible for the design of valuable machinery, for preparing estimates that are critical to the companies' survival, or simply for negotiating with manual workers about the daily practices of production. Some of these jobs require more technical skills than others, but all of them are important to the company and someone has to be trusted to carry them out without the close control that shapes the life of the typical manual worker on the shop-floor.

There are other workers, of course, who cannot be directly supervised. Some of the maintenance workers, even janitors, have the freedom of the factory, but they are relatively easily replaced, and the jobs with which they are entrusted are much less critical. What characterises engineers is that they are trusted with jobs which are important to the profitability of the firm.

Instead of understanding the hierarchical division of the technical workforce – craftsman, technician, engineer – as a hierarchy of skill categories, we need to see it instead as a hierarchy of discretion, a segmentation of employees by varying degrees of employers' trust (Fox, 1974; see also Kanter, 1977, ch. 3). Part of that discretion, the ability to carry out a piece of technical work without guidance, does depend on an employee's technical competence. But most workers, including engineers, have far more knowledge than they use on the job.[16] Even the most junior graduate engineer has as much formal technical knowledge as a senior engineer. What is missing in management's eyes is the responsibility to use it appropriately in a world where technical knowledge is only a small part of the skills necessary to be successful in getting things done.

Some autonomy can be forced on management. If employees are powerful enough, management may have no alternative except to 'trust' them. This was the source of the discretion and autonomy of the nineteenth-century artisan. But for engineers, that discretion is granted to a 'responsible' segment of the labour force, to get the tasks done as efficiently as possible. The deskilling of craft workers, so central to the development of the engineering occupation (Braverman, 1974; Noble, 1977), was an attempt to shift control of important production and design activities from little trusted workers to more trusted ones. The concept of management taking over the activities of conception and planning is misleading if taken to mean that these activities were carried out by managers. These tasks came to be carried out by workers tied to management by promotion prospects, by the material privileges of 'staff' positions, and the ideological constructs surrounding the difference between working with one's head rather one's hands.

How is such a trusted labour force secured? Partly by these kind of rewards, but equally importantly by selection and training mechanisms. Industrial training and internal promotion allow managers to create trustworthiness by controlling the motivational system and filtering out those they don't want.

Characteristics of the British System

The distinctive aspect of the British system is that British employers, unlike their American counterparts (Edwards, 1979; Pfeffer, 1979), are reluctant to let the university system pre-select 'engineers' to be placed immediately in responsible positions. In the United States, the professional engineer recruited from the university became the normal model of trusted worker. American employers willingly accept the products of professional schools because they assume that the process of self-selection and prior socialisation will already have developed 'appropriate' values (Blau and Schoenherr, 1971; Kanter, 1977). Consequently less external control is needed inside the company. In the United Kingdom a different system has emerged. British employers, having less faith in the educational system, prefer to see how technical staff perform on the job.

Most British companies recruit all engineers into junior technical positions. If junior staff are judged worthy, they can be promoted, given the pay and autonomy of an engineer, and have their work organised to suit. If not, then they can be kept longer in lower grades with appropriate supervision. The system permits the employer to promote only those technical staff judged both *technically competent* and *responsible*.

Employers seek not pure science but technical knowledge responsibly applied in their interests. That such knowledge is sometimes called 'science', as opposed to craft or technique, is a product of the way in which universities, particularly in the United States, legitimate the vocational training they offer. The professional strategy itself often generates science – educational science, nursing science, even management 'science' – but there is little hard evidence that exposure to such science is more productive than practical training on the job (Berg, 1970; Collins, 1971). Its acceptance as science simply confirms its acceptance as knowledge which significantly differentiates the labour market. The historical and social contingencies which led to the educational system becoming the source of trusted employees in the United States and France also ensure that such employees will legitimate their position in the rhetoric of science. In Britain, different circumstances led to a different pattern.

This is not the place to trace the historical relationship between British industry and the higher education system, but a number of points need to be made.[17] The relationship between academe and industry in England has never been so close as on the Continent or in the United States. The state in Britain did not use the universities as a source of a new industrialising élite as it did on the Continent (Crawford, 1984; Loveridge, 1983), nor were the business and professional institutions ever able to secure as much control over the universities as they were in the United States (Noble, 1977). Instead, British universities, particularly the older ones, have traditionally trained administrative and commercial élites rather than produce technical staff for industry.

The low status of industry in British life has served both to repel graduates and permit the universities to ignore the needs of industrial employers (Wiener, 1982), and British higher education remains consistently less vocational than comparable American or European institutions, even with the development of the polytechnics. In consequence, or perhaps in parallel, industrial employers have come to regard university education as alien to the practical needs of industry and to see its graduates as lacking appropriate training.

This is not to say that estrangement from the university system is the only factor encouraging British employers to resist occupational differentiation. There are significant advantages to a system which relies heavily on internal recruitment and promotion. For example, internal recruitment reduces the heavy costs of recruiting, screening and training technical and managerial staff.[18] Internal recruitment also gives flexibility to bureaucratic pay systems. Since job grading systems make raising wages to meet market demand difficult, salaries become one of the last factors adjusted to meet labour shortages (Mace and Wilkinson, 1977). In fact Metalco's technical unions resisted any attempt by the company's grading committees to consider market factors when grading a position. Internal labour markets mean that staff shortages can be met by promoting someone for whom the new position will automatically provide a pay increase.[19] Occupational differentiation would only weaken employers' flexibility.

On the other hand, internal labour markets have traditionally been regarded as inefficient unless a company needs job- or company-specific technical skills (Doeringer and Piore, 1971). A large company in a small and very specialised industry might have no choice but to grow its own engineers, but where an engineer's expertise is general, no one company should want to pay training costs when another might get the return. In the early days of the American electrical industry, General Electric was its own 'university' (Noble, 1977), but American industry rapidly externalised its training costs to the universities, where the costs are borne by the state or by potential engineers themselves. British industry, instead, has tried to externalise its training costs by reliance on industry-wide training levies which equalise the costs of 'general' industrial training. Given the mutual unwillingness of universities and employers to accommodate to each other's demands, such a system provides a functional alternative to the vocational training provided by the higher education system in other countries. Only reluctantly are industry and the universities developing a mutual accommodation.

This system of training and recruitment is maintained by employers for their own reasons, but their action is not entirely unilateral. Both shop-floor workers and many technical workers have also resisted occupational segmentation.

British shop-floor workers are well organised and have been able to constrain management's organisation of even its technical and supervisory staff. At one Metalco division, manual unions had won the right to reserve first line supervision positions for those promoted from the shop-floor, a practice fairly common in British industry (Finniston, 1980, p. 56). And the negative attitude of manual workers to the cultural styles of many university graduates also generated friction. UKAPE[20] recognised the problem in its report to the Finniston Commission when it argued that the shopfloor experience of a boy between ages 15 and 18 or thereabouts was absolutely vital. Not just because that was the age when he could pick up all the wrinkles quickly but that was also the age when the tradesmen would willingly, easily and proudly pass on their knowledge. Bring a young man back from University at age 22 and the magic has gone. Communication between the tradesmen and the graduate is very difficult, whilst that between the tradesmen and the school leaver happens more easily. (UKAPE, 1978, p. 16)

Apprentice-trained engineers not only share much common educational experience with apprentice-trained craftsmen, but are heavily recruited from the working class. Of the HNCs, 60 per cent had come from manual backgrounds, compared to 38 per cent of the graduates.[21] This necessity to get on with the shop-floor derives from the practical activities in which engineers engage. Only where engineers can be insulated from the factory, as is sometimes possible in R & D units, do British employers willingly engage 'high-powered' graduates without concern.[22]

Less qualified technical workers also benefit from a system which does not exclude them purely because of a lack of credentials. The occupational segmentation suggested by the professional associations and training establishments would mean career blockages for all employees not meeting the educational criteria, with subsequent loss of morale and potential discontent.

Under the present system, all technical staff at Metalco expect to be promoted to T4 after a suitable time: failure to promote would indicate the company does not trust them. Even at Computergraph, where the formal panoply of job evaluation is more visible, distinctions between grades reflect personal characteristics. In the test and service departments, for example, they are based on the number of machines an engineer is thought capable of handling. The system creates 'engineers' out of suitable employees regardless of the availability of 'engineers'' positions.

Any attempt to change this system would meet strong resistance from the unions, particularly at Metalco. TASS closely monitors the internal advertisement of positions and is very unhappy when its members are passed over in favour of outsiders. In fact, this issue was central to TASS' strategic change from a 'craft' union, defending the position of draughtsmen by controlling apprenticeship schemes and resisting 'dilution',[23] to an 'industrial' union, willing to recruit all grades of technical and supervisory staff. Since promotion prospects become crucial if occupational solidarity is not developed, TASS, ASTMS and other industrial unions have joined with employers in resisting occupational segmentation. Even when they have agreed to increased educational requirements, they have insisted upon the development of continuing educational opportunities for 'technicians', something very difficult under the present British educational system.

CONCLUSION

British technical workers are not divided up into technicians, technician engineers, and 'proper' engineers as the institutions and the manpower planners would have it. Identification of engineers by qualifications – while useful for certain purposes – says little about occupancy of positions in the division of labour. Rather technical work is an activity open to people with a range of experience and qualifications. Some of those qualifications are tickets that mark one out for an easier ride to the top, and the value of some of these tickets is probably increasing over time, but none has yet secured either a guaranteed or an exclusive trip. In consequence a single segment of the hierarchical division of labour contains a variety of workers, some at the end of a journey that started on the shop-floor or in a machine shop or toolroom, some with a strong chance of reaching the boardroom, some must be technical managers by the age of 35 or consider themselves failures, and some will be happy to retire as senior engineers.[24]

These career lines represent market positions, and they are important in locating opportunities for employees. They are not characteristics of individuals as is implied by some interpretations of Weber's discussion of market capacity (Giddens, 1975), but are socially structured labour markets with boundaries which are more or less permeable.[25] The extent of this permeability or 'closure' is an empirical issue. In Britain there is little closure between technician and engineer positions for employees with technical qualifications, and technical work experience is a substitute (partial at least) for qualifications. A considerable degree of social closure does, however, exist between manual and engineer positions for unqualified employees. Crossing that barrier involves individual social mobility.

The boundaries between labour markets are constructed around perceptions of trustworthiness as well as skill. Employers permit individuals to cross a market barrier if they feel they can be trusted to do the job; the presence of certification of one kind or another is only one indicator of this. The only knowledge that counts in the labour market is knowledge sanctioned by the employer. There is little evidence that engineers are becoming scientists, even in the new industry. And in British industry, at least, even the rhetoric of science is largely absent.

The boundaries of occupational labour markets are social formations which cannot be directly read off from the organisation of work and indeed, as we shall see in the next chapter, may directly constrain the organisation of work itself. However, the boundaries of labour markets are not fixed. Educational changes may force employers to place greater reliance on the educational system as a selection agent. Pressures for occupational closure from government and the institutions still exist, and in some circumstances occupational differentiation may be a more attractive strategy for collective struggle than the wider industrial alliances TASS is currently seeking. In Britain the labour market for technical workers remains a contested terrain.

4 The Organisation of Work

Although historians of engineering like to trace its roots to the civil and military engineering feats of the Romans and beyond (Armytage, 1961), the modern occupation has much closer links to the skilled artisans of the early industrial revolution. These mechanics, self-taught or apprenticed to a trade, were masters of the total labour process. It was they who knew the secrets of how to build an efficient steam engine, design a new loom, or smelt metal. It they were not artisans themselves, employers who wanted to manufacture such products had to hire a mechanic who knew the secrets.

In industries where the craft tradition was strong, metal working and engineering for example, the entrepreneur was often restricted to providing the factory, the machinery and the raw materials. The craftsmen themselves provided and supervised the unskilled labour under a system of internal contracting. Even when employers did hire their own labour and employed a foreman as a supervisor, craftsmen were still able to control the pace of their own work and pass on the secrets of the trade through their own apprenticeship schemes.[1]

The imposition of centralised employer control over the labour process developed gradually and unevenly. In industries such as brewing, soap-making and the chemical industry it developed out of the need to control a continuous-process manufacturing method (Littler, 1982). In others it grew out of a desire to mass-produce standardised items (Sabel, 1982). In still others it was part of a conscious strategy by employers to increase production by overcoming worker resistance to new methods or speed-ups (Brody, 1960; Braverman, 1974). The process often produced considerable worker resistance, and nowhere had the quality of inevitability that has sometimes been ascribed to it.[2] None the less the history of the capitalist labour process can still be read as the history of the gradual replacement of artisan control by a division of labour in which critical design, planning, and supervisory functions become concentrated in

66

the hands of employers' representatives, while execution is left to manual workers whose jobs are increasingly routinised and supervised. Engineers, of course, are those employers' representatives.

The separation of engineering from the craft tradition proceeded on two levels, involving a restructuring of both the technical division of labour and the social relations of production. Engineers, unlike craftsmen, became integrated into the management structure of the firm. As we saw in the last chapter, they are 'staff' not 'works' and the matrix of social relations clearly differentiates them from manual workers. At the technical level, however, the division is not always as sharp. A number of engineers begin their careers in manual work, many more share the early years of their training with craft workers. More importantly, the division is not always clearly maintained in practice. The line between mental and manual, conception and execution, does not neatly demarcate engineers from craft and production workers, at least in Britain.

The division is sharpest in production-oriented functions. Joe Brown's job is to plan work for others to carry out. Richard Taylor's job is to supervise the carrying out of such plans. At Metalco at least, the shop-floor unions protected their members' jobs with a strict ban on engineers working directly on machines, even for simple jobs. Instead they must give instructions to a craftsman or fitter to do the job.

Somewhat paradoxically it is in high-tech industry that engineers do more 'manual' work. R & D engineers, for example, carry out some of their own assembly. The first working prototype is generally put together in the R & D lab and though there is some help from technicians, most of the work is done by the engineers themselves. Test and service engineers also do work which differs only in its complexity and required training from that done by such 'manual' workers as car mechanics.

Most engineers do not see such work as unworthy of them. Many seek it out wherever possible. One evening, after Pressco's production workers had left and there was no one to enforce the union ban on working on machines, I was with two production engineers, their immediate superior, and his boss, as they clambered over one of the assemblies searching for the cause of a systematic defect of which a customer had complained. All showed more enthusiasm for this practical aspect of the job than they did for their regular routines. Even R & D engineers showed special enthusiasm for finally getting a prototype to work. As I suggested in the last chapter, engineers do not differentiate their work from that of manual workers by its intellectual content – non-manual versus manual – but by its skill level and the responsibility with which they carry it out. Many remain fascinated by the physical aspects of the work.

The extent of this engagement in practical activities derives in part from the absence of a clearly defined occupation of technicians working in support of engineers, but it also reflects the extent to which the engineering/craft distinction is a social distinction which is only partially and incompletely manifest in the technical division of labour.

SPECIALISATION AND THE DIVISION OF LABOUR

The division between conception and execution, incomplete as it is, is one form of specialisation, but there are other forms which are not institutionalised in this hierarchical way. As the sketches of engineers' work in Chapter 2 illustrate, engineers' work is very diverse. Richard Taylor's job as a Metalco line superintendent is very different from Alan Sullivan's work in Computergraph's R & D unit, and both are different again from Steve Smith's work in the test department.

In part this reflects their training. British engineers – like their US but unlike their European counterparts – specialise in a variety of fields: there are seventeen different professional institutions of the first rank, each catering to a different engineering speciality, and countless other minor institutions catering for special interests. But even when the skills required are quite similar – the engineers at Metalco are all mechanical or production engineers – British companies characteristically organise engineers into a relatively large number of small technical offices (Sorge and Warner, 1980).

From some perspectives, this specialisation should be a problem for engineers, reflecting, as it does, a falling short of the ideal of the engineer as a Renaissance figure (Florman, 1976). But in most cases engineers themselves do not object to specialisation. British engineers do not typically see themselves as polyvalent generalists, as many French engineers do (Crawford, 1984). Many actually see specialisation as an opportunity rather than a restriction:

> There is always a challenge in specialisation. One can become an expert and still have variety. Specialisation is necessary and requires a person dedicated to specialisation.

or more generally:

> There is a tendency to narrow things down throughout engineering. It applies in all disciplines. There is value engineering, quality engineering and so on. In general it's a good thing. Human knowledge is expanding.

Only 15 per cent of the engineers thought they were overspecialised. Specialisation becomes a problem only when it interferes with a sense of completion of a job. In the years immediately previous to the research, Pressco had divided up its production engineering office into four smaller specialised units: estimating, planning, shop-floor production engineering, and methods engineering, and this caused a number of complaints, particularly from estimators:

> I liked it better the old way. You could follow it through onto the shop-floor and see everything worked all right. You got the satisfaction of seeing it through from start to finish.

What defines completion of a job for an engineer varies. For mechanical designers it is doing a complete drawing rather than delegating it to detailers:

> Until 1972 we had a detailer section and that's not a good idea. When you design something you don't put it all down until you do the detailing yourself, and that leads to problems in explaining. And you miss the satisfactions of being fully involved in the job.

For others, it is signing off a newly tested machine in good working order. A new design, a tested machine, a new production method, a set of times, even an estimate, can all generate a sense of personal satisfaction in a completed product under the right conditions. A sense of completeness does not depend on producing a product for sale on the market, as the evaluative overtones of the Marxist distinction between the technical and social division of labour would seem to imply.

Specialisation is almost certainly increasing for some engineers and under certain circumstances it can weaken the engineers' market position by limiting the range of experience. This was partly the case at Massfas division where the nature of the product line limited engineers' usefulness in other industries. Just as often, however, specialisation can improve an engineers' labour market position, especially if expertise in that area is in short supply.

Whatever critiques can be directed at specialisation from the point of view of some idealised division of labour, specialisation needs to be differentiated from deskilling and proletarianisation, with which it is sometimes confused.

AUTONOMY OR DESKILLING?

Engineers, I argued in Chapter 3, are not trusted by management because they are engineers, they are engineers because they are trusted. The extent of this trust, however, and its manifestation in autonomous work conditions remains a contentious issue in the debate over the position of engineers in advanced society. There are those, like the post-industrial theorists, who argue that science-based industry will increase the number of employees who enjoy the favourable work conditions of the professional. But equally numerous are those who predict that employers will attack this autonomy to reduce labour costs and increase output, that technical workers are in the process of being deskilled.

In the pure 'professionalisation model', autonomy, high job interest and organisational freedom derive from the professionals' monopoly of the critical skills: professionals can dictate the terms of their working conditions to a management whose only function is to provide the support services. Chapter 3 showed that this is an unlikely prospect for British engineering. A modified version of the thesis is more plausible however. It argues that the typical conditions of science-based industry – high rates of innovation, rapidly changing product lines, unpredictability – themselves generate the conditions for increased technical involvement and organisational freedom: that autonomous work conditions are not forced upon employers, but represent the most efficient and profitable mode of deployment of skilled workers under high-tech conditions (Burns and Stalker, 1961; Scott, 1981, pp. 207–33).

The 'deskilling thesis', on the other hand, argues that control, not technical efficiency, is the critical issue in organisational design, and that the same increase in numbers and importance which post-industrial theorists see as marking a new era in autonomous work will cause employers to reassert their control over the labour process by fragmenting engineers' jobs, concentrating the detailed tasks into less technically complex and autonomous positions, and, ultimately, opening the labour market to a cheaper and more controllable labour force of lesser-skilled technicians (Braverman, 1974; Crompton and Gubbay, 1978; Oppenheimer, 1973). Thus the same rationalisation process which ultimately reduced the skilled nineteenth-century craftsmen to the twentieth-century semi-skilled operative will be applied to the work of engineers who were its initial beneficiaries (Stark, 1980).

THE ORGANISATION OF WORK AT METALCO AND COMPUTERGRAPH

There are two dimensions of work that are relevant to these issues: task involvement and organisational constraint. Work may be highly technical, involving and demanding, yet be performed in an intrusive organisational environment in which engineers cannot independently attend meetings, operate without knowledge of the rationale for their job assignments, and feel the organisational structure or their superiors get in the way of doing their job in a satisfactory manner.[3] Similarly the obverse is possible: a job can have organisational autonomy and none the less require little skill and be technically limited, even boring.[4]

Both the professionalisation and the deskilling theses suggest that these two dimensions should be congruent. The former assumes that engineers with high task involvement will work more efficiently under conditions of low organisational constraint. The latter assumes that increased control is necessary to counter the increased unwillingness of workers to cooperate when their tasks have been made more routine and deskilled.

Technical Involvement and Organisational Constraint

These dimensions of organisational life are captured in two scales constructed from the interview responses.[5] The first summarises responses to questions dealing with task involvement: utilisation of skills, the qualifications required to do the job, perceived task autonomy, variety and specialisation of tasks. The second scale deals with reactions to the organisational embeddedness of those tasks: the extent of delegated responsibility, whether the superior always gave reasons for assigned tasks, involvement in the organisation, whether engineers were ordered to do things they disagreed with, and the extent to which the division of labour was well structured. The components of the two scales can be seen in Table 4.1.

The components of each of these dimensions are not perfectly correlated. Test engineers, for example, though scoring high on most aspects of technical involvement, had little variety in their jobs which lowered their overall score. Metalco production engineers had considerable variety in their work, but used few of the skills they had learned in college. But technical involvement – one could almost say technical satisfaction, since engineers valued all of these items – is a complex phenomenon which is better caught by a scale such as this than by a detailed analysis of the separate items with a small sample. The same is true for organisational constraint.

TABLE 4.1　*Components of involvement and autonomy scales*

Scale of task involvement	Metalco	Computergraph
		(Mean Scores)
Feel skill fully utilised	.44	.61
Feel can do tasks own way	.59	.75
Feel free to innovate	.41	.61
Feel have variety of tasks	.52	.55
Feel not overspecialised	.86	.81
Feel no part of job could be done by less qualified	.59	.65
Task involvement scale (Maximum value = 6)	3.4	4.0

Scale of organisational constraint		
Not given reasons	1.37	1.29
Not involved enough	1.62	1.46
Not given enough responsibility	1.80	1.52
Told to do things disagree with	2.12	1.83
Feel have poor division of work	2.18	1.78
Organisation constraint scale (Maximum value = 15)	9.1	7.9

Modes of Work

Underlying the diversity of engineers' work portrayed in the sketches in Chapter 2, two distinct modes of organising technical work can be distinguished. Though the terms are not exact, I will call the first 'insulated involvement', where work is characterised by a high degree of technical involvement and a low degree of organisational constraint; and the second 'constrained standardisation', where there is greater organisational constraint and, at least for non-managerial staff, relatively low levels of technical involvement.

Insulated Involvement

Computergraph's R & D and service departments, and, to a somewhat lesser extent, its test unit, are good examples of a system in which engineers have a high degree of technical control over their own jobs, and are largely insulated from organisational constraints. Engineers in these departments get to use their skills:

> Yes, it's pretty demanding. You don't use all your skills, of course, no one ever does, but it keeps me fully stretched technically. (service engineer)

They are free to innovate:

> That's what they pay us for really. This company's pretty good like that. They encourage you to come up with new ideas. Not all electronics firms do. My last company tended to think that all new ideas should come from the top, but they did a lot of defence work, and they tended towards a civil service mentality. (R & D engineer)

And they are able to do their own job the way they think best:

> I like it that they don't interfere. Of course we have to go through the test manual, and it will get boring after a while, I'm sure, but you can just get on with the job. (test engineer)

As Andrew Hill put it: 'It's very loose here, provided things happen it's all OK.'

In this mode even the less complex tasks tend to be organised so as to maximise the number of technically involving jobs. In R & D, for example, seeing to production details and preparing minor updates are less complex than other tasks, but management resisted rationalising them into specific jobs. Engineers stay with a product through a complete cycle, from the interesting innovation to the more routine modification work. The more quickly new products are introduced and development work finished on old models, the more variety engineers enjoy. Similarly, in the test and service departments the company actively encouraged engineers to develop expertise on a variety of machines to permit flexibility.

> Routinisation and overspecialisation is not much of a problem within our [service] division. I do get the impression sometimes with R & D engineers that they work on a particular area and don't know how the machine functions. We have the opposite tendency. We try and train all our engineers on all the equipment to maintain flexibility.

Engineers do not choose their jobs, but in these departments they have a considerable degree of discretion over how to do them. Work is assigned to them in large chunks: R & D projects often last three years or more, service engineers may be on overseas assignment for months, and testing a machine may take five or six weeks. In such circumstances the prime criterion for evaluating engineers' work, individually or collectively, is whether it meets pre-defined objectives. Does the machine work according to performance 'specs'? Is the customer satisfied? Are the costs right? Can it be produced on time?

Such a system also provides for considerable organisational autonomy. Once peformance specifications, budgets and time schedules are decided engineers are left alone to meet them. Responsibility is delegated to those capable of doing the job whatever their formal position, as this R & D engineer indicated:

> Oh yes, you get given enough responsibility here if you want it. You can get things done and they'll leave you alone if you take the responsibility.

The organisational requirements that management does insist on – time schedules, budget, etc. – are built into the specifications that define the job. There is little need for managerial interference. In the service department, customers define the problems and the engineers solve them. In the test unit the problem is defined by the nature of the job itself. When R & D engineers define their jobs, as they do, as making things to meet specifications – or more colloquially, 'as making for one pound what any fool can make for ten' – they combine technical, cost, time and other specifications into a single set of demands to be met. Whether the company wants an 'all singing, all dancing' machine to sell at a premium price, or one with more limited specifications to fit another niche in the market, is all the same to most engineers if the task provides a significant technical challenge.

The 'space' granted to engineers in these departments does not arise because engineers have a monopoly of knowledge. Computergraph's managers are certainly as technically competent as their staff, but doing the job themselves would undermine the purpose of the division of labour. As one senior manager put it: 'Why employ engineers if you don't leave them to get on with it?' Research and development, service engineering, even testing, is to a certain extent an unpredictable activity. There is no way of knowing *in advance* what kind of problems will occur, or what the most appropriate solutions will be. What can be defined are the required results, and by building the desired results into the nature of the job, engineers can be insulated from day-to-day organisational interference.

Constrained Standardisation

In contrast to the involved autonomy of these electronics engineers, the work of Metalco's planning and design departments can best be described as constrained standardisation.

On the technical level, much of the work is subject to 'formatting'. Because drawings serve as basic records even the most minor modifications have to be re-drawn to meet standards embodied in 'style sheets'. In the planning and estimating department attempts were made to use modular procedures, called 'synthetics', which generate new estimates by combining a number of existing standards. Much of the work passing through the planning department requires only minor changes and the lack of new orders at the time of the research meant that the work was even less technically complex than usual.

Work performed by the most junior engineers is checked at each superior level. Knowledge is always presumed to lie at the top of the hierarchy and only there can authoritative advice be given. The consequence is that technical managers have *more* task involvement than the engineers under them (scale scores of 4.1 and 3.3 respectively), whereas at Computergraph they have the same (scale scores of 4.1). Thus technical autonomy almost always requires becoming a manager. As David Smith, a Massfas engineer, put it, 'I would like to take more decisions but position is important here and my boss often takes the decisions I could take.' An important new job that Pressco was tendering for at the time of the research was estimated almost entirely by the department manager and his senior assistant, to the chagrin of the rest of the department, who felt left out of a project that would have an important impact on the factory's order books.

This limited task involvement occurs in an environment of considerable organisational constraint. Many engineers complain that managers of other departments do not listen to their technical recommendations – only managers can persuade managers – thus staff engineers, however technically qualified or experienced, have to give their recommendations through organisational superiors. Despite Joe Brown's long experience and familiarity with the workings of the factory, his direct dealings with the quality and transport managers (see Chapter 2) were only possible because the problem was limited and didn't involve any major expenditure of resources, and even then he kept his manager closely informed.

This might not matter were the engineers' jobs insulated from the rest of the organisation, but they are closely involved in the main thrust of company production; their activities are intimately intertwined with those of other departments:

> We are supposed to discuss each job with each specialist department but that would take forever. You can't make progress now without interfering in other areas and if you involve them it makes everything top heavy. It leads to problems of coordination. (planning engineer)

Because each technical decision was tied to the functioning of the organisation, managers rarely delegated responsibility.

> My immediate supervisor interferes too much. I wish he'd leave me to get on with it. It usually ends up with a disagreement. ... I

don't feel I get the credit for the job sometimes, my supervisor does. They should let me go to other plants directly and not have supervisors as mediators.

They don't allocate enough responsibility, in fact they take it away from people. They should give them more and then people wouldn't leave at five. It leads to greater interest and responsibility. I don't mind doing extra work but people kick the feet out from under you and then say that you belong at that level. I'd like to work hard and carry the can. It'd be something to work for.

Even senior engineers and managers complain about this bureaucratic style. Andrew MacArthur, an assistant manager, said he lacked the necessary status to deal with other units; and George Wilkins, a technical manager at Pressco division, complained about meddling from above:

You tend to get a lot of detailed inteference. I feel the directors should give the project and let us get on with it, but they meddle and do your job and not their own. It wastes the time of highly paid people.

In comparison to the engineers working in Computergraph's R & D or service departments, these engineers lack both technical involvement and organisational autonomy. In comparison to manual jobs in the same factory, however, even these engineers' jobs are technically involving and have more autonomy. In terms of job satisfaction alone, none of these engineers would have swapped with the shop-floor.

Heterogeneity

These two descriptions represent the two extremes of engineers' work in the two companies, and there is in fact considerable departmental variety (Table 4.2). To visualise these differences they have been plotted, in Figure 4.1, on the two axes of organisational constraint and task involvement. This produces four quadrants corresponding to the boxes of the fourfold table that would be produced if the scales were dichotomised at their means.

The insulated involvement model best describes the upper left hand quadrant (with the test engineers included despite the fact that

TABLE 4.2 *Involvement and constraint scores by department*

| | Metalco | | | | | Computergraph | | | | | |
	Drawing office	*Method*	*Planning*	*Production engineers*	*Production managers*	*Drawing office*	*Production engineers*	*Production managers*	*R & D*	*Test*	*Services*
Total											
Task involvement	3.3	4.3	2.9	3.3	2.4	2.7	4.2	3.3	4.7	3.4	4.3
Organisational constraint	10.5	8.8	9.9	8.2	7.6	8.6	9.5	6.1	7.6	6.4	8.0
Engineers											
Task involvement	2.8	4.1	2.7	3.0		2.7	4.3		4.8	3.5	4.4
Organisational constraint	10.7	9.0	10.0	8.4		9.0	9.5		7.8	6.1	7.8
Managers											
Task involvement	4.0	5.0	3.4	5.0	2.4	3.0	4.0	3.0	4.4	3.0	4.0
Organisational constraint	10.2	8.0	9.8	7.0	7.6	8.0	9.0	6.3	7.3	11.0	10.0

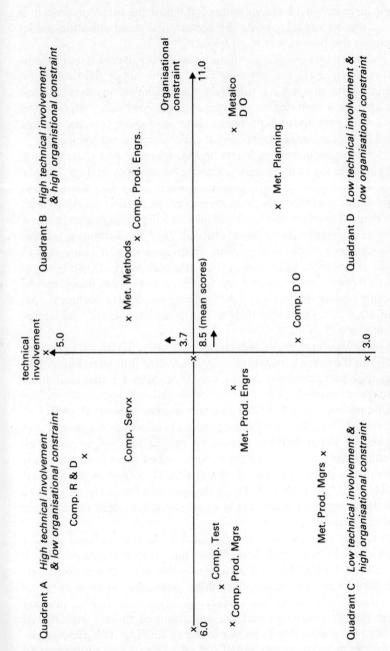

FIGURE 4.1 *Departmental distribution of technical involvement and organisational constraint*

their technical involvement scores fall below the mean because of a low score on variety), while the constrained standardisation model occupies the bottom left hand segment.

There are two quadrants where technical involvement and organisational autonomy are not congruent. In the upper right are those departments which have relatively high technical involvement but suffer from a high degree of organisational constraint, while at the bottom left are those departments who have more than an average level of organisational freedom but little technical involvement.

Metalco production engineers and both sets of production managers fall into the latter category. Having the mobility of their 'rounds' and the freedom to solve problems where they find them, these production engineers and managers contrasted their positions with the manual workers at their machines and the draughtsmen at their boards. 'I couldn't stick it in the office all day,' was a common refrain, referring both to the ever present supervision as well as the lack of physical mobility. As one production engineer put it: 'Down here I'm my own boss. I never see my manager for a week if I'm lucky, and he doesn't bother me anyway.' Not all engineers seek technical specialisation or regard using their technical expertise as the only source of satisfaction available.

For Computergraph's production engineers and Metalco's methods units, on the other hand, technically interesting jobs were losing their organisational autonomy as they were brought under increased direct managerial control.

Computergraph's batch production system generated plenty of interesting technical problems for its production engineers, but expansion depended on increasing production output, and increasingly production engineers were asked to coordinate their activities with the drawing office and R & D instead of 'firefighting' problems as they occurred. These changes, and the attention given to standardising procedures, made the organisation seem more visible and constraining.

A similar process was occurring at the Metalco methods unit, at Massfas division in particular. When the division retreated from a short-lived high-technology strategy to the mass production of its standard items, its expanded methods unit came to be seen as an expensive and overly isolated luxury. Money became tighter, projects more strictly controlled and the unit required to sell, literally, its ideas to the production units as a source of funding. This exposed the engineers to intra-organisational struggles over scarce resources and generated demarcation disputes with the small technical offices attached to the production units. It was this which accounted for the unit's sense of organisational constraint.

ORGANISATIONAL DESIGN

To talk either of the deskilling of engineers, or of their increased autonomy, assumes that the occupation is a meaningful unit of analysis for studying the technical division of labour. As we saw in the last chapter, it is not. In the absence of any strong professional or craft organisations able to insist on uniform privileges for 'engineers', conditions of work are the results of separate bargains worked out in many micro work environments.

One key element in shaping these arrangements is the socio-technical characteristic of each department. In Metalco's planning and design departments, the critical requirement was for standardised output. Plans have to follow strict formats if mass production is to operate successfully. Deviations from the norm need to be rare enough to require a decision by senior management. Strict controls are one way for management to ensure a standardised product. Similarly, mass production also encourages hierarchy. Metalco's managers' habit of 'interfering', or of keeping the most interesting jobs for themselves, was partly justified because few technical decisions can be made without an awareness of the current company policy *vis-à-vis* expenditures and production workers. They were also the most experienced engineers available, with the longest and widest knowledge of Metalco's operating procedures.

On the other hand, the design of Computergraph's new products cannot be profitably standardised, and the company's batch production encouraged flexibility. There is now considerable research evidence that in such conditions a more autonomous form of organisational design is a more efficient way of organising professional and managerial work. Computergraph's management, in fact, consciously tried to avoid bureaucratising its technical departments, not from any humanitarian motives, but because its management believed that this was the most efficient way to manage technical employees. As one very senior technical manager put it:

We try and run the place unbureaucratically if we can. I think the word you social scientists use is 'collegial'. That's probably putting it a bit strong, but all the managerial experts tell us that this kind of structure gets the most out of engineers, and I think it works.

To say that variations in organisational design are partly functions of the socio-technical environment is not to argue for a return to technological determinism. Not only are managers active agents in shaping design, as the quotation above indicates, but these socio-technical environments themselves are the consequence of managerial choice. The mass-production technology of Metalco's Massfas division stems from a marketing decision. A company run by engineers would have been unlikely to abandon its high-technology marketing strategy not least *because* it provided greater work satisfaction for engineers. Similarly much of the declining technical autonomy of the draughtsmen and planners at Metalco can be traced to the absence of new product development, something opposed vigorously by the engineers at policy-making levels of management.[6]

Organisational design is, to a large extent, a matter of political choice, in which socio-technical factors are only one element in the decision (Pfeffer, 1979), and supporters of the deskilling thesis have looked hard for examples of organisational design where management has routinised work for control purposes even when it was not technically efficient (Greenbaum, 1979). Computergraph's design office, however, provides an example where change in the structure of work was moving in the opposite direction.

At the time of the research Computergraph's design office had an organisational structure very similar to the drawing office at Metalco, and for similar reasons. The department's low scores on both technical involvement and organisational autonomy resulted from the increased documentation of design changes introduced in order to permit the subcontracting of increased production runs. But whereas this constrained standardisation style fitted Metalco's overall management style, it did not fit at Computergraph.

Management, therefore, made a conscious effort to minimise the problem. The company had recently disbanded a special modifications unit to share these tasks among the original design team.

It was just too boring to have designers doing modifications all the time. They couldn't sustain motivation and then if they were any good they would leave. So we now send the mods back to the original design team, that way everyone gets to do it. It probably saves time anyway, as the original designer tends to know what needs doing more quickly. (technical manager)

Five senior designers had been moved into R & D to maintain their technical interests and autonomy, and nine contract draughtsmen hired to work on the less complicated design and documentation work.

The innovation likely to have the most significant long-term effect in increasing the quality of the draughtsmen's work, however, is the computer-aided design (CAD) system, being introduced to make standardised documentation easier and less time consuming. Since it would not threaten their own jobs, and they dislike contractors on principle, most regular designers were pleased with the idea.

It looks very exciting. They took me to see a system in operation and I was very excited. It gives the designer a lot of flexibility but gets rid of a lot of the boring bits like modifications, nobody wants to do them. (design engineer)

The CAD system allows managers to build specifications and standardised formats into design parameters in the same way they can be built into R & D project specifications. The machine itself will take over the chore of producing standardised formats and will make minor updates and modifications a simple and speedy task. Though CAD systems are sometimes regarded as a source of deskilling, draughtsmen at the level of Computergraph's mechanical designers see the computer as freeing them of the organisational constraints currently in place to ensure standardisation.

DESKILLING AT METALCO?

To revert to our original discussion of the impact of high-tech industry on the organisation of engineers' jobs, it would appear that there is some support for the modified professionalisation model, that many of the newly created jobs in new industry do have considerable autonomy. It is the constrained standardisation model in place at much of Metalco that fits the deskilling model much better than Computergraph's emphasis on insulated involvement. However, before concluding that engineers working in the former system are in danger of being deskilled, there are two features of the labour market for British technical workers that repay attention: the absence of a clearly defined technicians' occupation, and the existence of career ladders.

The Absence of Technicians

While some jobs at Metalco, or in Computergraph's drawing office, might be characterised as routine and bureaucratised, the system of internal selection and promotion, described in Chapter 3, inhibits substitution of technicians for engineers since it is difficult to create 'technicians'' jobs without affecting the structure of the technical workforce as a whole. The whole rationale for the system of industrial training and internal promotions depends on the use of junior positions as the basis for recruitment. Should employers wish to substitute technicians for engineers, they would have to fail to make expected promotions, which would demoralise a cohort of future technical experts and managers; or lay off engineers and replace them with less qualified staff, something very difficult to do in the face of union opposition and the safeguards of the Employment Protection Act. To reorganise work to suit the characteristics of the incumbents is often easier, especially since British employers assume that work can be equally well organised with workers having various combinations of credentials and experience.

This willingness to adapt the characteristics of work to those of employees is illustrated by the jobs of graduate staff engineers at Metalco. Their task involvement and organisational constraint scores are comparable to their peers at Computergraph, rather than their own HNC colleagues (Table 4.3). This is partly because they are individually granted more responsibility, and partly because they avoid departments, such as the drawing office, which have the least autonomy.[7] In either case, it points to the willingness of employers to change the conditions of work to suit the occupant. In this respect British employers are closer to the Japanese model of flexible deployment of labour without change of organisational position than to the more rigid bureaucratic systems of American employers (Cole, 1979; Edwards, 1979).

Even if technicians were routinely available as an alternative, whether employers would prefer them to engineers would depend not only on technological conditions but on labour costs. Since flexibility is often a virtue, and flexibility implies the existence of surplus skill capacity, it may be worth paying for even if skill is sometimes underutilised. Replacing one category of labour with another is never cost free and is only undertaken if there are *significant* cost savings. If an engineer can be bought for £4650 per year, while 'technicians' have to be paid £3850 (Pressco division 1978 scales for the midpoint

TABLE 4.3   *Qualifications, involvement and constraint*

Qualifications	Metalco		Computergraph		Total
	Engineers only	Total	Engineers only	Total	
		(Mean scale scores)			
(a) Technical involvement					
Less than HNC	4.3	4.5	3.8	3.8	4.0
HNC and equivalent	2.3	2.6	4.0	3.9	3.2
HNC +	3.8	3.6	5.0	4.0	3.7
Professional qualifications	3.2	3.4	5.5	4.2	4.0
BSc (& +)	4.3	3.4	4.2	4.2	3.8
N =	35	56	37	54	110
(b) Organisational constraint					
Less than HNC	10.3	10.2	8.2	7.7	8.3
HNC	10.6	10.6	8.4	8.1	9.3
HNC +	10.9	10.6	11.0	8.7	10.0
Professional qualifications	9.0	8.6	5.0	6.8	8.1
BSc (& +)	6.0	7.3	7.7	7.7	7.5
N =	35	56	37	54	110

of the T4B and the T3B scales respectively), then the costs of instruction and supervision have to be very low to be outweighed by the small savings created by the substitution of labour. Because the costs of junior and senior technical staff are linked by bureaucratic wage systems this gap is not likely to be very wide. Attempts to understand the organisation of work which ignore the structure of the labour supply and the organisation of specific labour markets are bound to be inadequate.

The Importance of Careers

Even when technical reasons make the routinisation of positions profitable, the impact on engineers is not necessarily detrimental.

Management at both companies sought to alleviate routinisation by ensuring promotion possibilities are available so that occupancy of a routine position is only a temporary stop on a career ladder. At Metalco the planning department, which was used as an example of controlled standardisation, has been a traditional source for technical management, and the deployment of qualified engineers as production superintendents was an attempt to expose future general managers to the rigours of production. Computergraph deliberately employs 'overtrained' engineers in the test department with the expectation that they will develop as potential service engineers. Many engineers in turn understand their present position in career terms; as something that can only be evaluated in terms of its future prospects.

> The test lab must be a stepping stone. I get bored but a lot of people are content to stay. Anyone with any ambition would want to move. Most engineers now regard it as stepping stone, but then you need to recruit people who will stay long enough to justify their training.

Many production managers chose the job despite its low technical content because it had better career prospects. At Metalco in particular many engineers see their future in management rather than in greater technical involvement. Climbing the ladder is seen as a way of avoiding routinisation that might accrue to any particular position. Few even of those engineers who feel their skills are underutilised – less than one third – are actually bothered by this; many feel compensated by the career prospects.

John Chamberlain, a Metalco manager, seemed saddened that his engineers did not care more about the low complexity and autonomy of many of their jobs, but he also saw it in career mobility terms:

> Overspecialisation and routinisation does happen. I rode over that by promotions but it must be a real problem here. I see some whose job function has not changed for ten years and I'm amazed they put up with it. There just isn't [sic] the jobs available in a static economy. I got through my previous company quickly on an expanding area and I rode on that. But in a static company like this there isn't the opportunity and it horrifies me that people don't move. People do leave and it's the ones that don't mind that put up with it. It disappoints me that I can't improve it.

As we shall see in the next chapter, which deals with engineers' orientations to management and technical expertise, if technically-involving jobs are not available, engineers are often encouraged to seek positions in general management, even against their wishes. Where promotion does not occur, where individuals are found 'unsuitable' and left in less autonomous and involving jobs, the existence of such a career ladder makes failure an individual problem, rather than one requiring a collective response.[8]

As Chamberlain points out, however, one has to look beyond the individual company to the system as a whole, since careers can be made between companies as well as within them. The total opportunities for the individual engineer have to be seen in terms of the total labour market for technical workers, and it is this which determines whether an individual engineer will suffer the consequences of the routinisation of any particular position. Should particular industries or sectors face decline, or particular skills become obsolescent,[9] then prospects can be dim; if industries are expanding the opposite is the case. In either instance, the effect of a change in the labour process on individual engineers is mediated through the labour market.

The argument for the deskilling of technical workers proceeds by analogy from the case of the skilled craftsmen, but this misunderstands the different positions occupied by the traditional craftsmen and the modern engineer. The deskilling of the craftsmen was designed to *take away* the control craftsmen possessed by virtue of their special knowledge. That control was supported by an occupational organisation, the craft union, which ensured limited access to that knowledge and the way it was used. But British engineers are characterised not by possession of a particular training or set of skills, but by occupancy of a distinctive place in the division of labour. The nature of that place, access to it, even the qualifications, are controlled not by engineers but by employers.

In these circumstances management does not need to control engineers by deskilling and routinisation, since the processes of selection, training and promotion are all designed to ensure that engineers can be trusted to carry out tasks in management's interests. Engineers are part of the salaried workforce whose value to the company tends to be assessed over longer periods of time than are hourly-paid workers. They are treated as an 'overhead' rather than a variable cost. It is not in the employers' interest to deskill and routinise the jobs of employees who are part of the pool from which future high-level managers are to be selected. Though some of these factors originate in the social relations of production narrowly defined – the emergence of engineers is partly a consequence of employers' search for increased capital accumulation by the deskilling of craftsmen – the structure of work is now constrained by the segmentation of the labour market.

POTENTIAL SOURCES OF DESKILLING

Does this mean that there are no tendencies towards the deskilling of British engineers? No, but for the process to take place will require a redrawing of labour market boundaries as well as the standardisation of tasks. The pressures for standardisation of tasks are well understood. The influences reshaping labour market boundaries are of two kinds, the growth of technical unionism and the restructuring of higher education.

The Impact of Technical Unionism

I will discuss the growth of technical unionism in more detail in Chapter 7; here I want only to comment on its impact on the structuring of work. In the first place, it is noteworthy that both technical involvement and organisational autonomy are negatively correlated with union membership. Union membership is strongest among Metalco's staff engineers and Computergraph's design staff, all engineers with low levels of technical involvement and relatively high levels of organisational constraint. Such correlations have commonly been interpreted to suggest that deskilling leads to unionisation (Crompton, 1976), but it is equally likely that unionisation has itself helped contribute to such work conditions.

Though historical research still needs to be done, it is suggestive that it is the draughtsmen, the group with the longest history of unionisation, which show the most elements of rationalisation both at Metalco and Computergraph and elsewhere (Cooley, 1976). The long history of the draughtsmen's union, and its origins on militant Clydeside during the First World War, suggest that unions preceded deskilling rather than followed it. This unionisation, which posed a rare threat to total managerial hegemony over the organisation of non-manual work, may have encouraged management to keep control by transferring several of the more discretionary jobs to engineers located outside the traditional boundaries of the draughtsmen's collective bargaining unit, the drawing office.

Management can also do this more generally. The success of TASS and ASTMS in recruiting all the non-managerial staff at Metalco may be partly responsible for the strength of the company's distinction between management and engineers, and may have reinforced the latter's lack of autonomy by causing management to withhold the most responsible tasks from workers about whose trustworthiness unionisation may have caused some doubts.

On the other hand, much of this reorganisation of work has been terminological rather than deskilling. Many engineers who have benefited from the decline of the draughtsman are ex-draughtsmen now titled as 'design engineers' to fit the needs of bureaucratised grading schemes. The name, however, may be significant if it serves to designate a job as outside of a union bargaining unit, or to allocate other privileges that are attached to titles or grade levels. The old draughtsmens' union, the Association of Engineering and Shipbuilding Draughtsmen (AESD), recognised this when it became TASS, a union self-consciously designed for all technical workers.

The Impact of Educational Changes

Another source of change may be the transformation in training and recruitment that we discussed in the last chapter. If employers recruit university-trained engineers in greater numbers and these graduate engineers become unwilling to spend time in the 'technicians'' grades, 'learning the trade' and doing less responsible tasks, management may have no choice but to generate a whole new occupation of 'technician': an occupation willing to work in more restricted work environments, under greater control, and socialised to have lower expectations. If unions are then led to actively contest the organisation of work, employers might respond by restricting autonomous work even further, perhaps to management positions only.

If this occurs it will not be a response to technical developments but to a change in the mode of education, induced not by the industrial sector of capital but by pressures on the state from other sources. The organisation of the workplace is responsive to forces operating in the larger society – state encouragement of union growth, or the changing education system, for example. One of the major ways in which these external changes impact on the labour process is via the structuring of the labour market. This is not to reject the proposition that changes in class structure are ultimately rooted in changes at the level of production – the arguments for the 'graduatisation' of engineers are, after all, made in terms of improving productivity and employers' long-term interests – but it is to say that such changes do not always *emerge* at the point of production. It is also to say that the labour market position of engineers is a crucial mediating factor between the division of labour and engineers' location in the class structure.

CONCLUSION

There is no simple answer to the question as to whether engineers are gaining greater autonomy or being deskilled. Though Computergraph's engineers as whole had more autonomy than Metalco's, there were sufficient departmental variations to prevent drawing a clear conclusion. Increased autonomy and routinisation can go on at the same time, in the same company, for different groups of engineers. The lack of a strong occupational organisation prevents any collective resistance to deskilling should the latter take place, and attempts to create such organisations – such as the pre-TASS draughtsmen's craft unions – were easily circumvented by employers' capacity to transfer work to non-union groups.

This very lack of occupational control, however, is what makes much deskilling unnecessary from the employers' point of view, since there is little threat to their dominance over the work process. Engineers are useful to employers just because they are a trusted workforce, and attempts to deskill them undermine the mechanisms used to generate that trust. Even when the routinisation of positions is made profitable for technical reasons, such as the need for standardised output, individual engineers are still not necessarily deskilled. As salaried staff, engineers are treated as company employees rather than as the occupants of particular jobs, and their position in the company has to be seen in terms of the range of opportunities available to them. In many cases engineers are routinely promoted through low skill positions as part of the training process, in other cases they are expected to proceed through them as part of a career which stretches into management. Beyond the company, engineers have prospects in other companies and industries too, and their position depends as much on sectoral and industrial growth or decline, as it does on intra-company factors. Only by looking at the total labour market opportunities available can it be decided if deskilling is occurring. Temporary occupancy of a deskilled position as part of the career process is not enough.

5 Experts and Managers

Our discussion of the organisation of engineers' work has stressed the importance of career mobility for understanding their position in the division of labour. In this chapter I want to take that discussion one step further and look at the relationship between technical work and management. This is of central importance for any discussion of the class location of 'experts' in modern society. If engineers are regarded as management, they are usually unambiguously located on the side of capital. If seen as experts, simply a special kind of worker, their location is more problematic.

The question is especially relevant for British engineers since, as we have seen, they do not routinely engage in supervision. Unlike continental or American engineers they are not assisted in their tasks by subordinate technicians whom they supervise. They also differ from their accountant colleagues in finance departments. When qualified accountants in the production division of Computergraph were asked whether they regarded themselves as 'accountants' or 'managers', they found it difficult to answer. To fulfil their functions in financial administration most accountants have assigned to them a small team of clerical staff. To do their job they have to be accountants and managers at the same time. In contrast, at corporate headquarters there were a number of qualified accountants without assistants who self-consciously filled 'staff' positions, serving in an advisory or research role. These disclaimed any management activity. This is what is meant by the emergence of expert staff positions: highly qualified specialists in functions where they are the object of management rather than participants in it.

While it has been argued that engineers as staff specialists are a new phenomenon, dependent on the development of science-based industry (Carchedi, 1977), in fact this is the traditional mode of organising British engineers. As we have seen, junior staff rarely report formally to senior staff; instead, both are coordinated by an office manager. Both manager and staff have similar backgrounds, and while all technical managers, and some general managers, are recruited from technical staff, many engineers do not supervise others.[1]

Since many engineers do not routinely engage in supervision, they cannot be assigned to the middle class or petty bourgeoisie by that criterion alone. This point is important since many continental European writers, particularly Gorz (1976a, 1976b), Carchedi (1977) and Poulantzas (1975), assume that engineers are, or have been, routinely engaged in supervision, and this would seem to be the normal European practice.

There is a constructed history which accompanies most European writings on technical workers which can be summarised as follows:

* * *

In the beginning was the capitalist entrepreneur who ran 'his' factory without assistance. There was the boss, and there were the workers. As the workload increased the boss was forced to take on assistants who served as extensions of the entrepreneur himself. The owner's 'number one assistant' was *Monsieur L'ingénieur*, who needed to be highly educated and of similar, bourgeois background to the entrepreneur himself. He would probably have been trained in one of the state-supported technological institutes provided for such purposes.

With the development of the joint-stock corporation and the rapid expansion in size of the enterprise the entrepreneur's assistant was replaced by a bureaucracy. The size of the organisation meant that many employees no longer had a personal relationship with the boss; the division of labour increased and many of the staff began to fill some of the functions of the 'collective worker' as well. There were more of them, they were more specialised, but they were still linked by common culture, career prospects and function to the top positions of the company. Only in the third stage of industrial capitalism, with the development of ever more specialised and complex technology, does there develop the need for highly, though narrowly, trained specialists; no longer fulfilling any supervisory or coordination role, but simply engaged in collective labour. These are the jobs which are subject to the rationalisation and fragmentation process which is the fate of all such jobs under industrial capitalism. Engineers become technicians, and technicians *are* workers.

* * *

This particular version of the story is derived largely from Carchedi (1977), but a similar version is widely prevalent (Bain and Price, 1972). Whatever the accuracy of such a constructed history for France and Italy – and like many such sociological constructs it is not backed by much historical research – this history is highly implausible for Britain, and to a lesser extent for the USA as well. In both countries there is a long history of non-managerial expert work carried out by engineers.

Recognising the existence of such staff employees, Wright (1976, 1978) has argued that it is necessary to distinguish between 'experts', who differ from manual workers in possessing autonomy in the workplace and some control over the processes of production, and 'managers' who exercise control over subordinate labour. Similarly Poulantzas (1975) argues that emergent 'technicians' in France, while not supervisors, are not – *contra* Mallet (1975) and early Gorz (1967) – members of a 'new working class', but a 'petty bourgeoisie', distinguished from workers by the ideological structure of the manual/non-manual boundary.

Crompton (1976, 1979) has gone beyond these cross-sectional discussions to argue that it is not simply whether non-manual workers *presently* act as supervisors, but whether or not they have realistic *expectations* of doing so during the normal run of their careers that is important for understanding their class positions. Drawing on the work of Roberts *et al.* (1972), she argues that engineering technicians have been proletarianised by being cut off from promotion to managerial positions by the increased use of graduate engineers.

Erik Wright has raised the question of career trajectories briefly in a footnote (1978, p. 73), but failed to draw the appropriate conclusions. The issue is important, however. A career that stretches from lower level technician possessing little autonomy, to higher level staff engineer, to technical and perhaps general manager would pass through three of Wright's 'class locations'. If this were a rare event it would count as an example of social mobility, but as the normal career trajectory for whole categories of employees it would require a radical revision of Wright's argument (Stewart *et al.*, 1980; Spilerman, 1977).

The existence of careers linking 'expert' and 'managerial' positions is also critical for much of the professionalisation literature, which stresses the incompatibility between professionally oriented experts and adminstratively oriented management. The repeated finding that engineers experience low levels of strain has been ascribed to

American engineers' strong commitment to management rather than to their professional peers, a commitment contrasting with that of research scientists (Miller, 1967; Kornhauser, 1962; Perrucci and Gerstl, 1969a). The extent of this commitment to management is such that the creation of 'professional ladders' to reward experts without giving them managerial responsibility has been treated as a form of 'cooling out' for organisational failure (Goldner and Ritti, 1967). British management, however, has less technical training than that of most other countries and this may affect British engineers' orientations, especially in new industry, where technical involvement may offer countervailing attractions.

The choice of career orientation also has consequences for the individual 'equities' in which engineers invest. To become a manager, particularly if this means moving out of the technical function altogether, is potentially to sacrifice the equity built up in technical expertise, even to abandon the intrinsic pleasures of engineering, to develop a 'local' career with the company. However, to deny the temptation of organisational position so as to stay with technical activity is to remain committed to a vocation, to become a 'cosmopolitan', at the risk of being marginal to one's own firm (Gouldner, 1957).

Each strategy requires its own distinctive investment in 'human capital' (Becker, 1964), or equity. The educational certification, experience and personal characteristics that generate rewards in one situation may be different from those that provide returns in others. To put one choice simply and in American terms, should the engineer pursue his MSc in some technical speciality, pursue his MBA, or give his firm undying loyalty?

As 'professional experts' engineers are supposed to possess knowledge which does not depend on particular settings for its practice. This knowledge should enable them to seek advancement through inter-company mobility rather than by organisational career lines. As experts they are expected to have more of an interest in defending their occupational base than in defending their position within a particular company (Larson, 1977; Freidson, 1973; Johnson, 1972).

In contrast, pursuing a career in management supposedly demands a commitment to the organisation. The image of the successful manager has traditionally been that of the 'organisation man' who possesses knowledge of the company's administrative procedures and who sacrifices some of the possibilities of success on the external labour market for the rewards of organisational advancement.

Although company loyalty is no longer seen as the virtue it was in the early fifties (Whyte, 1956; Kanter, 1977), it is still generally assumed that managerial careers are more closely tied to organisational rather than occupational success.

These alternatives have been available to engineers since the beginning of modern industry. Indeed the modern occupation can only be understood as an attempt to keep them in harmony, but the growth of science-based industry is seen as threatening a delicately maintained balance.

From very different perspectives, both Mallet (1975) and Freidson (1973) also make a radical distinction between technical work and management. They assume that management and technical functions can be separated at the level of organisational structure and that either management positions are not available to technical workers, or are available so infrequently as to create only a sense of false promise. Or equally, that such workers have no interest in leaving their specialities for management positions. In contrast Galbraith (1967) sees engineers as attracted into management to secure increased control over technical resources, the facilitating power that accrues to those higher up in hierarchical organisations. Recognising that autonomy is not available to workers, engineers seek the control over productive resources, including labour, exercised by managerial agents of capital.[2]

In this chapter I look first at engineers' orientations to technical work and managerial careers, then at the varying equities and career strategies that accompany such orientations, and finally examine the effect these have on engineers' attachment to their present companies as loci for their careers.

MANAGERS OR EXPERTS?

There is a sharp difference between the two companies in the engineers' orientation to management. At Metalco most of the staff engineers, and all of those under thirty, have managerial ambitions, while at Computergraph only half have such ambitions. Only a third of Computergraph engineers were willing to consider leaving the technical departments to pursue a managerial career while three-quarters of Metalco engineers were willing to do so (Table 5.1).

TABLE 5.1   *Level and locus of ambition of staff engineers (per cent)*

	Metalco	Computergraph	Total
Level of ambition			
Senior engineer	17	54	36
Office manager	40	35	38
Senior management	43	11	26
Locus of ambition			
Willing to leave technical department	71	30	50
N =	35	37	72

Both differences significant at the .05 level (χ^2).

Organisational Engineering at Metalco

Metalco was not a company to find engineers committed to a life of intense technical activity. Though isolated pockets of technical innovation could be found – remnants from a previous marketing strategy at Massfas, potential harbingers of a new one at Pressco – a commitment to technical work *per se* was out of place at both factories. Engineers, *qua* engineers, are largely invisible to higher management: in Pressco division engineers are buried at the bottom of long managerial ladders and isolated in a number of small offices; at Massfas they are tucked away in tiny numbers in production units or isolated in separate profit centres. Non-managerial staff at Metalco are assistants helping to keep the main production business of the company going.

The low technology of both divisions resulted from deliberate marketing strategies, and as such reflected basic managerial assumptions about the role of engineering in the firm.[3] Higher management's attention was on production figures, sales and short-term costs. In none of these areas did engineers play a central role.

In any area of Metalco, but particularly in engineering, securing visibility meant acquiring managerial status. If the company wished to keep a technical specialist from leaving – a rare occurrence – it often had to create a new management position to do it. There was no such thing as a technical ladder. All the outward signs of company favour and status – special dining-rooms, reserved car parks, company cars, secretaries, offices and so on – were reserved for managers.

One young engineer, who was already making a success of production management, put the prevailing ethos this way:

> There is a feeling in this line of country and amongst these people that promotion is natural, that every few years one is expected to expand one's area of responsibility. First that means management, then it means higher management.

For some engineers management offered its own job rewards, though Sam Young is unusual in liking paperwork:

> I'd like to be a manager someday. I like the responsibility and I like writing up reports, I actually enjoy it.

Paul Radley and David Smith were more typical in seeking the authority attached to the job.

> Managers get to see what's going on from beginning to end and are able to do something about it. I like that. If you aren't a manager you get chewed up if something goes wrong and you can't do anything about it.

> I'd like to be a manager. It's running one's own show. It's the challenge of running the whole thing, the responsibility.

Others sought managerial position because they did not want to spend their lives in technical work. Paul Higgins, a young graduate, thought he was better suited to managerial work than to technical specialisation.

> I'd like to be a manager so I can have more say over my immediate environment. I'd prefer to have influence over an area I can control than a technical job I couldn't do well. I don't want to be stuck purely on the technical side. I'd prefer to be involved with people who make things.

Such comments were particularly common among engineers such as Ken Watkins, who had already moved away from technical specialisation into production management.

I went into production management because I prefer working with people and the priorities of production to simply solving technical problems.

Management has it own joys and for many it is an activity desirable in its own right. Engineers are not scientists.[4] An engineering training, even a university education, is no guarantee of a technical commitment. For many engineers it is simply an entry ticket to a good job in industry, one with the possibility of career advancement. Only 33 per cent gave 'interest in mechanical work or science' as their primary reason for becoming engineers. Far more said they had done so because they had friends or relatives in industry who recommended it. Others simply saw it as a good career. These were the engineers who saw themselves as the general staff of industry. What they wanted was a good job with prospects of promotion, preferably, though not necessarily, in a technical area.

Wanting to be manager does not mean that engineers preferred managerial activities *per se*. Though the 'professionalisation' of management has reinforced the British tradition of generalist administrators with little functional expertise, management and technical work have not become entirely separate functions. Though management is considered a distinct kind of work – with the social distinctions surrounding managers at Metalco it could hardly have been otherwise – at the level of departmental manager the labels 'engineer' and 'manager' can coexist.

As we saw in the last chapter, one reason that Metalco engineers wanted to become managers was that being a manager was a necessary prerequisite to getting even *technical* things done, since managers at Metalco had more technical involvement than their staff. As one assistant manager put it:

No, I don't think I'd prefer a technical staff position. I like to be involved and be able to present opinions and like to hear the issues.

Technical management positions, however, are in short supply, and above that level management loses its technical flavour. As a senior technical manager at the company remarked:

A good engineer in this company is an ex-engineer. If you make it into management then you have to learn to forget the past or you get stigmatised. In Germany the technical director has a drawing board in his office. In England you have to keep convincing them [the other executives] that you know more about the company than simply how to fix its machines. They don't ask the senior accountants to forget their skills. In fact they put them on the Board because of them. Not with engineers. Not here anyway.

Steve Head, who had recently left the methods department for a production control manager's job in the mills, thought that this was a problem that extended further than Metalco.

One of the crying shames for all engineers in all companies is that it's a dead end job. It's very interesting, it's a taxing job, but there are very few opportunities for advancement. The company can only support a limited number of development engineers. There is no progression. Some of the engineers are content with the job satisfaction and the life-style but I wanted to control what projects are done and I couldn't do it in the technical sphere though I would have liked to. Metalco doesn't recognise professional engineering qualifications. I was the top engineer in the methods department at Massfas at 29 and I was paid less than a colleague who was a foreman. Production is the kingpin at the end of the day. R & D is considered a nuisance.

Fifteen per cent of the engineers, however, did resist the temptations of managerial promotion and had a career orientation to technical work. Most of these were found in the methods department, which had the highest levels of technical involvement. Matthew Berry was one of them:

The problem with being promoted here is that it means being an administrator 80 per cent of the time and I'm not interested. I'd like to organise but not do all of the administration. I like designing machines, it's the pay that's the problem. I thought at one time that it would be nice to be a manager, but I didn't know what it meant. Now I know and I don't like it. I can't understand what all this ambition to be a manager is about. You just need an incentive to do the job, just a fair wage. It seems a shame to have to do a job where there is less value to the company just for the reward.

Tom Stockbridge, the union representative in the department, put it even more strongly:

> I don't want to go into management. [Metalco] have made mistakes in the past in creating management positions to satisfy salary demands but now they are cutting back on those positions. To progress you need to be in production. Of the sixteen technical apprentices I've seen here ten have reached high management positions in production. A lot go into management for the money but you lose satisfaction. In my twenties I wanted to be a manager to give the public impression of success but now I realise that to be a manager just for the money isn't worth it.

These were the technical experts who found the administrative and people orientation of managerial positions alien to their interests. This is what many consider to be the 'typical' engineer's mentality – but it was rare in this form at Metalco.

Berry and Stockbridge were not rationalising away a failure to be promoted. Many others with much less chance of promotion held strong managerial ambitions, and there probably would have been more engineers with this technical orientation were it not for the general dissatisfaction over pay. Ninety-six per cent of Metalco engineers felt badly paid compared to 30 per cent at Computergraph, and many sought managerial positions as the only way of securing a pay rise.

To assess the extent to which managerial ambitions were created purely by the distribution of monetary rewards, engineers, both staff and managerial, were asked if they would prefer to be technical experts rather than managers, if they could be rewarded adequately. Forty-four per cent responded positively to the idea of technical specialisation, but most found the possibility of being rewarded for staying in a technical position somewhat hard to imagine:

> It's difficult to think of being given the pay for staying in technical work. I'm used to the attitude that after technical work comes management, but if we did have the structure then I would be interested. It would be a challenge to improve the situation. You need the job interest and job content to match the salary but there are possibilities, it's not as low as it looks or is treated.

Certainly management was seen to have some disadvantages, even for those hoping to manage some day (Table 5.2). The responsibility was seen as burdensome, and nearly a quarter of those with managerial ambitions expressed some concern about the consequences for their relations with friends and colleagues. The common recruitment pattern and the undifferentiated labour force generated a sense of 'comradeship' which created ambivalent feelings about promotion. None the less these were not strong enough to divert their aims.

Metalco engineers are not extremely ambitious, but they do routinely seek management positions as part of their definition of a successful career. They see the organisational structure granting autonomy, power and extrinsic rewards only to these who 'make it' on the organisation's own terms – to those who become managers. Except for the few in the methods department, Metalco engineers are organisational employees for whom management is simply a more desirable job.

The selection process is too restrictive and the social boundaries surrounding the positions too great, for management to be treated as

TABLE 5.2   *Disadvantages to management: Metalco staff engineers (per cent)*

Disadvantages to management	Favour technical work over management at equal pay			
	No	*Ambivalent*	*Yes*	*Total*
Time away from family	6	20	0	9
'Responsibility'	28	40	0	28
Prefer technical work	6	10	100	19
Dislike 'political' activities	6	10	0	6
Not enough pay or job security for management	11	0	0	6
Problem of social mobility	22	10	0	16
None	44	10	0	28
N =	22	10	4	36

NOTE   Columns may add to more than 100 per cent because of multiple responses.

the vertical extension of the engineering ladder, but in a sense it is. For most of the staff engineers, becoming a manager is the desirable next step. The bureaucratic structure of Metalco makes such orientations inevitable.

Technical Experts at Computergraph

At Computergraph there is a different story to tell. Engineers are not ancillary to the main production function – there are almost as many engineers as manual production workers. Far from being simply aides to management, technical staff helping accomplish the major task of production, engineers, especially those in R & D, design, test and service, are central objects of company concern. They *are* the workers who get things done.

It is possible to achieve financial and status rewards in a technical function at Computergraph in a way not imaginable at Metalco. The valued technical specialist who is not considered 'management potential', or who does not want the job, is a fairly frequent phenomenon. Only 55 per cent of the engineers had managerial ambitions, only a third were willing to pursue them outside technical departments, and half of these were in production engineering. Outside the production units, only service engineers were willing to leave technical work in any number (40 per cent) – and then to go into the technically oriented sales function.

Technical work provides a powerful competitor to managerial attractions, especially for R & D engineers. Alan Sullivan, who had previously been project manager but who had voluntarily given up the position, commented:

> I wouldn't want the chief engineer's job. I don't much like having to get people to do things and being in the middle of chaos all the time. I was once the project manager of the — but I left to do the software. The project manager's job involves dealing with too many fools. Each engineer should be made responsible for a small section of a project and deal with the drawing office and other departments directly. There is not enough delegation of responsibility. I'd much rather be a technical consultant. I like to do my own thing and not have my tail wagged the whole time. I like to be buffered from autocratic despots.

Increased responsibility was the prime cause of negative reactions to management positions (Table 5.3). 'Being responsible', taking responsibility for other persons' actions, was the main function of management in most engineers' eyes and, where their own work was sufficiently absorbing they did not wish to be blamed for the activities of 'fools'.

Some engineers rejected management out of a dislike of dealing with interpersonal relations, confirming the classic image of the engineer as preferring to deal with 'things' rather than people.

> I'd like to be a technical consultant, to stay on the technical side not the managerial side. It's a personal thing, I'm not capable of being responsible for a lot of people's work. I'm competent technically but not with dealing with people. It *shouldn't* be a disadvantage, a firm needs people on both the technical and people side, but in practice they reward managers, those who are good with people and those who are good politically. (Tony Stevens, R & D engineer)

TABLE 5.3   *Disadvantages to management: Computergraph staff engineers (per cent)*

| Disadvantages to management | Favour technical work over management at equal pay | | | |
	No	Ambivalent	Yes	Total
Time away from family	8	0	9	3
'Responsibility'	42	60	47	49
Prefer technical work	0	10	53	24
Dislike 'political activities	17	10	7	11
Not enough pay or job security for management	0	0	7	3
Problems of social mobility	0	0	0	0
None	42	30	7	24
N =	12	10	15	37

NOTE   Columns may add to more than 100 per cent because of multiple responses.

Dealing with people is central to the managerial project, while dealing with things is the major focus of technical work.

But rejecting management for technical work does not mean that such engineers are entirely happy with the alternatives available to them. Bob Johnson was an older technical specialist on the same team as Alan Sullivan, and a recognised company expert in his field:

> I've got to a dead end in my career and I don't like it. I can't go any further on the technical side of engineering and management doesn't interest me. I could do some of it, the planning, the costing etc., and do it effectively, but it would bore me. I would like a more senior position in a technical capacity but it doesn't exist in this country. When chief engineers were technical people, then I wanted to be chief engineer. But now it's purely administrative and managerial. I don't know, it's a problem. All engineers ask themselves the same question, whether they want the administration.

Others, however, accepted the reality of their limited prospects, and saw the value of low-level management positions in pragmatic terms:

> Ideally I'd still like to be an engineer but paid accordingly. There shouldn't be a big difference between management and the technical side. Chief engineers are involved technically as well as doing management. One wants some management. I'd like some control, but I don't want to avoid all engineering activities. Chief engineer is the highest I could or would want to get. At the other companies it may be different but here it's political. There's more emphasis on memos and propaganda than on the technical aspects. Stabbing people in the back gets you ahead. (senior project engineer, R & D)

This technical orientation on the part of highly educated electronics engineers involved in high technology projects might have been expected. But engineers who had developed their mechanical design skills through experience also shared this orientation.

> I don't want to become a manager. I've no ambition for that. You become divorced from the job you're trained to do and become a politician. You ponce [pimp] on other people's ability. You meddle in design. I only get satisfaction from creating something. (Jim Thomson, mechanical designer in R & D)

However, designers with similar training and experience to Thomson but who remained in the drawing office were more likely to have managerial ambitions than were the electronics engineers. Like the engineers at Metalco they sought autonomy and power which only management could provide in their departments. Ray Braithwaite was a union representative in the office but he none the less harboured a yen to be a manager.

> I'd like a position of responsibility like a section manager. I'd like to control people, and make things work and sort out problems.

Even these designers, however, restricted their ambitions to the technical function. Only a very few (17 per cent), almost as few as the R & D engineers (10 per cent), were willing to leave the technical function to achieve their goals.[5] On the other hand, 86 per cent of the production engineers were willing to leave technical work to achieve their ambitions. In departments where technical involvement or organisational autonomy were least available, Computergraph engineers, like those at Metalco, sought managerial positions.

Although many of Computergraph's technical staff had a very different attitude to management than those at Metalco, managers did not. Only two would have preferred a technical position at a similar level of pay, and both were in R & D. The rest had either consciously chosen management for its intrinsic satisfactions, or had come to prefer it with experience. Keith Simpson, a project manager in R & D, had consciously chosen a managerial career:

> I wouldn't want to be a technical specialist, I'm not cut out for it. I like to be involved with people and organisations, not just the technical side.

Others regarded it as a new challenge, or had learned to appreciate its pleasures.

> I prefer management to the technical side. I've got more to learn. I learnt a lot about electronics in the test lab. I used to work long hours to learn things. It helped me get promotion as well. I always felt I was learning and now I want to learn about management. When I joined Computergraph I had no plans to be a technical supervisor. I thought ambition would lie in the training department when I'd picked up the background [he had spent some time

as teacher], but that changed after a couple of years. Circumstances change attitudes.

Thus Computergraph's management was considerably more ambitious than its engineering staff as a whole. Fifty-nine per cent of managers aspired to top positions in the company as opposed to only 11 per cent of the staff engineers.

This difference in type and level of ambition, which did not exist at Metalco, is particularly paradoxical since Computergraph's senior management had more technical training than those at Metalco. R & D, whose engineers had the least ambition for management, was also the department which served as the breeding ground for new management talent. In new industry trained engineers are acquiring more and more influence and a technical background is becoming essential for top executive positions.

At the same time, however, there is even more opportunity to practise technical skills and become a technical specialist. It is this which creates the dilemma. As Tim Williams, a production engineer who had gone back to college to obtain a degree after starting his career with an HNC, put it:

I don't know about the future. One side says 'go on to be chief production engineer and higher'. The other side says 'specialise'. You have to specialise highly or go into management otherwise there is too much competition from younger people.

At Computergraph the distinction between management and technical work was seen as one between occupations rather than between levels of control. Consequently many engineers talk about 'sides', and emphasise the individual choice involved. Computergraph's electronics engineers can have technical responsibilities and control over their work without being a manager. They can also be well paid in a technical staff position. This is not because Computergraph had a technical ladder – true only in R & D – but because, in comparison to Metalco, it not only paid staff well,[6] but granted most of them technical involvement. Thus many of the pressures that pushed Metalco engineers towards management were absent at Computergraph. Another, perhaps more revealing, indicator is that none of Computergraph's staff engineers wanted to be anything higher than head of a department, most often of their own department. Only managers had higher ambitions. At Metalco, on the other hand, nearly 50 per cent of the staff engineers had ambitions to reach company director, if not higher.

Engineers at Computergraph also make a sharp distinction between management and technical activities. Both are seen as having their place, both as having their attractions. They are 'sides', not hierarchical relations. It is possible to envision an occupational career in technical work as an alternative to an organisational one, even though it will not be as well paid. At Computergraph, therefore – though not at Metalco – there is the clash between the technical interests of the engineers and the reward structure of the company predicted by the 'professionals in a bureaucracy' literature, and observed by Gerstl and Hutton (1966) for their sample of members of the Institute of Mechanical Engineers. However, it is not the engineer's possession of formal skills in high technology that is responsible for this clash, but the organisational structure of the company.[7]

Managers and Experts

The prediction of a potential conflict between the engineers' 'expert' orientation and company reward structures that define success in managerial terms assumes that engineers possess a fixed orientation to technical work which conflicts with organisational needs. There is some of this conflict at both Computergraph and Metalco, but more typical is a *congruence* between the personnel needs of the companies and the orientations of the engineer. At Computergraph, where the company needed technical expertise, engineers were more committed to its practice; at Metalco, where the company professed a need for more technically-trained general managers but fewer 'experts', its engineers seemed happy to oblige.

What accounts for this congruence? One possible explanation would be self-selection. There is no sure way of knowing this, since retrospective questions about reasons for becoming an engineer are undoubtedly contaminated by present orientations – though, for what they are worth, they do indicate that some degree of self-selection does take place. And surely no engineer would join Metalco expecting a career at the frontier of technological development. In addition to self-selection, however, engineers' orientations are shaped by the organisational structure. Both companies deliberately organised work to motivate engineers in their desired direction. Metalco's hierarchical structure offered those who moved into management the rewards, not only of money and status, but of technical autonomy as well. At Computergraph, on the other hand, technical satisfaction and autonomy were available to many staff engineers and so, to a degree, were material rewards.

The assumption that technical and managerial orientations are somehow incompatible involves the same kind of error incurred in treating knowledge as an autonomous source of labour market power. Engineers seek, among other things, job satisfaction from their employment. While predisposed by their training to seek it first in technical work, they can readily be persuaded to seek it in managerial positions. Engineers have to respond to a market dominated by the interests of employers. Technical orientations are not so fixed as to be impervious to employers' distribution of rewards and advantages, particularly when conditions of work, task autonomy and so on, vary as part of the rewards being offered. Engineers are no more resistant to the blandishments of such rewards than any other kind of employee.

Achievements and Expectations

So far we have looked at orientations and ambitions. I would also like to have assessed the realistic chances of these ambitions being realised, particularly for the different educational categories in the sample. The declining rate of return to certain low-level qualifications – the 'dequalification of labour' in Carchedi's terminology – and the blockage of promotion prospects for such labour has been widely assumed.[8] The projected decline in prospects for technicians – in which draughtsmen and others with HNCs are included – has been seen as part of the general proletarianisation of lower-level non-manual labour (Crompton and Gubbay, 1978), and as a cause of increased militancy (Roberts *et al.*, 1972). Although the discussion in Chapter 3 suggested employers have resisted the closing of entry to engineer positions, it might still be the case that prospects for promotion to management are declining in the face of increasing graduate recruitment. While to assess such structural changes would require a different kind of study from that undertaken here, a number of observations can be made using the material available.

Although I have no way of measuring the objective chances of the various groups actually reaching their goals, the changing educational structure itself makes it unwise to infer the experiences of the present cohort of young engineers from the experience of their elders. Though there is an increase in the graduate intake for junior engineers – all of Metalco's graduates were under 35 – and there is no doubt that the company treated them as high-flyers, it does not follow that this will affect the promotion chances of previous cohorts of technical staff with lesser qualifications. It is just as true to say that many of those now obtaining degrees would, prior to the sixties' expansion of formal education, have received HNCs. Given employers' general unwillingness to accept formal qualifications at face value, the mere possession of a degree is unlikely to assure success.

Moreover the increased recruitment of graduates is causing companies such as Metalco to widen their vision of the areas in which engineers might fruitfully be employed. There were signs that the company was encouraging engineers to move into sales departments and other areas where they had not previously been engaged. Engineers often made such moves as managers or with good expectations of a managerial promotion.

Certainly the HNC engineers felt that they had reasonable chances of reaching their managerial ambitions, though they were somewhat less sure than their graduate colleagues. At Metalco, for example, 79 per cent of the HNC engineers who hoped to reach managerial positions thought they had a fair or good chance of achieving their ambitions (Table 5.4). At Computergraph the impact of education for those seeking management positions was somewhat stronger. Only 18 per cent of those with HNC qualifications or less felt they had a good chance of achieving even a middle-level managerial position, while all of the graduates did so. (However, these are quite small percentages of the total numbers in each category since many did not want to leave technical work at all.)

Success

All this is not to say that education does not make a difference in successful achievement, particularly if we look at organisational positions as a single ladder rather than a dichotomy of technical and managerial positions. To measure relative success in climbing such a ladder a three-value scale of success was constructed describing those engineers who were doing significantly better than other members of their age cohort, those who were doing about average, and those who

TABLE 5.4 Effect of education on career expectations of staff engineers (per cent)

	Staff engineers Metalco						Staff engineers Computergraph					
	Less than HNC	HNC	HNC +	Professional qualifications	BSc	Total	Less than HNC	HNC	HNC +	Professional qualifications	BSc	Total
No ambition	0	14	43	50	0	20	64	72	100	50	58	65
Poor expectations	67	7	29	25	0	17	18	9	0	0	0	8
Fair expectations	0	29	0	0	29	17	9	9	0	0	8	8
Good expectations	33	50	29	25	71	46	9	9	0	50	33	19
N =	3	14	7	4	7	35	11	11	1	2	12	37

were doing significantly worse (Kanter, 1977; Rosenbaum, 1979).

Differences in education did make a difference. Fifty-nine per cent of graduates were doing better than their age cohort, as compared to only 22 per cent of the HNC group and 12 per cent of those with lesser qualifications. The proportions were similar at both companies.

Such results indicate that graduates achieve high positions more speedily than do their non-graduate colleagues. At the two extremes are the young graduate production managers at Metalco, and the older draughtsmen at Computergraph. Lack of education acts not only to delay the age at which senior positions are reached but also puts a lower ceiling on the career climb.[9] Experience can be used as an alternative to education, but it takes longer to acquire. However, there is no evidence from these companies that graduates have secured a monopoly on access to managerial positions. While it is unlikely that totally unqualified technical workers any longer have access to technical management positions – though there may still be room for them in management jobs in less technical areas – for those with HNC or similar qualifications access to management is still open. It is too premature for claims about the dequalification of such labour to be taken seriously, even in high-technology industries.

EQUITIES

If qualifications neither determine orientations to management nor, for those with at least some qualifications, determine ultimate success, what kinds of factors do engineers consider important for their careers? From the individual engineer's perspective, the variety in career structures and orientations creates the possibility of different kinds of investments to maximise rewards. A PhD in materials technology, while the knowledge might be useful, would hardly pay off in success in Metalco's production divisions; similarly, the kind of attributes looked for in production managers might not be useful for success in R & D.

Different kinds of resources may also generate different rewards inside and outside the company. Knowledge of a company's administrative procedures may pay off in an internal labour market but have little value outside. Consequently possessors of different kinds of 'equities' – marketable resources – have different positions in the market, positions which cannot always be directly inferred from the possession of educational certification. Upon such equities rests the engineers' dependence or independence from the company.

The difference between the two companies is immediately noticeable (Table 5.5). Metalco engineers felt that their past career and future advancement depended on having the 'right attitude', or being in the right place at the right time. Computergraph's engineers placed much more reliance on their own skills or experience. This is not an unexpected result given the differences in the engineers' orientations, but it confirms the view that engineers' sense of investment in the labour market cannot be 'read off' from their qualifications or training.

Organisational Equity: Metalco

One senior engineer at Pressco, Jim Jackson, put his view of the talents required for advancement at Metalco, this way:

> I think you have to be as brassy as the buggers at the top. It helps if you've been an officer.

A similar point was expressed more decorously by David Smith, a high-flying graduate engineer at Massfas,

> They always have a lot of of schemes to move people around but it tends to boil down to being in the right place at the right time. It's easy to get left behind. You need the same here as anywhere else to get on, a fair amount of cheek, initiative, being positive. If you get on quietly and do your job well then nothing will happen. You have to make yourself felt.

Brian Morrison explained how he got to be a senior estimator in graphic terms:

> By not showing signs of being fed up, not complaining, giving the impression of being keen and being polite. The same things will help me in the future.

Only 20 per cent mentioned qualifications as being of use to them in the past and only 6 per cent thought they would be of any use to secure future promotions.

Table 5.5 Perception of equity in career (per cent)

Past career

Equity	Metalco			Computergraph			Total		
	Engineers	Managers	Total	Engineers	Managers	Total	Engineers	Managers	Total
Qualification	15	30	21	14	44	23	14	36	22
Experience	18	25	21	56	38	50	38	31	35
Technical skills	24	40	30	36	50	40	30	44	35
Management skills	0	0	0	0	0	0	0	0	0
'Right' attitude	46	55	49	22	25	23	33	42	36
Organisational developments	42	30	38	8	0	6	25	17	22
N =	33	20	53	36	16	52	69	36	105

Future career

Equity	Metalco			Computergraph			Total		
	Engineers	Managers	Total	Engineers	Managers	Total	Engineers	Managers	Total
Qualification	6	5	6	0	17	6	3	11	6
Experience	9	10	9	39	28	5	24	18	22
Technical skills	23	30	25	24	28	25	24	29	26
Management skills	9	30	16	15	50	28	12	40	22
'Right' attitude	31	50	38	24	22	24	28	37	31
Organisational developments	74	35	60	39	33	37	57	34	49
N =	35	20	55	33	18	51	68	38	106

NOTE Columns total to more than 100 per cent because of multiple responses.

On the less positive side, there was a widespread feeling, at Pressco in particular, that family or social connections were what really mattered.[10]

> You can get on if your face fits, if your father is high enough, that's evident.

Failing these, if promotion was to come at all it would be as a consequence of organisational processes rather than individual initiative or virtue.[11]

> Promotion is limited. It's just a question of time, it's deadman's shoes.

Graduate engineers were not exempt from this emphasis on organisational virtues. The graduates differed from their colleagues only by emphasising even more strongly the importance of having the 'right attitude' for achieving future promotion (71 per cent to 31 per cent for the rest of the sample). In the parochial communities of Pressco and Massfas, the graduates' exposure to university life, even when company-sponsored, gave them outside experience and new ideas. But these new ideas were regarded as products of personality and attitude rather than technical knowledge. The graduates were thought to have a more 'progressive' attitude than the non-graduates, and what the company looked for was not technical innovations but an 'attitude of mind'. To have the 'right attitude' was, at the least, to take a positive stance towards promotion rather than adopting a passive reliance on seniority or nepotism.

Equity in Skill: Computergraph

In contrast to Metalco's emphasis on organisational virtues, engineers at Computergraph felt that their past and future careers depended on their skills. These skills, the ability to do things, were much more highly regarded even by departments which differed extensively in the backgrounds of their engineers. Engineers in the drawing office and the R & D lab both stressed the importance of skills, although they defined their claims in different ways – the drawing office in terms of experience, R & D in terms of education and technical skills.

In both the drawing office and test lab experience was seen as a genuine alternative to qualifications.

I'm not terribly qualified so the only thing that will help me is the experience and background to compensate for that. I can't compete with degrees to get interviews but I'm OK once I get the job. I can do the job because of my experience. If you get it right you get noticed and can work your way up. Qualifications don't count much in this field, especially after a few years, it's the experience that counts.

Everyone at Computergraph felt that technical ability of some kind was of major importance; they simply varied in the basis of their claims to that ability. The older, less qualified engineers made claims based on experience, the younger, more qualified ones on technical ability, and managers on managerial ability. Few mentioned the attitudinal or organisational equities so common at Metalco, and they invoked qualifications no more often than Metalco engineers (Table 5.6).

Engineers' equities, like their technical and managerial orientations, are strongly influenced by company needs and organisational structures. Engineers assess what attributes employers value, and act accordingly. It is therefore a mistake to assume that engineers' orientation to technical work, not to say science, is somehow imprinted by education and remains unchanged thereafter.[12] British engineers lack the independent occupational base which would allow them to bargain from a position of strength with employers. As employees, they learn to sell themselves in the terms the market requires.

LABOUR MARKET ORIENTATION

How do these variations in orientations and equity affect engineers' attachment to their present company as the most appropriate loci to pursue their careers? Fairly predictably, it would seem. Metalco's engineers project their careers internally, while Computergraph's have a more cosmopolitan orientation, though the difference was not quite statistically significant (Table 5.7).

TABLE 5.6 *Equity in career by department (per cent)*

Past equity

	Metalco					Computergraph						
	Drawing office	Methods	Planning	Production engineers	Production management	Drawing office	Production engineers	Production management	R & D	Test	Service	Total
Qualifications	10	6	36	17	43	0	25	83	12	20	22	22
Experience	10	0	36	50	29	57	63	50	29	60	67	35
Technical skills	80	31	7	17	14	29	13	33	71	40	22	35
Management skills	0	0	0	0	0	0	0	0	0	0	0	0
'Right' attitude	40	38	50	67	71	43	13	0	12	40	44	36
Organisational development	10	63	21	50	43	0	25	0	6	0	0	22

Future equity

	Metalco					Computergraph						
	Drawing office	Methods	Planning	Production engineers	Production management	Drawing office	Production engineers	Production management	R & D	Test	Service	Total
Qualifications	11	6	0	17	0	0	0	29	0	20	0	6
Experience	11	6	12	0	14	67	38	29	19	80	22	22
Technical skills	33	24	31	33	0	17	0	14	50	40	11	26
Management skills	11	12	13	0	57	17	25	29	50	0	11	22
'Right' attitude	22	47	31	17	71	50	13	29	6	20	44	31
Organisational development	56	65	69	83	14	17	63	57	25	20	44	49
N =	9	17	16	6	7	6	8	7	16	5	9	106

NOTE Columns total to more than 100 per cent because of multiple responses.

'Locals' at Metalco

Engineers at Metalco had predominantly 'local' careers: most had held only the one job and most expected to continue to pursue their careers within the company. Less than a fifth of the Metalco sample saw their future as lying elsewhere. Seventy per cent said they had ties to the community – 60 per cent mentioning family or relatives – which inhibited their job search. The graduates were potentially more mobile, only 40 per cent claiming strong local ties and 20 per cent feeling limited by family connections.

This localism was strongest among staff engineers at Pressco. Most of Pressco's younger engineers were locally born and bred, even its graduates.[13] The local community had a strong inward-looking tradition – the consequence of two centuries as a mining and minor industrial centre surrounded by an agricultural region. Though it is only thirty miles from the Black Country, few engineers saw themselves as belonging to this neighbouring labour market. By defining their labour market so narrowly they restricted employment opportunities. Only 8 per cent at Pressco division (compared to 24 per cent at Massfas and 21 per cent at Computergraph) thought that jobs outside the company would be easy to get.

At Massfas division many of the engineers were reluctant to see a future outside the company because they felt their experience was restricted by the nature of their industry.[14] Matthew Berry, a designer:

> It's doubtful if I could trade on my experience here. Who else makes —? I could sell myself as a designer of special purpose tools but they might not accept this. I do have a general engineering background.

Massfas is a large producer in a limited UK market.

Despite their localism most Metalco engineers believed that mobility would help them get ahead *if* they pursued it. Sixty-six per cent of Metalco's engineers, including those at Pressco, thought that external mobility was the best way to secure career advancement.[15] Terry Nixon, a Pressco planner, had no doubts on the matter.

> You've definitely got to move. You've got to be prepared to move and take the chances that are offered. Does you good as well, it brings out your confidence and a broader attitude to engineering and to life.

Table 5.7 *Labour market orientation by company (per cent)*

	Metalco			Computergraph			Total		
	Engineers	Managers	Total	Engineers	Managers	Total	Engineers	Managers	Total
Internal	43	40	42	23	29	26	33	35	34
Ambivalent	40	40	40	44	41	43	42	41	42
External	17	20	18	32	29	31	25	24	25
N =	35	20	55	34	17	51	69	37	106

Table 5.8 *Labour market orientation by department (per cent)*

	Metalco					Computergraph						
	Drawing office	Methods	Planning	Production engineer	Production management	Drawing office	Production engineer	Production management	Test	R & D	Service	Total
Internal	56	53	38	50	0	14	14	33	20	29	33	34
Ambivalent	44	41	31	33	57	43	57	50	60	41	22	42
External	9	6	31	17	43	43	29	17	20	29'	44	25
N =	9	17	16	6	7	7	7	6	5	17	9	106

This faith in the advantages of mobility was perhaps a consequence of the depressed state of the industry. Metalco engineers were very distressed about their pay, and though they claimed not to be overly concerned about job security,[16] the past experience of redundancy at both divisions must have generated some insecurity.

Though the desire to become a manager may have led engineers to tie themselves to the company, once a managerial position had been obtained some managerial skills were transferable. In fact it was production managers who were most likely to see their futures as lying outside the company (43 per cent). None of them saw their futures as definitely committed to Metalco (Table 5.8). One technical manager compared his own prospects with those of the production managers:

> You do tend to get very specialised. You need to break out at an early age otherwise you get beyond the point of no return. The experience here is only really useful in a relatively small number of firms, whereas production management is saleable anywhere. The technical track is more difficult especially after 35. Before that the experience is useful but after that alternative jobs become more difficult.

The production managers in the sample are not typical of British production managers as whole, but probably do represent the 'wave of the future' of technically trained production management. To a degree their marketability was a consequence of their distinctiveness. As technically trained graduates in a function dominated by people promoted from the shop-floor they stand out. They also stand out as high flyers: most of them had been encouraged to go into production management because they were ambitious.[17] But there are structural factors, too, which encourage their mobility. British production management has had technical functions pared away from it, leaving only the supervision of manual workers. By limiting the range of responsibilities it has encouraged the belief that man-management is a specific and transferable skill (and reinforced an emergent ideology of managerial professionalism).[18]

More surprisingly, neither type of ambition nor education had a significant impact on labour market focus. Only age significantly varied the pattern. There was a steady rise in internal orientation in each age group. None of the 15 to 25 year olds saw their futures limited to Metalco, compared to half of the 35 to 45 year olds, and all of those over 55.

'Cosmopolitans' at Computergraph

Engineers at Computergraph had more cosmopolitan attitudes. Not only were they more likely to have worked at other companies, but they expected to do so again in the future. However, it was not the R & D engineers who planned to be the most mobile, but the designers. They had the most experience with other companies and had the least intention of staying at Computergraph (Table 5.8). They also felt that new jobs would be easy to obtain. Forty-three per cent thought that they could get another job easily compared to 6 per cent of the electronics engineers at R & D. In direct contrast to Metalco, production managers were the ones who felt they would have the most to gain by staying with the company.

Computergraph engineers had also had more personal experience with forced lay-offs: 28 per cent, all designers or production engineers, had been laid off at least once. None the less over three-quarters of the engineers felt their jobs were secure, including those with previous experience of lay-offs. Feelings of security are rooted in perceptions of the company's present prospects, rather than in past labour market experience.

As at Metalco, education had little effect on market orientation. The multiple paths of recruitment and the specialisation by function meant that educational qualifications did not identify different labour markets. Function was more important. Mechanical designers, whatever their qualifications, all shared more of a common job market than did, say, graduate mechanical designers with graduate electronics engineers. While different educational backgrounds predominated in some functions – graduates are comparatively rare in mechanical design – it is the education–experience–function package that determines appeal in the labour market.

More surprising is the fact that an engineer's managerial ambitions had little impact on where he planned to pursue that career. At Metalco most engineers felt that attitude and contacts – their organisational equities – would help them, regardless of technical or managerial interests. At Computergraph individual skills were seen as important in determining career outcomes. The type of skill was less important than the fact that it was seen as the property of the individual, not a function of position in the organisation – contacts, luck, organisational growth and so on – or dependent on arbitrary evaluation by superiors concerned with attitude or personality. Individual skills – whether experience, technical skill or managerial ability – are widely marketable because they are not dependent on a particular organisation.

Once again, company structure had a greater impact on engineers' orientations than their education. The distinction between local 'managers' and cosmopolitan 'experts' is a real one, but these orientations are organisationally created. Metalco's system of rewards was structured to produce managers and kept engineers tied to the company. The involvement in the organisational division of labour, which manifests itself in the seeking of managerial positions to secure autonomy, also undermines the engineers' sense of having transferable skills independent of the organisation in which they are practised. Computergraph rewarded 'experts' and accepted a much greater degree of mobility.

CONCLUSION

This chapter has mapped out the career orientations of the technical workers at Metalco and Computergraph and has confirmed the distinction between technically oriented workers and those who are committed to organisational success.

Though a technical orientation is more common in the new industry it does not stem from university training, the possession of formal knowledge, nor even the possession of distinctly new skills – the designers in the drawing office at Computergraph were the most occupationally oriented of all the groups. Rather, new industries – any industry dependent on extensive product or process innovation – are able to utilise the skills of much larger numbers of such people, and employers are therefore able to provide a structure in which they are willing to function.

However, organisational structures are also capable of *producing* different orientations.[19] The reliance on industrial training and experience as crucial components of the production of engineers, and the willingness of British employers to treat experience as a substitute for formal education, provide a number of means by which employers can channel orientations. For example, the Computergraph structure, which insulates technical staff into units where they practise sophisticated technical work with autonomy and are rewarded for it, can *create* a situation in which technical activity is seen as a practical career *per se*. In the past Massfas had deliberately set out to do the same thing when it had built up its methods department as a separate unit and insulated it from the rest of the company, but when it no longer wished to support a staff of development engineers it tried to integrate them into a more general pool by encouraging them to move into management.

Since engineers are organisational employees, their investment in equity depends on the returns available in the labour market. Within a range laid down by individual preferences they maximise what sells best: some expertise, some managerial virtues. Lack of job satisfaction in technical positions intrinsic or extrinsic can be compensated for by promotion to management. Not only can this solve any problem resultant from the deskilling of positions, but it ties engineers firmly to management by making the latter a career extension of the former. At Metalco they became part of the same labour market. On the other hand, where job autonomy is available without such promotion it is not necessary to generate such orientations to retain engineers' loyalties.

Engineers are not *either* technical experts *or* managers; they can be induced to be either by the right combination of rewards and organisational design. Both experts and managers have relatively privileged careers, and both carry with them their distinctive responsibilities. The ease with which such goals seem to be substituted one for another, or combined into a single career, suggests that to see differences between them as marking different class positions is treating the relationship between position in the division of labour and class structure in too mechanical a fashion. These positions are held together by recruiting from the same pool.

It is necessary to see individual positions in the division of labour as a phase in a past and future career. This is central for the study of individual orientations to the company and the strategies of job control and participation. It is equally central for the analysis of the class structure. An engineer's normal career will pass through technician, engineer, and manager positions. It will therefore pass through positions of low pay, of low autonomy and relatively small skill requirements – positions hardly different from those of manual workers except for status – through positions of high technical autonomy which have been characterised as being 'contradictory' between worker and petty bourgeoisie, and may also pass through management positions implicated in the 'global function of capital'. Being an engineer potentially involves *all* these things in different measures at different times, and in different companies.

6 Authority, Profit and Participation

So far we have been concerned with the social location of engineers rather than with their distinctive ideology. Much of the discussion could have been applied in a similar fashion to many 'expert' groups in modern society; for example, accountants or personnel managers. But, as we saw in Chapter 1, engineers raise special questions because of the potential conflict between their technical expertise and the profit-making aspects of capitalist enterprises. Juxtaposing the rationality of 'science' and 'technology' against the logic of profit maximisation raises the question of how technical staff can be ideologically integrated into the capitalist firm (Galbraith, 1967; Gorz, 1967; Gouldner, 1976; Mallet, 1975; Veblen, 1922).

In part, of course, this integration is secured by the 'production' of the right kind of employees: professional technical staff are socialised and selected from the beginning to accept the legitimacy of both bureaucratic authority and the dominance of business values. In part it is secured by career structures which reward trustworthy behaviour. Both these processes are important since they provide the basis for treating engineers as trusted employees in the first instance. None the less the tension between technical expertise and profit maximisation is continuously generated *within* the structure of the capitalist firm. It emerges from the pressure to develop new technology and at the same time to maintain profitability, and is not solved by simply recruiting an appropriate workforce.

Questions still need to be asked, therefore, as to whether technical workers accept the legitimacy of commands from managers often no more, and sometimes less, technically qualified than they, and if so, whether they also accept the right of the company to maximise capital accumulation rather than technical elegance or social utility. If their interest in technical excellence does come into conflict with demands for capital accumulation, will engineers respond by demanding increased control over the running of the firm? And if so, what forms will such demands take?

PERSONAL AUTHORITY

Recent Marxist scholarship has tried to isolate the productive features of the managerial function from its exploitative features: to
distinguish those features of the management role which contribute
directly to production because they arise out of an 'unforced' division
of labour, from those which arise only because of the need to
discipline alienated workers (Carchedi, 1977; Marglin, 1974; Noble
1977).[1] It has not been an easy task, and fortunately we do not have
to solve this structural problem here. What concerns us is how the
managerial role is perceived by staff engineers, since if engineers view
managers as doing something useful and necessary, their activities
will not be seen as an imposition, or in need of extensive justification.
If, on the other hand, engineers see managers' work as necessary only
because of the firm's hierarchical structure, or because employers
seek to maximise profit, they may question the legitimacy of
management's role.

Managers as Supervisors

Despite complaints about managerial interference in a number of
Metalco's departments, one of the engineers' essential functions as
trusted workers is to operate without the close minute by minute
control that is imposed on many manual workers by the flow of the
assembly line or direct supervision. When asked what they saw as
being the major functions of their own manager, only about a quarter
of the engineers even *mentioned* supervision as one managerial role
among others (Table 6.1), and many of these did so in terms of
leadership or motivation. 'Everyone needs someone to keep them at
it', as one engineer remarked. This is the language of facilitation not
imposition:

> He's there to ensure that I am doing my work correctly, to give me
> my work, supervise it and then evaluate it. To give technical
> advice and a mutual generation of ideas with the details left to me.
> Everybody needs some kind of guidance. People rarely function
> on their own. You need some sort of stimulation.

This is not too surprising since most managers do not actually do
much supervising. When asked how their work was checked, only a

TABLE 6.1   *Perceived functions of management (per cent)*

	Metalco		Computergraph		Total	
	Engineers	*Total*	*Engineers*	*Total*	*Engineers*	*Total*
Advice	21	24	28	31	25	28
Coordination	52	35	75	67	64	51
Policy setting	42	50	28	31	35	41
Organisation linkage	30	41	11	20	20	31
Supervision	30	30	25	18	28	24
Don't know	3	4	3	2	3	3
N =	33	54	36	54	69	108

NOTE   Columns may add up to more than 100 per cent because of multiple responses.

quarter of the engineers reported that their boss directly observed them working. For most engineers 'bad work' is discovered only by results: when machines fail to work, or designs are not produced on time. Most often it is engineers in other departments who discover it first. Computergraph's service department is the first to notice any mistakes made by test engineers, the service engineers expect the customer to spot their failures; while R & D engineers say that the test and service departments would be the first people to complain about their errors. Immediate superiors hear of such failures only indirectly, and not at all if the engineers in the various departments are in close contact with each other.

Since few engineers are supervised directly and continuously, the real variance is in the size of the 'chunk' of work allocated before 'results' are assessed. When chunks are large, supervision tends to become invisible. When asked how anyone might know whether he was doing a good job or bad one. Greg Williams in R & D had trouble responding:

I don't know in practice. I think the project manager keeps the closest check but maybe the field engineer does, and then that comes down to the chief engineer and down through the project manager to me.

In part this consequence derives from the nature of the job: many engineers, particularly those in production, go on 'rounds' which, like the activities of the service engineer, render them invisible to management. But the absence of supervision is also one aspect of the autonomy that engineers receive by virtue of their trusted position. If management wanted to supervise directly it would not need to pay for engineers.

Only in the most organisationally constrained departments, the two drawing offices and Metalco's planning unit, for example, did engineers emphasise the supervisory role of management, or claim that their work was directly checked by their supervisor. In general, direct supervision is an indicator of lack of trust. Thus 58 per cent of Metalco's junior engineers reported that they were directly supervised compared to 36 per cent of their senior colleagues. As engineers are accepted as responsible employees, their level of supervision diminishes.

Managers as Organisational Linkages

Instead of being perceived primarily as supervisors, managers are seen as the experts who link technical work to commercial and organisational ends, either by coordinating the different technical specialities or as a source of organisational or commercial information. This is seen as a distinctive and rare expertise, what Perrow (1979, p. 55) has called 'administrative–technical competence'. 'I'm not sure I could do his job' was a common remark by engineers, particularly junior ones, and it was said with a degree of admiration.

It's not the technical skills, I can do that, it's keeping everything in the air at once that I admire; the technical specs, the organisational politics, and he seems to have a nose for what will sell in the market, or at least for what he can convince top management will sell. That takes real expertise. I admire him for it.

To this extent, non-technical authority can also be seen as the exercise of expertise.

Coordination, in particular, was mentioned by at least half the engineers, particularly in those departments with high levels of technical autonomy. As one R & D engineer put it:

He coordinates projects together and allocates time and doesn't allow personal interests to dominate all one's time. He's necessary, the department wouldn't run as well without it, and people would pull in all directions.

Although not allowing 'personal interests to dominate all one's time' might sound like supervision it is a recognition of the need to coordinate the division of labour in a collective project. The greater the degree of insulation that individual engineers have from the direct line authority, the greater the need for coordination by management. When engineers are left alone to 'do their own thing', someone is necessary to pull all the separate pieces together. Thus, at Metalco, where autonomy was handed out sparsely, the more successful engineers were more likely to mention coordination (70 per cent compared to 35 per cent for the least successful), and so were the graduate engineers (83 per cent compared to 45 per cent of those with HNCs or equivalent).

When the bureaucratic structure is more visible, as at Metalco, engineers emphasise management's role in the articulation of organisational structures. Managers either set policy and channel it down from higher positions, or, working in the reverse direction, act as departmental representatives to the rest of the company. As one Metalco designer put it graphically, 'the boss is there to join up the organisational tree, at the point of the join of ladders and branches'. The organisation exists and managers hold the bits together, and because of their superior position they can get things done.

> It's a position of power. He has access to high places where there is a greater chance of getting things done. I have to invoke him to get things done over someone else. There are certain levels above which I cannot go. I can go up to the line superintendent level, and possibly up to manager level to put my case but not above that. I have to take it to the boss and he'll take it above.

> He can see how the pattern fits into the overall sub-group position. For example, the overall use of manpower in this department. He's a heavyweight prod when the units are slow. He has an overall view, and can develop new markets. And he has a directional role, he takes a broad view and sets overall policy.

These organisational linkages are so taken for granted at Metalco, that when they are absent engineers feel so isolated from the organisational structure that they complain about it:

I feel undermanaged. I should be given more direction. You need someone to sort out longer term priorities. It's not done. I'm not in a position to reject demands.

Management engineers, as the most organisationally involved of all, are particularly likely to see *their* bosses functioning in both these organisational roles.

The contrast between these organisationally embedded engineers and those who are more insulated is illustrated in the following comments from two engineers at Computergraph. The first is a production superintendent and the second an R & D engineer:

His function is to act as a cornerstone. If I have a problem I go to him to defend me from attack, to provide advice. He's even more necessary in a job like this where I'm dealing with senior management and lack experience. He's a good buffer between me and X [the manager two levels above]. X is too senior a level to report to. I don't want to keep going for advice and getting direction from X. He's channel between us. You can't talk things over with X. He doesn't have the time, he's too senior. I wouldn't feel relaxed to make criticisms of people.

It never really crossed my mind what his function is, because within very broad limits I do what I like. I get the specifications at the very beginning and it's up to me to do what I want. I don't have too many technical superiors in my line.

The R & D engineer operates in an environment where his linkages to the organisation are restricted to getting the specifications and meeting them. The production manager on the other hand is involved in organisational matters continuously.

Though these organisational features of management's role dominate engineers' perceptions, they are not entirely unaware that a boss is a boss. Even the role of technical adviser still contains elements of hierarchy since the distinctive feature of a manager's advice is its authoritative nature.

I don't know exactly what his function is, he keeps the administration away from me and gives advice if needed. It's nice to know he's there. When he give advice it's authoritative advice. He can take the responsibility.

Some degree of authority is seen as necessary for the coordination function to work, but it is facilitative rather than coercive. Thus managers are seen as experts in organisational knowledge. Control functions are largely invisible to most engineers, and those that do exist are often seen as organisational necessities. Much of the predicted conflict between technical expertise and managerial authority is absent because of the organisational embeddedness of the engineers' work, and their position as trusted employees. Given the organisational structure of the firm, the engineer cannot function alone and therefore needs coordination. The ratio of coordination to supervision is very high for such workers, and as long as engineers continue to accept the goals of the company the manager is seen as a special kind of expert and as performing a necessary role in the organisational division of labour.

Managerial Authority

Given these matter-of-fact descriptions of managers' functions, engineers might be expected to have conventional views of the sources of legitimacy of their bosses' decisions. In fact over half of them (58 per cent), equally distributed across both companies, felt that the rights of their manager to supervise them derived from his organisational position, from the fact that somebody even higher up had chosen him for the job.

Metalco engineers were the most articulate in developing this conventional bureaucratic argument. Designer Matthew Berry:

> Somebody, somewhere, has promoted him and given him the right. Whether he gets my respect and earns the right is something else. I respect him because he's good at his job but ultimately it's his position.

Berry, like many other engineers, made the distinction between 'right' deriving from organisational position, and 'right' deriving from the respect of subordinates. The former is what Scott has called 'authorised' power, the latter 'endorsed' authority (Scott, 1981, pp. 281–3). Even 'bad bosses' can have authorised power.

A few engineers were strong supporters of the principle of hierarchy:

It's a question you just don't ask. He's the head of the department. It's in the terms of contract that you work in a particular place, department and company. Kids are like that nowadays. That's one of the problems, they ask questions like that. That sort of thing can lead to a breakdown of discipline. A loss of respect for private property. Not in this country, don't ask it.

Much more common, however, were the flat responses of Paul Higgins and Jim Cready, both young methods engineers at Massfas:

The system. I accept the idea of the hierarchy of organisation to get work done therefore I accept him because of his position. It's easier because I also respect his abilities.

Don't know really, I just accepted that I report to the manager and that it's part of the job to do it. It's just the accepted way of doing things.

Cready's comment, 'It's just the accepted way of doing things', could stand as a summary for most of the engineers' comments about authority.

Though organisational delegation is the most common justification given for managers' right to tell them what to do – with another 30 per cent mentioning another organisational characteristic, responsibility – half of Metalco's staff engineers justified their boss's position in terms of his expertise. In Metalco's bureaucracy knowledge and expertise increased with position whereas at Computergraph technical expertise, at least, did not.

That engineers see their manager's right to give orders as a function of his position might seem trite, but it is the very matter-of-factness that is important. Both the engineer and manager are deeply embedded in the organisational division of labour from which both technical and managerial jobs derive.

ENGINEERS AND BUSINESS

If personal authority is rooted in the everyday operations of the firm; if it is accepted because it derives from the organisation, then what legitimates the firm itself? Management may be experts in bringing things together, but to what purpose? Much writing about technical experts, from Comte through Veblen to Galbraith and Mallet, has suggested that the relationship of technical rationality to commercial goals is itself problematic: that the subjection of engineers' talents and expertise to profit cannot be taken for granted, most particularly for those with the greatest technical involvement.

Business as Constraint

All engineers are constrained by their company's needs to make a profit. No engineer is given a blank authorisation to pursue their work without regard to costs and marketability. The question is not whether engineers experience business constraints, but the extent of these constraints and how they are interpreted.

Objectively engineers experience most business constraints at Metalco. The company was experiencing tough times and this directly affected the engineers' work. Production engineers did not have the manpower or time to do the methods assessment they would have liked. Methods engineers were not asked to develop interesting new machinery as much as before. Jobs tendered for in the automobile industry were small and rarely won. Money was not available for new machinery or risky product development. No engineer could ignore these effects of Metalco's profit and loss situation.

At Computergraph, on the other hand, engineers were encouraged to be innovative. The new corporate owners were encouraging R & D expenditures. The market situation was such as to encourage high mark-ups on product costs. In fact the only time I heard an engineer spontaneously use the term 'professional values' was when Ted Bryant, the chief engineer, told Alan Sullivan's project team: 'My professional values are offended when we sell something for eight-times cost, we need to design a Rolls-Royce for this market, not a Mini'. The effect of this market difference, however, was simply to adjust the standards by which technical freedom is assessed, and only 18 per cent of the engineers, evenly divided between both companies, felt totally unconstrained by pressure stemming from their company's business concerns (Table 6.2).

At Metalco, most of the business constraints were simply accepted as part of the job.

Yes, sales and business considerations always get in the way of doing the best technical job, they always have done. But it doesn't

TABLE 6.2   *Constraints on technical work (per cent)*

	Metalco	Computergraph	Total
None	17	20	18
Part of job	46	13	30
Organisational constraints	13	44	29
Commercial constraints	24	22	23
N =	54	54	108

NOTE χ^2 significant at the .05 level.

bother me. It's part of the job. You can always spend more money but you have to finish a project at the point at which you can sell it for a profit. I accept the fact that we are in it for the money. You can only design things that sell. The company needs to make money for the shareholders and I support that. Our aim is to make something to sell.

Metalco engineers readily agreed that they sometimes had to be coerced to meet commercial pressures, but they did not resent this. Some saw such pressure as a major managerial function.

The dangerous thing for people in our situation is that we get involved in the job and enjoy it. Yet it's the managers' job, my managers, to put those restrictions on us in the interests of profitability. Profit, not our happiness, is the point.

Few, if any, engineers believe in engineering for engineering's sake, or that their technical activities are self-grounded and need no further justification than technical excellence.[2]

The only time Metalco's engineers found business constraints a problem was when they were not explained.

Business constraints only bother me if I don't know the reason. If it's purely political then it's a bit frustrating. For example, on a machine purchase, if they don't accept my recommendation for non-economic reasons that can be frustrating and they don't tell you why. Basically it boils down to things that aren't explained.

As long as decisions could be rooted in market 'realities', the engineers were willing to accept them as 'just part of the job'.

At Computergraph, in contrast, the engineers were much less accepting of constraints on their work. They were seen as unnecessary, and often based on 'political' organisational decisions, rather than business pressure *per se*.

> There is always the constraint that we are never given enough time. We are the last in line and therefore our time gets cut. It's better to meet deadlines and get cash flow than to maximise profit by doing a good production engineering job. It doesn't bother me personally but professionally it does. My professional vanity takes a minor knock.

In fact such constraints were as much a consequence of business concerns, as were the far more numerous pressures at Metalco. Computergraph was doing well commercially, and the pressure was often the result of attempts to keep up with sales demand, or to sell a product early to keep ahead of the competition. However, the strategy that the company practised with respect to its engineers' work, deliberately insulating them from the outside market, meant that most such commercial pressures reached the engineers only via organisational decisions. Whereas at Metalco such constraints seemed to stem from market constraints external to the company, and therefore were seen as 'inevitable' and 'part of the job', at Computergraph they were seen as decisions made by some manager or some department within the company and thus, in the widest sense, *political* decisions.

As long as the number of such constraints remains small, their politicisation is of little concern. But should a changed market strategy or increased cost constraints lead management to restrict technical autonomy, then engineers are likely to place the blame for this directly on management's shoulders.

The Relevance of Finance

As a matter of principle, Metalco deliberately chose to expose its engineers to commercial pressures rather than insulate them on the Computergraph model. Although the financial difficulties of both Pressco and Massfas divisions were real, Metalco as a corporation had the option of minimising the impact of this on its engineering departments if it had wished to. It had once done this with Massfas' methods unit, and continued to do so with departments in other divisions whose work it wished to encourage. Instead the company wanted its engineering function to share in the constraints imposed by the difficult business climate. It did not, however, want to create the kind of atmosphere that André Gorz foresaw arising whenever long-term research was cut back in favour of the manufacture of simple but profitable items (Gorz, 1967, p. 104). It therefore adopted a sophisticated policy of what I will call 'internalising the market'.[3]

This involved the company in a number of strategies. The first required a major decentralisation of operations. At Massfas, where the process had been carried the furthest, the original production unit had been divided up into three separate operating divisions, one for each of the main product lines. A separate technical methods unit was established, along with a tool and die unit, a unit to deal with site maintenance, security, and personnel matters, and a product-finishing unit. Each operated under a separate management and was responsible for its own financial well-being. Each treated the other units as 'external' companies: companies with whom they were expected to trade only on commercial terms. To ensure competition, the companies were expected to compete for business with non-Metalco companies and bid for their orders. At Pressco the operation had not been carried as far, except for the toolroom, which was increasingly being constituted as a separate business. None the less each department was its own cost centre and profit unit, and the beginnings of Massfas-style decentralisation could be seen.

In addition to this restructuring, the company distributed extensive financial reports to its employees, along with other material designed to expose the staff to the commercial world as management saw it.

The effect of this on engineers was most visible at Massfas methods unit. Under the old regime, it had been deliberately insulated from the market by the provision of block grants from sub-group funds. Under the new system, however, in order to receive money to develop new machinery, the methods unit – and this often meant the assistant manager or the designer himself – had to sell the concept to one of the production units. The poor market situation of the production units themselves translated into an unwillingness to engage in projects that could not guarantee direct financial benefit. Nor were they under any obligation to deal only with the methods unit for new machinery. Project costs therefore became crucial, and designing to a competitive price became of direct relevance to the individual designer.

TABLE 6.3   *Financial knowledge and technical work (per cent)*

| | Metalco | | | Computergraph | | | |
	Engineers	Managers	Total	Engineers	Managers	Total	Total
Possess extensive knowledge of financial situation of the firm	29	71	45	5	59	22	34
Think financial knowledge is relevant to own job	69	75	71	22	65	35	53
N =	35	21	65	37	17	54	110

NOTE   Both χ^2 significant at the .05 level.

The success of such practices can be seen in Table 6.3. Engineers at Metalco thought they possessed greater knowledge of the financial position of the firm and, more importantly, nearly three-quarters thought that financial and commercial knowledge of the company was directly relevant to their jobs as engineers.

Tom Stockbridge, a confirmed trade unionist and a technical specialist without managerial ambitions, expressed a typical Metalco attitude:

Now we get quite a bit of financial information. In the last two or three years in any case. We get a newspaper sent round with the whole of [Metalco] information and since the new government regulation we get it itemised by site. It's part of any person's job to be interested in the financial structure of the company. I have a vested interest in the success of the company. I may help find ways of decreasing its problems. It's the prime object of the company to make money, though not at the expense of the workforce.

For many engineers, particularly those in methods development and production engineering, cost saving and helping the company's financial situation were part of the job. Geoff Sanders, Massfas graduate engineer:

Financial knowledge is definitely relevant to the engineer's job because it's part of the function anyway. You need to be able to relate costs to savings and the technical side. They are all related. It's all concerned with the rate of return to capital. We get enough information for our purpose but I would like more to back up the statistics. They are easily fiddled. I'd like to know more about the monetary position, the exact breakdowns of expenditures. We could use the information in salary negotiation. We are always told there is no money and yet we see plenty of waste.

The traditional reason for management to protect its books from employees is to improve their relative bargaining position in salary negotiation. As Geoff Sanders indicated, engineers were not oblivious to such possibilities. But these disadvantages for management have to be weighed against its integrative role. The more the engineers can see the difficult market position the company is facing, whatever its cause, and whoever is to blame, the more likely they are to accept as inevitable the constraints placed upon their technical work.

This financial interest is not an antagonistic one, but shares the basic managerial perspective on the rules of the game. Engineers want to join in the game not change it. Even when they offer a distinctive technical perspective on the company's problems, their goal is to improve the company's profit position. Thus Arthur White, production engineer at Massfas, was critical of the failure to develop new technology, but didn't criticise the profit motive:

Engineers have got to be in on the discussion. All successful companies make a product, something that others cannot make as well or at all. [Massfas] division depended on its own new technology back in 1926 [*sic*], for example. I'd like to be involved in policy questions over financial decisions. For example over selling our technology.

Few challenged the basic assumption that the market to which the divisions were being exposed was anything other than natural and inevitable. Metalco was able to successfully defend itself from being seen as a single corporate group allocating resources to its various divisions according to corporate management's conception of potential profitability. Instead, engineers accepted the inevitability of the financial constraints which restricted their ability to practise their craft.

The success of Metalco's campaign is most clear when these responses are compared with the attitudes of the Computergraph engineers to financial matters: only 22 per cent of the high-tech company's engineers thought that financial knowledge was relevant for engineering practice. And indeed by large it was not. Engineers did not have to deal with the company's market situation in their everyday work. Cost constraints were not crucial and long-term development work was a possibility. In Computergraph's high technology atmosphere, getting the technology right is the most important factor. When costs did concern the engineers they focused narrowly on their own product cost. Martin Wood was one of the senior designers in the company and rejected any notion that its wider financial affairs were any concern of his:

> No, I've not got the time to be involved in company finance. It's my job to be concerned with product cost but not with overall profit, that's someone else's job.

Even those who were exposed to the company's attempts to disperse financial knowledge were not overly concerned with the issue. Bob Crawford was a new R & D engineer:

> I've just been on a company course for all new graduates and we were taught how to read a balance sheet. I think I could read one now. It's important to be aware but not to devote too much time to it. It's a specialist's job.

It is not that Computergraph hides its financial situation from its engineers, but that they are not of pressing concern for engineers' day-to-day practical activities.

For Computergraph managers, however, the situation is different. It is here that commercial and technical matters combine, since it is managers who lay down budgetary parameters, understand market pressures and monitor deadlines. Ted Bryant (R & D project manager): 'It's the name of the game to make money, not serve as a social service. All managers need to know and not leave it to the accountants.' Similarly, those staff engineers who did think financial knowledge relevant, saw its usefulness for managerial positions, as helpful for promotion, as did Tim Simons, a service engineer:

> If you want to go up the ladder you have to be concerned. I'd like to know policy and ideas for the future. Particularly on the commercial and sales side. I see myself as management potential.

In fact all of the financial interest variables are significantly correlated with managerial ambition.[4]

Participation

A similar pattern was found when engineers were asked whether they would like to be involved in other aspects of their firm's affairs. Nearly half of Metalco staff engineers were eager to participate in general policy decisions in their company, compared to only 12 per cent of their Computergraph equivalents (Table 6.4). Computergraph engineers were as uninterested in getting involved beyond their specialty as they had been in financial knowledge. Joe Altherton, a senior mechanical designer in R & D, claimed this lack of interest was a trait common to engineers:

> No, I don't want to be involved in more decisions. I'm not trained in other subjects and I prefer not to be involved if I don't know anything about the subject. That's a trait common to engineers.

He found plenty of support, from unqualified designers in the drawing office to graduate production engineers.

> No, there has to be some sort of framework where you have to stop and have someone do it. It wouldn't improve efficiency. I wouldn't want to get involved above my head, you have to rely on the expertise of management. (draughtsman)

> No, I don't think it's the responsibility of people like me to make other decisions. If I'm left alone to do the job that's O.K. (production engineer)

Computergraph's engineers rejected participation because they thought it was not their business, or because they didn't think they had the expertise.

In contrast, those engineers at Metalco who rejected participation did so not out of lack of interest, but because of a strong commitment to hierarchy. While not all of them agreed with Jack Greenhough, who was a 'firm believer in master and man', a number of older engineers such as Sam Stone did have very traditional views on the subject:

TABLE 6.4 Desire for participation (per cent)

Would like participation in:	Metalco			Computergraph			Total		
	Engineers	Managers	Total	Engineers	Managers	Total	Engineers	Managers	Total
Not interested	12	5	9	29	12	23	21	8	15
Involved enough	12	14	13	9	35	18	10	24	15
Personnel matters	6	5	6	18	18	18	12	11	11
Technical matters	24	19	22	32	6	24	28	13	23
Business and policy matters	47	57	51	12	29	18	29	45	35
N =	34	21	55	34	17	51	68	38	106

NOTE χ^2 for comparisons between staff engineers, and total samples both significant at the .05 level.

I'm not in favour of participation personally. I'm in favour of letting people in command get on with it. I disapprove of committees, properly trained people should do the job. For example, the Royal Family. You should leave it to senior positions in management, the hereditary principle has a lot to be said for it. My son has been brought up to take an interest in management, while someone who has been a machine operator couldn't learn it in ten years.

But even a young graduate engineer such as Simon Jacobs was willing to defend the hierarchical structure:

No, democracy at work is bad. It's a different structure in industry. It's a dictatorship in industry. You can't elect a boss. It wouldn't work. You wouldn't get the right people in the right job. You need leadership from the top. Industry is to make money. People put money into it and they should have a say. Society is different.

None the less most Metalco engineers did seek increased involvement in the running of their firm, but it was not the radical kind that Gorz and Mallet thought might emerge from the conflict between high-technology skills and the constraints of the capitalist firm. Engineers did not want to take over the company and run it on radically different principles. Even someone like Tom Stockbridge, whose extensive union activism made him a radical by most engineers' standards, discussed the issue in these moderate terms:

I do like to be involved earlier in meetings, in projects or other technical involvements. The situation is changing. We used to have separate trade union negotiations with managers and now we have a site Works Council, and a [methods unit] Works Council which has a wider scope to discuss policy. It's not fully utilised by management but I hope that management will come at an early stage and discuss policy with the reps. I hope it will deal with really important discussions.

This is hardly a call to the barricades!

Legitimation by the Market

Contrary to certain 'new working class' arguments, increased technical involvement does not encourage a greater concern with the commercial position of the company or a demand for a greater say in its running. At least not when the company's position is strong enough to be able to protect its engineers from direct cost-squeezes. Such interest was most developed at Metalco where technical involvement was lowest and the market situation weakest. This was not inevitable, but the result of a deliberate company policy of exposing its engineers to the 'authority of competition' (Pignon and Querzola, 1976, p. 79).

Metalco deliberately placed its staff engineers in a position similar to that of its managers by exposing the engineers to the cost and commercial constraints that management itself faced. Edwards and others have drawn attention to the strategy of controlling organisational employees by bureaucratic rules which depersonalise authority and allow management to claim universality for its procedures (Edwards, 1979; Perrow, 1979). But the rules of the market economy which bind managers and staff employees alike are even more resistant to challenge than bureaucratic rules.

It is a mistake to assume that the maintenance of the capitalist system is based on hiding from employees the way the system works. It might be a useful strategy for certain employers to hide their profits from the workforce during collective bargaining, or to hide incompetence, but the legitimacy of the system is not grounded at the level of the firm but at the level of the system as a whole. Neither capitalism nor socialism can exist in one firm alone. Engineers observe management managing the relationship of their company to a market which operates according to rules not significantly affected by the decisions of a single management. It is not mystification to talk of the discipline of the market, unless one argues that there are no alternative systems.

To challenge this arrangement would require not only a challenge to the legitimacy of Metalco's management but a challenge to the legitimacy of the system as a whole. The ability to expose or shield various subdivisions of the corporation from market pressures is an extremely valuable managerial tool of control.

Metalco risked raising expectations for involvement that the company could not deliver, but for a group such as engineers, already being encouraged to seek careers as managers, the risk is small. The overall effect was simply to increase engineers' adherence to a vision of themselves as committed employees who could be trusted with a greater say in the firm's affairs.

Worker Directors

The conservative nature of engineers' interest in greater participation can be seen in their attitude to greater participation by manual workers. Just prior to the time of the research, employee participation received wide public attention in Britain as a result of the publication of the report of the Bullock Commission on Worker Directors (1977). The commission was set up by the government to study workplace democracy and included one of Metalco's very senior excutives. Its report recommended – over the dissent of its management representatives – that the boards of directors of large companies should have the so-called XXY composition, consisting of one-third directors elected by the shareholders, one-third by the employees acting through their union representatives, and one-third jointly elected by the other two groups of directors.

Only 11 per cent of the engineers supported these recommendations. Another 35 per cent gave support to some kind of further participation by employees, while 54 per cent were opposed to the increased involvement of manual workers altogether. There was no difference between the companies or between education groups, but being a manager at Metalco did have an impact: they were significantly more opposed than other groups (Table 6.5).

Those supporting some variety of increased participation for all employees, about half the sample, did so for one of three reasons (Table 6.6). There was a desire to bring employees together and reduce the alienation of manual workers from the firm.

> Yes I think they [manual workers] should have more say. I think it would give them a greater commitment to the company if they were more involved. I think that's one of the problems we have now, they are not involved. I think if they were consulted more, we'd have less of a problem.

Nearly half those in favour of greater participation gave this reason, particularly at Computergraph.

TABLE 6.5 Attitudes towards worker directors (per cent)

	Metalco			Computergraph			Total		
	Engineers	Managers	Total	Engineers	Managers	Total	Engineers	Managers	Total
Favour	15	5	11	14	6	11	14	5	11
Favour with reservations	38	20	32	27	65	39	32	41	35
Opposed	47	75	57	60	30	50	53	54	54
N =	34	20	54	37	17	54	71	37	108

NOTE Differences between engineers and managers for each company separately are both significant for χ^2 at the .05 level.

Another 46 per cent argued that employees had some knowledge of the operations of the company that was hidden from senior management and they could usefully contribute this to the running of the firm.

> Oh, yes, I think they should be consulted a lot more. After all it's the shop-floor that actually makes things and they often know a lot more about what's going on than the directors in their offices.

However, only a few conceived of such employee participation in terms of democratic rights. Overall, staff engineers emphasised the knowledge that employees could contribute, while managers stressed the integration advantages.

Most who opposed such participation did so because they thought manual workers did not have the knowledge to participate adequately in the running of the company (Table 6.7). As we have noted, engineers often see managers, particularly senior managers, as performing a specialised role in the division of labour, and assume that this requires training and experience not available to most employees.

> No, I don't think they should be involved any more. If they knew how to run a firm then they would already be doing it. How can somebody off the shop-floor know how to run a firm like this? And if you sent them off to training courses, they wouldn't be representative anymore. They should leave it to the experts.

Another quarter argued that most manual workers did not have the company interests at heart. Computergraph engineers were most concerned with a militant union leadership, perhaps because of the company's past record. Managers often argued that employees did not share the company interest.

> I think most workers are only interested in the wage packet. I don't think they have the company's long-term interests at heart. They would be only in it for what they could get out of it, and that's no way to run a company.

All engineers rejected strongly the notion that unions should provide the vehicle for any participation that did occur.[5]

TABLE 6.6 *Reasons for supporting increased participation of manual workers (per cent)*

	Metalco			Computergraph			Total		
	Engineers	Managers	Total	Engineers	Managers	Total	Engineers	Managers	Total
Bring people together	32	44	36	56	67	61	42	57	48
Special knowledge of manual workers	50	33	45	56	33	46	53	33	46
Employee rights	27	22	26	6	0	4	18	10	15
N =	22	9	31	16	12	28	38	21	59

NOTE Columns total to more than 100 per cent because of multiple responses.

TABLE 6.7 *Reasons opposed to worker directors (per cent)*

	Metalco			Computergraph			Total		
	Engineers	*Managers*	*Total*	*Engineers*	*Managers*	*Total*	*Engineers*	*Managers*	*Total*
Workers lack experience	68	63	66	52	79	61	59	70	63
Workers have opposing interests	12	42	25	21	21	21	17	33	23
Militant leadership	12	11	11	35	7	26	24	9	18
Only know their own job	16	21	18	17	0	26	17	12	15
Union provide representation	20	16	18	0	0	0	9	9	9
N =	25	19	44	29	14	43	54	33	87

NOTE Columns may sum to more than 100 per cent because of multiple responses.

There is certainly no indication of any generalised commitment to a democratised workplace. Only when engineers feel that manual workers can contribute something useful to the efficient running of the firm, or when they feel that increased integration might improve productivity, are they willing to consider greater participation for them.

MANAGERS AND MARKETS

Questions about authority are often assumed to be questions of value, or normative legitimacy. Indeed it is normative legitimacy which conventionally distinguishes authority from power. The problem with this conventional model, however, is that it permits only two alternatives: an order is either legitimate or it is not. It does not allow for a third possibility, that no value judgement is passed at all, that it is simply considered a fact of life.

For example, when a manager gives an order to cancel a project, the engineer can either cooperate or not. On what grounds is the latter's decision made? He can fear the consequences of non-cooperation, in which case it becomes an exercise of power. He can consider that the manager's position gives him the 'right' to give orders. This is authority. He can also ask for a reason and accept the decision because he accepts the reason, or because he assumes he would find the reason satisfactory if he did ask. This too is a kind of authority, but it differs from the former in being grounded in knowledge or claims to knowledge. A rejection of the decision on these grounds entails the argument that the decision is mistaken, that the claim to knowledge is false.

Most knowledge claims in organisations are not claims to knowledge about the natural world – engineers make those kind of decisions all the time and they are rarely the stuff of hierarchical decision making – but claims about the social world, about markets, expected profits, governmental policy or company policy. Since these claims are about the social world, it is sometimes denied that they are knowledge claims at all, but rather are disguised positional claims, whose acceptance implies some moral commitment to the social world of the market or the firm. For example, a managerial claim that a project must be cancelled because it is unprofitable will only be accepted as legitimate, it is argued, by those who accept the moral legitimacy of the profit-making system. This argument is mistaken.

The acceptance of the decision implies only that it is seen as the right one given the rules of the social game currently being played. The engineer or capitalist who chooses to make unprofitable decisions because he disapproves of a profitable alternative will go broke and be in no position to make further such decisions.

Of course some of the participants might prefer to play a different game under different rules, and this preference may be grounded in moral values and preferences, but to accept a decision as correct under the present rules does not imply a moral commitment to them. That the structure of the firm and the operations of the market are simply taken for granted is sufficient to generate the acceptance of managerial knowledge.

The personal authority of management is grounded in the matter-of-factness of the organisational structure, but the operations of the market provide the ultimate grounding of management decisions. At Metalco, in particular, the two sources of compulsion in the modern capitalist firm – management's control of employees and market constraints on the firm – become inextricably interrelated in engineers' eyes because managers only exert constraints that seem to stem from market exigencies. It is because nationalised industries are insulated from the 'realities' of the market by government financing that most engineers reject them as inefficient: management cannot make efficient decisions because the market does not provide the discipline. As long as management decisions are shown to be reasonable given the market conditions under which the company is operating – or, as in the case of Metalco, is seen to be operating – then this is a sufficient grounding for their decisions.

However, the extent to which the market is seen to determine managerial decisions is a variable over which corporate management itself has a good deal of control. By deliberately 'internalising' the market, management can seemingly 'depoliticise' decisions which have an unfavourable impact on employees. Companies can choose either to expose or to insulate their various sub-units from the 'authority of competition', and this is a legitimating tool of great power, since it appears to place the source of any constraints on engineers' work beyond the reach of managerial decision-making.

Under normal conditions of operation a least, if a company wishes to insulate its most technically involved jobs by setting wide enough parameters around them, this will ensure that 'experts' focus only on their tasks. On the other hand, where such technical involvement cannot be provided, or management does not wish to provide it, the company can encourage increased interest in finance and company policy. That this is essentially a managerial kind of participation is indicated by engineers' rejection of wider employee participation. Engineers wanting to participate as managers is not the kind of radical involvement the theorists of the new working class had in mind.

Because the organisational structure of the firm and the ultimate rationality of profit seeking are imbued with such facticity, engineers see greater involvement in company policy as just another form of job satisfaction. Metalco engineers, largely deprived of technical involvement and encouraged to see their careers in organisational terms, were interested in their company's commercial position and sought out increased involvement. Computergraph engineers thought such participation was largely unnecessary extra business which would interfere with their pursuit of technical satisfaction. At Computergraph, only managers were, or had to be, interested in such things.

Engineers' interest in participation, in anything like the radical form predicted by the French theorists, requires a sense that the world can be somehow other than it is. The French tradition of radical syndicalist white-collar unions offers such a radical vision. British management works hard at emphasising the 'reality' of the present situation and there is little to challenge it. Least of all a commitment to the higher rationality of science.

What could instigate challenges to such managerial authority? A sense that decisions that affect engineers directly are somehow arbitrary or political: when it is clear things 'could have been otherwise'. This is why increased state involvement often leads to protests. If a decision to close off a project is made in a nationalised or state-related industry then that decision is clearly political in its widest sense, and is not legitimated by the facticity of the market.

A sense that management is incompetent or deviant in some way may also be radicalising. Decisions to invest overseas in search of profit are not so legitimate in engineers' eyes as decisions to invest in other sectors in the British Isles, even if the consequences – a decline in their own companies – are the same. Metalco's activities overseas were often criticised by engineers as 'creating jobs abroad'. The 'national interest' in the form of 'keep jobs at home' provided a framework from which to criticise the decision. Failing any of these challenges, only a crisis of legitimation of the whole system is likely to be sufficient, and this is not likely to be generated at the level of the firm.

7 Collective Organisation

A crisis of legitimacy within the firm is, of course, only one possible consequence of a changing consciousness of engineers. There is also the possibility of increasingly radical forms of collective organisation. In particular a good deal of attention has been paid to the recent growth of trade unionism amongst technical staff (Carter, 1979; Roberts *et al.*, 1972).

Trade unions and professional associations are often treated as very different forms of collective organisation (Blackburn, 1967; Millerson, 1964; Prandy, 1965). Trade unions have been seen as the traditional organisational arm of the working class: conflict-oriented organisations struggling to secure better wages, better work conditions, and organisational power for their members. Professional associations, on the other hand, are usually said to complement a middle-class status view of society, stressing not conflict but consensus, not class struggle but the maintenance of status and market position for non-manual workers (Johnson, 1977; Prandy, 1965). In the absence of research on actual changes in the structure of the workplace, technical workers' attitudes towards unions and professionalism have sometimes been treated as a sensitive indicator of their developing class consciousness (McLoughlin, 1981).

It is, of course, too simple to treat collective organisations as directly derivative of the attitudes of the employees, and the latter as derivative of position in the social relations of production, although this kind of argument has often slipped into the cruder versions of what has been called the 'stratification' model of unionism. Trade unions and professional bodies have histories of their own which are affected by changes in government legislation, business cycles, the changing organisation of collective bargaining at national, industry and company level, and changes in the education system.[1] None the less changes in the workplace might be expected to shape engineers' orientations to unions and professional associations to some degree, and it is this I want to examine in this chapter.

PROFESSIONALISM

We saw in Chapter 3 that the occupational base for engineers' claim to professionalism is very weak. British engineers have failed to restrict entry to the occupation or to gain control over the organisation of work. There are, none the less, a large number of professional institutions to which engineers specialising in the various disciplines might choose to belong.[2] The three most relevant to the engineers in the sample are the Institution of Mechanical Engineers, the Institution of Electrical Engineers and the Institution of Production Engineers.

The primary function of professional engineering institutions has always been to publicly certify engineers who acquired their education by the part-time route (Millerson, 1964), but – unlike their accountancy equivalents – they have never been able to restrict the allocation of jobs to their members. Although there are no exact figures, less than half of all qualified engineers are members, and this figure is likely to be even lower in the private sector.

In recent years the institutions have attempted to bid up the status of engineers by raising academic standards, and as a result the number of memberships awarded by the institutions to other than degree holders declined from a peak of nearly 6000 in 1965 to just over 1000 in 1975. Although there have been attempts to set up institutions for 'technician engineers' they have met with little success.

Professional Membership

Less than one-third of the sample belonged to one or more of the major institutions.[3] There were slightly more members at Metalco than at Computergraph, and many more technical managers were members than staff engineers (Table 7.1). In part this managerial predominance reflects the managers' greater age. Many had obtained their qualifications at a time when the linkage between professional membership and the part-time acquisition of an HNC or other qualification was easier than it has become in recent years. In part, membership is itself a qualification which may have played some role in their having reached their present position.

Engineers join professional associations for very pragmatic reasons. Sixty-eight per cent of the members had joined to improve

Table 7.1 Professional memberships (per cent)

	Metalco			Computergraph			Total		
	Engineers	Managers	Total	Engineers	Managers	Total	Engineers	Managers	Total
Major professional association	20	62	36	19	41	26	19	53	31
Minor professional association	9	0	5	8	6	7	8	3	6
Managerial associations only	3	0	2	0	6	2	1	3	6
None	69	38	57	73	47	65	72	42	61
N =	35	21	56	37	17	54	72	38	110

NOTE The difference (x^2) between engineers and managers is significant at the .05 level.

their careers, while less than a third mentioned either the institutions' learned society role, or what might loosely be called 'status' reasons. For most, membership is simply another credential:

> It's a piece of paper that's all. It gets you in the door for a job. It looks good on the résumé, especially if you don't have a degree.

The highly trained mechanical engineers in Metalco's methods units had a high percentage of professional qualifications because most had begun their training as apprentices. Their electronically trained equivalents in Computergraph's R & D had BSc's and did not belong to the institutions (Table 7.2) But these differences reflect different methods of education rather than a different orientation to professionalism. Seeing professional associations as qualifying institutions does not reflect a status orientation. These engineers do not see membership, or other credentials, as honorific devices. As we have seen already, they rarely used their qualifications to legitimate their position. Membership is simply an instrumental device to help them get a job. Only a very few, such as George Wilkins, a technical manager at Pressco, saw membership in status terms and even he saw a university degree as being a partial substitute.

> I joined to support the institutions. I hoped they would gain prestige for engineers which is down here compared to other countries. It's good to meet other engineers and see how they tick. As I've only worked in one company that is important, and I go on visits. I'm not sure everyone need join. It's important to have institutions and therefore they need support to encourage professionalism and in so doing give pride and status to the engineer. They have professional bodies for solicitors and doctors where you have prestige for the jobs and we need that for engineers to help keep up standards, to be looked up to. I'm proud to be a professional engineer. I would have liked to have been a university graduate. There is a certain feeling of achievement, and a certain amount of status.

However, though it appears rarely in the formal interviews, a status-oriented view of institutional membership was expressed by high-level engineering managers in a number of the traditional companies I visited. When distinctive engineering expertise was challenged, as it sometimes was at high levels of traditional British

Table 7.2 Professional membership by department (per cent)

	Metalco					Computergraph						Total
	Drawing office	Methods	Planning	Production engineer	Production manager	Drawing office	Production engineer	Production manager	R & D	Test	Service	
Major professional association	10	47	31	33	57	14	38	57	28	20	0	31
Minor professional association	10	6	0	17	0	0	25	14	6	0	0	6
Managerial association only	0	6	0	0	0	0	0	14	0	0	0	2
None	80	41	69	50	43	86	37	14	67	80	100	61
N =	9	17	16	6	7	7	8	7	18	5	9	100

companies, the status claims of professionalism could be usefully invoked to defend the managers' position as an *engineer*. One of the complaints made by a number of the most 'professionally' oriented managers at Metalco was that qualified accountants were accepted as being *distinctively* expert on financial matters, whereas professionally qualified engineers were not given such respect in their own fields. For most engineering staff and their technical managers, however, their position as engineers was not threatened and more pragmatic responses prevailed.

Neither company officially encouraged professional membership, as often occurred in the nationalised industries. Management was as unaware of professional memberships among its staff as it was of other forms of qualification. As Ronald King, a Metalco planning engineer, put it, 'They don't pay for qualifications here. It means nothing. If there had been money in it I might have joined.' A few engineers had begun their careers with higher expectations of the institutions but had become disillusioned with them, both as qualifications and as protectors of engineers' positions. Tom Stockbridge of Metalco's methods department was now an active unionist.

> I joined the professional institute at the time of my apprenticeship when I thought I would end up in management and I thought membership would help with the career. It's useful in job applications but at interviews I found that people were not interested in membership and it wasn't useful. I look at the BMA [British Medical Association] and the Law Society, who seem to have done more for their members. It could do more to improve the lot of the engineer. I'd like to have seen them fight more, for improvement in job prospects and pay.

Many of the younger engineers in particular regarded the institutions as antiquated organisations, with little to offer the practising engineer. They seemed irrelevant.

A long-standing source of debate within the professional institutions has been the extent to which they could improve their members' material and social status without engaging in the collective bargaining prohibited by their charters (Prandy, 1965; CEI, 1975b). Though the debate filled the editorial and letter pages of newspapers and the institutions' journals, fewer than 15 per cent of the engineers I talked to were interested in the topic. As one of them said, 'If you need a union, join one'; 81 per cent thought that the primary purpose of the associations was to serve as learned societies, a function they showed no personal interest in.

Being a Professional

This is not to say that the rhetoric of professionalism struck no responsive chord with engineers. It did, but in a much weaker and less institutionalised form. Nearly 80 per cent of the engineers considered themselves professionals, but only 5 per cent thought the term had anything to do with institutional membership, and only 12 per cent connected it to qualifications. Instead professionalism was seen as a function of special skills (25 per cent) or a responsible attitude towards one's work (38 per cent).

Specialised skills were cited most often by Metalco staff engineers:

> Yes, I'm a professional. I have professional skills. I have special skills and training that the production people don't have.

These skills were what most clearly differentiated engineers from the manual workers with whom they incessantly compared themselves.

For the rest, the concept of 'being a professional' was closely tied to the idea of having a 'responsible job' and a 'responsible attitude' towards it:

> I'm a professional. I have a professional attitude towards my job. I care about getting it right. I feel responsible for it. That's what being a professional is all about, being responsible.

Professionalism, in this sense, has become a generalised defence of position divorced from any institutionalised base. It does not have the all embracing character it has taken on in the United States, where professional standing is claimed by all non-routine white-collar occupations and many other besides; but as a way of differentiating themselves from manual workers and bolstering their middle-class status, engineers are anxious to be considered professionals. The institutions, however, are no longer – if they ever were – seen as its institutionalised expression.

In all, there seems little reason to view institutional membership as an expression of a particular ideology, status or otherwise. Engineers view professional associations purely in pragmatic terms, and primarily as a source of qualifications for those who need them. There is certainly no reason to think that the growth of high-technology industry will encourage institutionalised professionalism in Britain. To the contrary, if they employ more graduates, or give engineering managers more centrality in the organisation, professional membership is likely to become less important. Only if companies encourage membership, as is done in the nationalised industries, are more engineers likely to join, and then for the very pragmatic reason that there would be money in it.

Professional institutions serve a useful role as learned societies, but this is a long way from seeing them as representative of a particular form of class consciousness. If they continue to serve a status function, it is as much to reinforce functional claims within management as hierarchical ones between engineers and lesser mortals. Professional membership seems to become more important to managers the more divorced they become from actual technical practice. It is this, as much as any affinity with the organisationally powerful, that accounts for the correlation between position and membership.

TRADE UNIONISM

Although professional associations have not benefited from the growth of high technology industries, there has been a rapid growth of engineering unionism in the sixties and seventies, a growth which has sometimes been treated as a sign of the developing proletarianisation of technical work.

Engineers have, however, a variety of unions from which to choose, not all of a kind that would make membership a likely indicator of working-class consciousness. It is necessary to examine this institutional structure before we examine the variations in membership and attitudes in our sample.

In their analysis of the growth of white-collar unionism in the early sixties, Blackburn and Prandy (1965; and see Carter, 1979) developed the concept of 'unionateness' to describe the extent to which the proliferating staff associations and quasi-unions approached the typical style of manual worker unions. The concept incorporated seven elements (Blackburn and Prandy, 1965, p. 112):

1. Whether the organisation regards itself as a union.
2. Whether it is registered as a union.

3. Whether it is affiliated to the TUC.
4. Whether it is affiliated to the Labour Party.
5. Whether it is independent of employers for negotiation purposes.
6. Whether it regards collective bargaining and the protection of its members as its major function.
7. Whether it is prepared to be actively militant.

Engineers have gone beyond staff associations and other quasi-unions for which the concept was originally developed, and Blackburn and Prandy have been criticised for using manual workers as some idealised point of comparison (Crompton, 1976; Carter, 1979), but the concept does draw attention to the fact that not all bargaining associations, not even all unions, are alike. Unions, particularly white-collar unions, pursue a variety of different industrial and political strategies, and it is useful to typologise them based on the strategies they emphasise. Engineers have three from which to choose.

The first is the one adopted by most manual unions: recruit as many employees in the workplace as possible and use the strength of numbers to bargain with the employer. For engineers this is the strategy adopted by the Technical and Supervisory Staffs section of the Amalgamated Union of Engineering Workers (TASS).

TASS has emerged as the largest white-collar union in the engineering industry after having undergone a series of transformations from its roots as a craft union for draughtsmen, the Association for Engineering and Shipbuilding Draughtsmen (AESD).[4] While its leadership gives lukewarm acquiescence to the demands of many of its members for differentiated bargaining units reflecting their status in the workplace, the union is ideologically committed to being a single staff union – ultimately to a single union for all employees. TASS practises what Parkin (1979) has called a pure 'usurpationary' strategy: i.e. it is more committed to mobilising its collective strength *vis-à-vis* employers than it is in maintaining distinctive privileges for sections of its membership. In this respect TASS is closer to being fully 'unionate' than any of the other technical unions.

A second and very different strategy is the attempt to control the labour market for engineers in the manner of the craft unions and professional associations, a strategy Parkin calls 'exclusionary'. The United Kingdom Association of Professional Engineers (UKAPE) is a pure type of such union, since it accepts for membership only those who meet the qualifications for chartered engineers laid down by the professional associations (Dickens, 1972). The old draughtsmen's union, AESD, began as such a union for draughtsmen, and indeed often came close to turning itself into a professional association before finally becoming an industrial union as TASS. UKAPE is small and still struggling after more than ten years in existence, but its importance lies in the kind of union it tries to be, and the support it has received from the professional associations, rather than in its membership figures.[5]

The third group of unions adopt a mixture of each of these strategies. Both ASTMS (the Association of Scientific, Technical and Managerial Staffs)[6] and the EMA (the Engineers' and Managers' Association)[7] are fully fledged industrial unions in the sense that employee status is the sole criterion for membership, but both are much happier than TASS with the idea of segmented bargaining units for different grades of staff. Unlike TASS, which is more concerned with the homogenisation of its membership, both ASTMS and EMA strongly support differentials. They are both more than willing to set up separate negotiating units for each grade of staff, and EMA, in particular, has set itself up as a union for managers. Both are happy to exploit status differences in the workplace when they are to the advantage of any of their members.

Not only do these unions have different negotiating strategies, but different styles and images as well. UKAPE and EMA both emphasise their non-political images, particularly their lack of affiliation with the Labour Party, and UKAPE – though not EMA – is also a vociferous non-member of the Trades Union Congress (TUC). TASS, on the other hand, has strong left-wing leadership, while ASTMS leadership has projected a strong middle-class image, coupling considerable verbal aggressiveness to an emphasis on professional bargaining.

These unions themselves now offer the variety of strategies that once differentiated professional associations from trade unions. In what follows, therefore, we have to look not only at membership patterns and attitudes towards unionism in general, but also at attitudes towards these different modes of unionism.

Engineers and Unions

Forty per cent of the total sample were members of trade unions of one kind or another, but this membership is unevenly distributed between the two companies and between the staff and managerial engineers (Table 7.3).

Eighty-three per cent of Metalco staff engineers were union members, and between them TASS and ASTMS had secured bargaining rights for all grades T3 and T4 on both sites. Nearly a quarter of the Metalco managers were also members, but these were not represented by a bargaining unit, and two out of the five belonged to UKAPE.

At Computergraph only 24 per cent of the engineers and 6 per cent of the technical managers were currently members: all, except one mechanical designer in R & D, located in either the drawing office or the production engineering units. A somewhat larger proportion (60 per cent) had had experience of union membership at some time in their careers, including 50 per cent of the engineers and 38 per cent of the technical management. No union had secured bargaining rights at Computergraph, though the company did recognise TASS' right to be consulted on matters concerning its membership.

Though less extreme, a similar pattern emerges when attitudes rather than membership is looked at. While overall the engineers were split almost evenly into three groups, with slightly more favouring unions than were either opposed or were ambivalent, negative opinions were strongest at Computergraph and among managers (Table 7.4). The biggest difference of all was between Computergraph staff engineers and their Metalco peers. While over a third of the former expressed some hostility towards unions, only 6 per cent of the latter did so.

In explaining their need of unions, Metalco engineers stressed security, pay, and a general need for collective representation (Table 7.5).

Unions are a good idea for people like me in the present situation because we're having our differentials eroded.

I'm no lover of unions but you need them for the security.

A union is the only way to get things from the company. Only union awards got anything. Pay, holidays, all have been improved by the union. Management doesn't do anything without union pressure.

Even Bill Stafford, one of Metalco's production managers, shared this view:

Table 7.3 Trade union membership (per cent)

	Metalco			Computergraph			Total		
	Engineers	Managers	Total	Engineers	Managers	Total	Engineers	Managers	Total
Member	83	24	61	24	6	19	53	16	40
Potential member	14	71	36	41	59	46	28	66	40
Hostile to membership	3	5	4	35	35	35	19	18	19
N =	35	21	56	37	17	54	72	38	110

NOTE Comparison between companies, and comparisons between engineers and managers at Metalco and for the overall sample, all significant at the .05 level for χ^2.

TABLE 7.4 *Attitudes to trade unionism (per cent)*

| | Metalco | | | Computergraph | | | Total | | |
	Engineers	Managers	Total	Engineers	Managers	Total	Engineers	Managers	Total
Positive	56	38	49	38	6	28	47	24	39
Ambivalent	38	29	35	24	53	24	31	40	34
Negative	6	33	16	38	41	39	23	37	28
N =	34	21	55	37	17	54	71	38	109

NOTE Differences between companies, and between engineers and managers at each company and for the total sample, all significant (χ^2) at the .05 level.

Unions are a good idea. The position of the engineer has become critical. Workforce and staff unions have improved wages and conditions for their members. Engineers must have bargaining power via unions if they are to maintain their position.

Other engineers joined because 'everyone else did', and still others because they wanted to be more involved, whether it was to improve 'bad management', or have a voice in running the union. Few joined because they supported the principles of trade unionism and wanted to see them advanced. Brian Morrison's strong principled support is interesting mainly for its rarity:

Everybody should join a union. The companies have a union, the Engineering Employers' Federation. Many managers who object to unions are Masons, and that's a union of sorts. It's the union's job to see that justice is done. Without unions we wouldn't get pay awards. Companies don't dish out money because they want to, and they would be quite happy to keep people on the poverty line. Companies always show a low profit when they think wages are coming up for discussion.

TABLE 7.5   *Reasons for joining a trade union (per cent)*

| | Union members only | | |
	Metalco	*Computergraph*	*Total*
Pay	12	0	9
Insecurity	35	0	27
Collective representation	24	30	25
'Everybody did'	21	10	18
Closed shop	3	10	5
Wanted to stay in the union	6	20	9
Support principles of unionism	3	30	9
Other	12	10	11
N =	34	10	44

NOTE   Columns sum to more than 100 per cent because of multiple responses.

Not surprisingly, this kind of general ideological reasoning was much more common at Computergraph, where membership was an individual choice and there were few immediate rewards for joining.

A similar level of practicality was shown in the reasons given for *not* joining. Over half thought they offered no particular advantages (Table 7.6). These comments were fairly typical.

As long as I'm doing well and can look after my interests better myself I won't join. I'd join soon enough if I lost confidence or I felt my career prospects were threatened. (Computergraph)

I'm not a trade union member. I like to think I can argue my case better than someone else can. I'm not against them in principle. If I wasn't getting attention or the satisfaction I ought to be, or if I had a grievance or felt insecure I would join. I'd probably join the local staff union, TASS. There's no point in being the lone member of a remote organisation. (Metalco production manager)

Most of these engineers saw 'bureaucratic individualism', pursuing their own careers, as a viable strategy for looking after their own

TABLE 7.6 *Reasons for not joining a union (per cent)*

| | Non-members only | | |
	Metalco	Computergraph	Total
No personal benefit	59	52	55
Union too weak or unavailable	14	11	12
Management disapproves	5	0	2
Not good for management	14	9	11
Dislike union politics	5	14	11
Anti-collectivism	18	18	18
Militant leadership	5	16	12
Unions do not share company interests	0	5	3
N =	22	44	66

NOTE Columns may sum to more than 100 per cent because of multiple responses.

interests and saw unions as unnecessary. Others would have liked a union like UKAPE but thought it was too weak to be worth considering. R & D engineer Tony Stevens thought the problem lay in engineers' inability to organise:

> The trouble with engineers is that most of them are fairly interested in what they are doing and don't do it just because it's a job but because they enjoy it and therefore they are not really in it for the financial gain. It's more interest than money and therefore they are unlikely to unite for a really strong union.

Given this pragmatic attitude it is not surprising that less than a fifth of the total sample – most at Computergraph – were so opposed to unions that they could never see themselves joining. A majority, including managers, would join a union if they felt the need of it (Table 7.7). Future insecurity was seen as a likely reason to join, particularly at Metalco – naturally enough given its recent history and market position – and many engineers commented on the features of the Employment Security Act which made it particularly advantageous to be in a union in a lay-off situation, even if the union could not prevent them. Of these 'potential members' about a quarter wanted a 'professional' union of some kind, though preferably one with more teeth than UKAPE. This figure rose to nearly half for Computergraph management.

TABLE 7.7   *Reasons to consider union membership in the future (per cent)*

	Non-members only		
	Metalco	*Computergraph*	*Total*
Security	36	14	21
Collective representation	27	16	20
Pay	5	7	6
Moderate union available	5	11	9
If everybody joined	18	9	12
Never	9	43	32
N =	22	44	66

NOTE   Columns may sum to more than 100 per cent because of multiple responses.

Unionism and the Labour Market

For engineers, unions offer security and some protection against attacks on their salaries. An obvious reason for Metalco's greater unionism, therefore, is the different labour market positions of engineers in the two companies.

Metalco engineers were clearly worse off than Computergraph's in terms of pay and security. In 1978 the average pay for the sample at Metalco was £4300 and for staff engineers £3700, while at Computergraph it was £5900 and £5300 respectively.[8] Only 4 per cent of Metalco's staff were satisfied with their salary as opposed to 70 per cent of Computergraph engineers.

Not only were Metalco engineers worse off than Computergraph's, but they were worse off in comparison to their prime reference group, the company's production workers. The average earnings of mechanical engineers as a percentage of average male manual earnings declined from 155 per cent of parity in 1971 to 149 per cent in April 1977. More dramatically, at Pressco the T4 minimum declined from being 117 per cent of average piece-rate pay for the production workers in 1972 to 88 per cent in 1977. This change was largely the result of government incomes policies which stressed flat-rate increases that had lowered differentials across the board, but which had been easily avoided by Metalco's piece-rate workers. Though few engineers gave pay as their own reason for joining a union, half thought that declining pay differentials were the primary reason for the national growth of engineering unionism.

Dissatisfaction with pay and a greater sense of insecurity would itself account for the difference in unionisation rates, but they were compounded by other market factors. Metalco engineers in general tie their fate more closely to the company than do Computergraph's, and within Metalco the engineers most likely to see their future with the company were the ones most likely to favour trade unions. Conversely those that thought they could easily find another job outside their company had the most negative attitudes to trade unions (Table 7.8). If TASS or ASTMS were still occupationally based craft unions they might be more useful to those who seek their careers on the external labour market, but this is not their present role. Neither provide their members with a ticket to employment, as an AUEW (Amalgamated Union of Engineering Workers) apprenticeship card does for a tradesman, or an AESD card once did for draughtsmen.

TABLE 7.8　*Labour market perception and attitudes to unionism (per cent)*

Attitude to trade unions	Perception of availibility of jobs in other companies			
	Not looking for a job	Hard to find a job	Easy to find a job	Total
Favourable	56	37	5	39
Ambivalent	21	46	35	34
Opposed	23	17	60	28
N =	39	20	46	109

NOTE　χ^2 significant at .0001 level.

Instead what they offer is a substitute for the market: the setting of wages and benefits by collective bargaining (Prandy, Stewart and Blackburn, 1983).

Proletarianisation?

But differences in labour market position cannot entirely explain the pattern of variations, particularly the sharp difference between managers and staff. Wage differences, certainly at the margin, are not great and many managers felt themselves threatened, both financially and in terms of security. We need to look more closely therefore at other features of the organisation of work, and in particular at the claim that the 'proletarianisation' of technical workers is responsible for their increased unionism.

The manager/staff boundary is obviously important for collective bargaining purposes. Metalco, for example, had come to accept the unionisation of its engineers, at least *ex post facto*, but many managers thought the reaction would be very different if managers unionised. Phil McIntosh was a technical manager who was leaning towards unionisation:

The only problem might be a sense of resentment by senior management. There's a lot of 'us' and 'them' syndrome in industry, and if we joined we'd be one of them rather than one of us.

But the issue goes beyond company hostility. As we shall see below, managers, even if willing to consider unions, show a consistent preference for moderate action.

By itself, however, this difference between managers and staff engineers tells us nothing about the 'proletarianisation' thesis, since the division between technical staff and management has been a long-standing feature of British technical work. Nor did these engineers see unionism and managerial ambitions as alternatives. In fact managerial ambition strongly correlates with membership. As we saw in Chapter 5, Metalco engineers have a strong orientation to management and yet are highly unionised and pro-union.

> I'm a union member because of what it can do for me now. I don't know whether I'll need it when I get to be a manager, but it's certainly useful in this job. I think in some companies they might hold union membership against you, and I don't think I want to be too active in sticking my neck out, but as long as I'm an engineer along with all the others I think it's necessary. (graduate engineer, Metalco)

Crompton (1979), however, claims that the critical issue is blocked mobility into management positions, since she considers that all white-collar workers were once intimately involved in managerial work at some point during their careers. Roberts *et al.* (1972) also argue that blocked mobility into management positions is responsible for the 'reluctant' militancy of their sample of technical workers,[9] and there is some limited support for this argument. Seventy per cent of those engineers who felt they had only a poor chance of achieving their managerial ambitions were union members. However perceptions of blocked mobility had no impact at all on *attitudes* towards unionism.

The relationship between a sense of blocked mobility and union membership diminishes, however, if each company is considered separately (Table 7.9). Metalco engineers – the most unionised – were the more ambitious, and the most pessimistic about their future prospects. Similarly Metalco staff engineers were more disappointed in their careers than other members of the sample, and this too produces an overall correlation with union membership which disappears when the groups are considered separately (Table 7.10). The relationship is at the organisational level rather than the individual.

TABLE 7.9   *Ambition and union membership*
(percentage of each ambition category who are union members)

Per cent union members	No ambition	Ambitious with poor expectations	Moderate ambitions with good expectations	High ambitions with good expectations	N
Total sample	28 (N = 11)	70 (N = 7)	47 (N = 8)	41 (N = 18)	44
Metalco engineers	71 (N = 5)	100 (N = 6)	83 (N = 5)	81 (N = 13)	29
Computergraph engineers	21 (N = 5)	33 (N = 1)	67 (N = 2)	14 (N = 1)	9

NOTE χ^2 significant at the .05 level for total sample.

In a company such as Metalco where managerial ambitions are encouraged but there is a low rate of promotion, where many engineers and staff have a sense of a disappointing career, the atmosphere is likely to be favourable to unionisation.

Blocked mobility is only one element in Crompton's explanation of union growth. The other is loss of autonomy in the workplace. What we find, however, is that a similar relationship exists between the organisation of work and unionism as between unionism and perceptions of blocked mobility. Individual attitudes to trade unions are not associated with low involvement or autonomy but there is a rela-

TABLE 7.10   *Career satisfaction and union membership*
(Percentage in each category of career satisfaction who are union members)

Per cent union members	Career satisfaction			
	Disappointed	Satisfaction	Pleased	N
Total sample	64 (N = 21)	29 (N = 11)	32 (N = 12)	N = 44
Metalco engineers	94 (N = 15)	60 (N = 6)	89 (N = 8)	N = 29
Computergraph engineers	40 (N = 4)	13 (N = 2)	25 (N = 3)	N = 9

NOTE   Only total sample signficant at the .05 level (χ^2).

TABLE 7.11 *Organisational constraint and union membership*
(Percentage in each category of organisational constraint who are
union members)

Per cent union member	Organisational constraint		
	Low	High	
Total sample	30 (N = 18)	52 (N = 26)	N = 44
Metalco engineers	79 (N = 11)	86 (N = 18)	N = 29
Computergraph engineers	22 (N = 5)	29 (N = 4)	N = 9

NOTE χ^2 significant at the .05 level for the total sample.

tionship between organisational constraint and membership at the contextual level (Table 7.11). Metalco engineers have less organisational autonomy than do those at Computergraph, and the two departments at Computergraph with low organisational autonomy, the drawing office and production engineering, are also the departments where unionisation is the strongest.

Unionism and Trust

We cannot decide with this kind of data which of these three factors – poor market situation, blocked mobility, or low levels of organisational autonomy – are causal in increasing unionism.[10] Not least because the precipitating factor for membership occurred in the past, and none of these factors correlated with present *attitudes*. There is obviously a relationship between Metalco engineers' greater sense of discontent with all these features and the company's increased unionism. As engineers say, 'if you need a union, join one,' and in comparison to Computergraph engineers at least, Metalco engineers did need their union.

Despite this, I think there is also evidence that the causal relationship between work conditions and unionism does not only run in the direction that the conventional model allows. There is some evidence that unionism may itself serve to shape the work conditions of Metalco engineers. In Chapter 4 I showed how Metalco had structured work in such a way that autonomy was largely reserved for its managerial employees and that it encouraged its employees to seek work satisfaction in management rather than technical positions. In a non-expanding company, however, there were not enough managerial positions to go around, and there was plenty of room for engineers to become dissatisfied with their positions.

But why did Metalco not grant discretion to its staff engineers? In part because socio-technical features of the work environment did not always make it profitable, but also in part, as I argued in Chapter 4, *because* its staff engineers were unionised. Rather than deskilling causing unionisation, unionisation may itself have encouraged the development of low autonomy jobs.

A number of factors speak in favour of this interpretation. There is the testimony of the engineers themselves. Most of them see threats to differentials and job security as triggering unionism rather than declining work conditions. Of course such changes in market capacity can be seen as reflecting prior changes in work position, but there is no real evidence of this occurring. Certainly loss of supervisory positions cannot explain the increased unionisation among staff engineers, since there is little evidence of any change in this respect.

There is also the role that engineers see unions as playing. Crompton sees unionism as an indication of worker consciousness, whereas most engineers see it as a device to defend whatever privileges they already have. Unions can be just as exclusionary as professional associations, and serve a function for employees who might be far from proletarianised.

We need at least to recognise that the development of unionisation, whatever its *immediate* precipitating cause, may feed back on to the structure of work by rigidifying boundaries between bargaining units, by causing management, if it has the power, to withdraw 'trust'. One of the dilemmas of unionisation for privileged employees is that they may indeed have something to lose by this withdrawal of trust.

AMBIVALENCES

When necessary most engineers will join a union to protect their interests, but this does not imply a commitment to full-scale support of 'usurpationary' unionism. Though, as we have seen, there was a choice of unions to join, choice of union is not always a matter of individual preference. There is a widespread perception that, however appealing UKAPE's programme might be, it was too ineffectual to be seriously considered. Thus engineers often found themselves having to join, or consider joining, a union while disapproving of its official policy. The fact that engineers are willing to join unions such as TASS when they see them as providing the best immediate answer to their problems – 'if you need a union join a strong one' – is no testimony to their support of the leadership programme.

There are three dimensions of union organisation over which the potential for conflict between membership and leadership is strong: political involvement, collective militancy, and relations with manual workers. Each of these are areas where traditional middle-class attitudes potentially conflict with the ideology of most union leaderships.

Political Involvement

Nearly three-quarters of both members and potential members opposed union involvement in 'political issues', by which they meant social and economic policy which did not affect the membership *qua* members. A further 15 to 20 per cent felt that involvement should be restricted to work-related issues. Tom Weaver was a TASS member at Metalco:

> The principle of a union is a good idea but they should look after their own members and see their members get a fair deal. I disapprove of being run by the subversive Left for their political ends, or of going in for politically motivated sympathy strikes.

Jim Padget, a technical manager at Computergraph, agreed:

> I wouldn't touch TASS. It's weak and so Red, especially in north London. If a branch of EMA recruited here then I might join, especially now. The company has to consult with AUEW over pensions but not with me, and I would like to have that say. So I may need recognition, and UKAPE is a non-event.

Many therefore preferred a 'professional union' because they disliked the politics of the TUC-affiliated unions, most particularly TASS.

Disliking TASS politics, however, often left engineers and managers with no choice they felt would be effective. Peter Chamberlain, technical manager, Metalco:

> I wouldn't join TASS. It's bloody communist. It represents all levels and so can't adequately represent the higher levels. I wouldn't want a union official to know my business. ... I've toyed with the idea of joining UKAPE but I haven't seen it could offer anything to justify the expense. For the first time it seems that an organisation represents professional engineers. I'm sitting on the fence at the moment to see if they succeed in establishing themselves, but at my level they couldn't do much to help my interests and therefore I'm not inclined to spend money. If I was further down the ladder I would do so. Management take more notice of organised labour than unorganised. It's regrettable but it's a fact and therefore engineers need it. Problem is that UKAPE couldn't dominate here. In a large organisation, with a large number of professional engineers then maybe it could make advances, for example at GEC or ICI, but not here.

Similarly Nigel Lewis, also a Metalco technical manager:

> It's difficult to sort out my feelings. I feel they are generally a good thing and good for companies. The union is more often right than wrong and are good for conditions etc., and force management to act over safety; some managers wouldn't give a damn. I'm pro-union in this sense and I think people should unite together to protect the weak, and that's a good thing. But it all gets linked up with politics and gets led by the left wing. I don't like that. Therefore I'm all mixed up at the moment.

It was only the more highly educated engineers, and in particular the graduates, who favoured this political activity. Geoff Sanders, a graduate engineer at Massfas, put it this way:

> Unions must be involved in politics. They are political institutions. American unions have done a superb job in the plant but a deplorable one outside, whereas the British unions have extended beneficial pressures on, e.g., pensions and welfare. They should restrict their activity to social issues.

Similarly only a third of the union members overall paid the political levy, but half the professionals and graduates did so, again perhaps indicating a greater political commitment amongst the proportionally fewer graduate and professionally qualified members.

Collective Militancy

Unionist staff engineers were split 50/50 in support of a closed shop. But even those in favour gave only reluctant support, seeing it as sometimes necessary in a precarious bargaining position. Managerial engineers opposed it almost unanimously, and potential members were also overwhelmingly opposed to the idea. There was little difference by educational category, though the non-graduate 'professional' engineers were the most opposed.[11]

Strikes were less controversial although none of the engineers interviewed had ever been on strike. When asked whether they were likely to support a strike, many engineers distinguished between a strike itself and the conditions under which the strike would be called. While 58 per cent of the staff-engineer unionists said they would support a strike if their union called one, another 34 per cent said they would only support it if they personally favoured job action on that issue. For example, many said they had opposed a TASS call for a sympathy strike with craft workers in the car industry. The insistence on personal agreement with the strike issue was strong amongst prospective members of all kinds (Table 7.12). Managers in particular had difficulties with the idea of strike action. Metalco's George Wilkins' comments were typical:

> No, I couldn't support a strike. It's an old-fashioned attitude I know. They pay you and if you don't like the conditions and you've tried every way to change it short of strikes, then leave. I know it's old-fashioned but a lot of unionists are like that and get worried. That's why I don't really want to join a union because I wouldn't like to strike. If you're in a union they have to take action and if they aren't strong enough to win a strike then they have to back down and they lose anyway.

There is a clear relationship between willingness to participate in strikes and having expectations of achieving managerial ambitions (Table 7.13). Those who think they have reasonable expectations of achieving their managerial ambitions are much less likely to be willing to strike on issues with which they disagreed, than those with no managerial ambitions or those who felt their chances to achieve them were poor. This relationship held for both companies.

TABLE 7.12 Attitudes to strikes (per cent)

	Trade union status					
	Metalco		Computergraph		Total	
	Members	Potential members	Members	Potential members	Members	Potential members
(a) Total sample						
Would strike	47	5	70	12	52	9
Would strike if personally approved	38	30	10	40	32	35
Would not strike	15	65	20	48	16	56
N =	34	20	10	25	44	45
(b) Managers only						
Would strike	20	0	0	0	17	0
Would strike if personally approved	20	0	0	40	17	28
Would not strike	60	100	100	60	66	72
N =	5	15	1	10	6	25

TABLE 7.13   *Managerial expectations and willingness to strike: staff engineers only (per cent)*

	Managerial expectations						Total
	None or poor			Good			
	Metalco	Computer-graph	Total	Metalco	Computer-graph	Total	
Yes	75	50	61	32	25	30	45
Maybe	8	31	21	64	25	53	38
No	17	19	18	4	50	17	22
N =	12	16	28	22	8	30	58*

* Asked only of those who were not irrevocably opposed to unions.
NOTE Differences for the total sample and for Metalco engineers separately are significant (χ^2 significant = .05).

Relations with Manual Workers

Though TASS is affiliated to the AUEW – the manual-worker union at both Computergraph and Pressco, and for many at Massfas – 60 per cent of engineers at both companies thought that relationships between staff and shop-floor unions were poor. Furthermore, more than half the engineers at both companies had a hostile attitude to the manual-worker unions.

Whatever solidarity might have existed at Computergraph had been destroyed by the management/AUEW conflict of the mid-seventies which had resulted in a sit-in at the company. TASS members had refused to honour the AUEW pickets and relations had been hostile ever since. Few of the engineers showed any concern for the threatened lay-off of manual workers if the company moved more of its production outside London. The strike had also caused dissension within TASS, between those who felt the staff should have supported the machinists and those who did not, and it is significant that all of the staff engineers at Computergraph who claimed they would never join a union were hostile to manual workers.

At Metalco, and particularly at Pressco, relations were poor because of the continuous decline of engineers' differentials over production workers, which had been caused by the company's claimed inability to pay its engineers more during a pay freeze while being unable to restrain manual workers' wages because of 'creepage' in piece-rates.

Rather than being seen as political allies manual workers serve as a negative reference point, the group whose fate engineers do not wish to share and over whom they feel they should possess a significant pay differential to reflect their skill, responsibility, and qualifications. None the less union members did have a less hostile attitude to manual workers than non-members, so it is possible that membership had some effect in developing employee solidarity, although self-selection may also have played a role. A TASS representative at Computergraph expressed his views this way:

> Relations could be a lot better; you don't get cooperation. We exchange views but not activities. In theory we should work in conjunction but the views of the shop-floor and the staff clash and pull different ways. TASS members think differently and act more responsibly. They are less likely to do something rash and therefore take a broader view of activities, looking at things as a whole and not just at your own interests.

It was not only Computergraph's TASS membership who 'saw things differently' or who 'took a broader view of things' and were unlikely to do anything 'rash'. In general engineers feel themselves to be responsible and trustworthy members of the company, who might need a union to protect their interests when they are in danger of being overlooked in the struggle between employers and manual workers, but who certainly do not share the collectivist vision of the trade union activists in TASS who see themselves as workers in a class struggle with employers. Even when engineers see themselves in opposition to management it is often expressed in language that appeals to their common concern for the good of the company:

> It's important that people don't get messed about by management and have to do everything they want. Unions can ensure that jobs don't die overnight because of new techniques, can enforce retooling rather than closure. It's a way for people to have a say in how we work and how the company runs. Management shouldn't be weak and bow down to the union. You need a compromise between union and management to reflect company interests. (Computergraph D.0)

Paul Higgins, a young graduate engineer at Metalco, offered similar sentiments:

I believe in unions for anybody who is in a subordinate position. You need some way of passing ideas back up the system. It's difficult to criticise management direct. The firm's interests and the workforce's interests are not yet close enough for historical reasons. There is no trust, therefore they cannot talk and therefore need a union. It bothers me that the union is only interested in money.

This is the kind of language engineers also used when they sought 'involvement' in the running of the company.

Members' Attitudes and Union Policy

I have no way of assessing whether experience of unionism is as radicalising as the TASS leadership assumed. Certainly union members are closer to the leadership views on political involvement, collective solidarity and relations with manual workers than are non-members (Table 7.14). How much this is an effect of membership, and how much a reflection of the various factors leading to membership, is impossible to assess from this data. It is probably both.

However, there does not have to be a close relationship between the individual engineer's attitudes and the policies of the union leadership as long as a mutually acceptable arrangement can be

TABLE 7.14 *Membership and union policy (per cent)*

	Members	Potential members	Hostile to membership	Total
% support union-called strikes	52	9	5	26
% favour union involvement in politics	12	2	0	6
% not totally opposed to closed shop	48	11	0	24
% not hostile to manual unions	55	27	0	33
N =	44	45	21	110

NOTE χ^2 significant at the .001 level.

made. If engineers are willing to grant union leaders the political autonomy they need, whether agreeing with their ideology or not, in return for strong union leadership, active protection and an improved market position, then the consequences of increased engineer membership in trade unionism can be independent of the attitudes of the engineers themselves. TASS' influence on the political scene is a function of its membership numbers and, with a considerable degree of leeway, that influence can be used according to the needs and wishes of the union leadership. There are limits, of course, but in the political structure of the United Kingdom, where involvement of unions and other organisations in the affairs of state is a matter of arrangements made between élites, then the influence of engineers' unions can be considerable without engineers themselves seeking increased involvement.

THE GROWTH OF TECHNICAL UNIONISM

The opposition between professional associations and trade unions often posited by those who see them as surrogates for variations in class ideology is weak or absent for most engineers. Both are viewed in largely instrumental terms, and each has its different function.

Professional associations are seen as qualifying associations, useful if they serve to get a job. The cutting-off of the part-time route to full professional membership has deprived the associations of a major function, and most graduates see them as having little purpose other than as a source of sometimes useful technical advice. Only if employers provide career or monetary incentives for membership will it appeal to most engineers. Professional membership serves to make status claims only as a visible form of functional differentiation for senior management. Even here the claims are made *vis-à-vis* such groups as accountants, rather than *vis-à-vis* lower echelons.

Trade unions are similarly seen in instrumental terms. Those engineers who feel they need them for monetary or job security reasons join, whereas those who think they can do equally well on their own by individual negotiation with the employer do not.

Engineers' approach to unionism is different from that of manual workers because their position in the firm is different. The reasons which in the past have led many engineers to prefer professionalism as a strategy to improve their collective position now lead to concerns about the appropriateness of various union strategies. There is a general feeling that only unions can improve market position, but the type of union and the acceptable bargaining strategies are still problematic.

If engineers' attitudes could be directly transcribed into institutional form, there is little doubt that a union approximating to UKAPE, though without its overly restrictive membership criteria, would have been closest to their wishes. Engineers are reluctant to support UKAPE, however, for two reasons. First, they are unwilling to accept the exclusionary principles on which it is based. Although they often talk admiringly about the British Medical Association, or the Law Society, they are not in favour of the credential-based exclusion which is such institutions' strength. Second, engineers see unionism in instrumental terms, and they are realistic about the institutional framework with which they have to deal: UKAPE is not big enough; engineers are not a large enough block within most firms to stand alone; employers will not recognise UKAPE. In sum, UKAPE lacks teeth and without teeth it cannot serve their purpose.

Though TASS does have teeth, many engineers find its political stance uncongenial. None the less, because of its historical strength in drawing offices, it is often the union that has a presence in the company, and employers are reluctant to fragment bargaining situations. On the other hand, ASTMS' strength among foremen, and the fact that it is not the representative of the technical staff, gives it strength when it comes to management. When engineers need a union it is to one of these they are likely to turn. Their membership, in many cases, will be *despite* the unions' political stance rather than because of it. In terms of national rather than workplace politics, however, this matters only a little, since engineers are in effect exchanging their tacit support for a union politics of which they often disapprove, for the strength of the union in the workplace.

Engineers' willingness to turn to unions, however, is more a function of changes that have been occurring in the British economy and polity than a direct consequence of changes in the workplace. The close relationship – albeit a stormy one – between the Labour Government and the manual trade unions during the nineteen seventies led both to a national pay policy which engineers thought discriminated against staff employees, and to several other pieces of legislation which made union membership more advantageous. As the TASS recruiting literature says: 'the law gives members of trade unions important rights that other employees do not have', one of which is the increased lay-off rights given to union members by the

Employment Protection Act.[12] Given the importance of security for many engineers, this legislation has proved a valuable recruiting tool. The same law also made it easier for unions to claim collective-bargaining rights and thus some anti-union engineers joined non-TUC affiliated unions such as UKAPE to escape the predatory attentions of ASTMS and TASS.[13]

Unions also promoted the advantage of membership for involve-ment in the employee participation schemes which were much discussed in the late seventies. Though these have received little implementation in private industry they remain important in the nationalised industries. Involvement of unions in 'corporatist' econo-mic planning also played a role, at least amongst the politically aware. Although many engineers strongly object to this aspect of the unions' role, there may also be an element of 'if you can't beat 'em, join 'em', and EMA, TASS and ASTMS all include in their literature the number of national institutions on which they are represented – from education bodies to the National Economic Development Council.

In this social context, even the professional associations came to recommend that their members should join unions to protect their salary and status (CEI, 1975b). The institutions initially recom-mended only UKAPE and two other small non-TUC affiliated unions, and partially accepted the EMA, which was affiliated with the TUC but not the Labour Party, but these recommendations were met with outrage by TASS and ASTMS, and with considerable reserva-tions by employers who were not keen to have yet more unions to deal with. The institutions eventually backed down and admitted that membership in a union such as TASS is not incompatible with being a professional engineer. The outcome has been to increase the respec-tability of all unions. As the TASS representative pointed out, and as it became obvious from the interviews, once engineers begin to think that a union is desirable at all, they look for one with some power.

These factors have helped to change the national climate of opinion about while-collar unionism and made unions the first choice of all employees who feel they need collective protection.

CONCLUSION

Engineers see professional institutions and trade unions as pragmatic tools to solve immediate and pressing needs. Attitudes to them can no longer, if they ever could, be used as indicators of class or status consciousness. As traditional craft unions have long known, unions can maintain privilege as well as empower the weak. This is particularly true for the kind of segmented unionism common for British white-collar workers which, despite the ideological convictions of many union activists, serves to maintain distinctions and differentials.

Engineers in principle prefer the kind of craft or professional union that could improve their position by controlling the labour market rather than directly confronting employers, but they lack both the power and the will to support a credential-based exclusionary strategy. If unions cannot control entry, however, the only other source of bargaining power available is numbers. Hence engineers are caught in a potential dilemma. Joining a union with sufficient numbers – TASS for example, which is willing to organise all white-collar staff in industry – risks the loss of differentials.

Engineers' ambivalences about conventional collective bargaining strategies are also rooted in a real sense of having something to lose, not only as individuals, but as a collectivity. Engineers are concerned to be seen as responsible, trustworthy employees, and emphasise how much the union can be an aid rather than an hindrance to management. They are generally reluctant to support any union action other than defence of their job security and pay differentials.

Engineers in management positions face these dilemmas even more strongly, since managerial unions are still relatively rare in the private sector. In particular, what employers seem to dislike most is their managers *seeking* unionism, since they see this as a major breach of trust. It is possible, however, that if the threats to their positions as employees continue, managerial unionism will spread and employers will come to accept it as part of a bureaucratic system of industrial relations. Unionisation will then cease to be a negative indicator of trustworthiness.

8 The Social Production of Technical Work

This book's initial interest in engineers stemmed from a conjunction of two concerns, each deriving from a separate tradition of intellectual discourse. On the one hand engineers have received attention as bearers of a special kind of knowledge, knowledge critical to production in high-technology industries. A knowledge expected to generate a crisis of organisation and legitimation in profit-oriented busienss, as control over the dominant force of production – now no longer capital or labour, but knowledge – fell into the hands of technical experts.

On the other hand engineers are representative members of an expanding middle strata of company employees. They are neither high level management, manual workers, nor even deskilled administrative workers, and sociologists, Marxists included, have found it increasingly difficult to understand them with categories developed in traditional industries, where their small number meant they could readily be lumped with one or other of the big battalions of capital and labour.

These competing traditions of discourse occasionally interpenetrate, as they did to produce Mallet's discussion of a 'new working class', but most often they talk past each other. The former, with talk of professionals and knowledge workers, focuses on engineers themselves: their training, their knowledge, and how organisations adapt to accommodate them. It concentrates, in other words, on the 'production' of labour. The latter tradition talks about positions in the division of labour; positions derived directly from the organisation of production. It is concerned primarily with the 'consumption' of labour power. The social production of technical work, however, involves *both* these processes. Production and consumption meet in the labour market and shape each other in an ongoing process of dialectical interaction.

THE SOCIAL PRODUCTION OF TRUSTED LABOUR

John Westergaard has perceptively described the existence of two broad groupings of employees in the modern workplace:

> The larger group are those whose lives are confined within the resources and horizons of routine *jobs*. This is work which, even if skilled, involves neither autonomy nor authority on the job; allows little discretion or variety; carries with it no increments in pay and few claims for promotion to better things after the early years; leads often to hardship in old age; and is relatively vulnerable to redundancies in recession.
>
> The other group are those whose lives centre on *careers*. This is work – now or within realistic prospect – of a significantly different kind: it promises regular increments in pay to take income well above job wage levels after the early years; offers visible opportunity, though no certainty of promotion beyond that; carries some authority even at subordinate levels, while allowing discretion and variety in the application of skills and experience; demands (and tends to elicit) more commitment than goes with merely working for a wage; offers security in retirement; and, while not immune from the risks of redundancy, is much less exposed to it than routine work and provides better resources to cope with it should it happen. (Westergaard, 1984, pp. 31–2)

This is the phenomenological reality of class in the workplace and, although the boundary between these two groups is drawn in different places and goes under different names, they are both immediately visible in the workplaces of all industrial societies. In France, for example, the key boundary is between *cadre* and the rest; a distinction that is drawn quite far up the organisational structure. In the United States, the distinction is marked by the less socially resonant labels of 'exempt' and 'non-exempt' employees, referring to the collective bargaining provisions of the Taft-Hartley Act, but the dividing line is equally clear; even, as Kanter (1977) shows in her analysis of the different worlds of secretaries and executives, in non-industrial employment.

Engineers are first and foremost part of the world of Westergaard's second group: employees with autonomy, authority, career expectations, a monthly salary, fringe benefits and a certain security. They may not always be privileged members of that world, particularly in Britain, but it is their membership in it which is the defining feature of their existence.[1] This is the world of what I have called trusted workers, and what Goldthorpe (1982), following Renner, has called a service class. The key features of this world are the twin characteristics of discretionary work and an employment matrix of careers, contracts, salaries and fringe benefits.

Employers' need for trusted workers arises because there are a number of activities – design, supervision, planning among them – which require the delegation of a considerable degree of discretion to employees and where mistakes are potentially costly. It is this shared 'responsibility' which ties together such diverse positions as production supervisor, planning engineer, development engineers and test engineers, which by other criteria – authority, training, function – might seem to have little in common, and it is this responsibility, and its twin, accountability, which plays such an important role in company grading and selection schemes.

But the conjunction, in Westergaard's description, of characteristics of work and conditions of employment is not accidental. The career prospects, salaries, fringe benefits and job security which Westergaard describes are not simply quantitively different from the hourly wage of the manual worker, but are part of the matrix of social relations in which such workers are embedded. These features of the employment contract shape the relations of engineers to the firm, in the same way that the cash nexus relationship of the hourly wage helps define the position of manual workers. Graded salary increases, benefits, careers, even the notion of salary itself, are designed to secure responsible behaviour. In positions where supervision cannot be carried out directly, or results evaluated immediately, and where the consequences of a mistake are important,[2] it is necessary for employers to ensure the trustworthiness of their employees.

However, although employers have a functional need to have such discretionary tasks carried out, this by itself does not tell us much about how these tasks will be structured into jobs or careers. Neither a 'logic of industrialism' nor a 'logic of capitalist accumulation' provides a 'one best way' of organising production. Although an occupation to carry out discretionary technical tasks exists in all industrial capitalist societies,[3] the way technical work is socially organised, the boundaries which define the service class, and the nature of the career linkages within it, vary significantly.

In this concluding chapter I want to examine some of these variations – in particular the organisation of technical work in France and the United States – in order to illustrate the distinctive features of the British case. But first it will be useful to summarise the basic features of the organisation of technial work in Britain.

The Organisation of Technical Work in Britain

British engineers, as we have seen, are products of a recruitment and training system strongly controlled by employers. Many are recruited direct from secondary school and pass through company-controlled training schemes, earning non-degree qualifications by part-time education. Others, though earning degrees, often do so under employer auspices and in a manner – the sandwich degree – which emphasises industrial training. Even after qualifying, both types of engineer are recruited into low level technical jobs, which they often share with ex-manual workers who have been recruited off the shop-floor towards the end of their careers. Only after working their way 'through the grades' do they become 'engineers', a term which describes no more than a hazily defined set of positions at a particular point in the company hierarchy. This weak differentiation of engineers from other technical workers is the cause of the general public's ill-defined image of who they are, and what they do. It also severely limits the extent to which academic knowledge and qualifications can be used as legitimising or exclusionary devices.

Unlike their accountant colleagues, British engineers do not normally have a team of 'technicians' to supervise. Rather, junior and senior engineers work side by side, both reporting to a departmental manager. This supporting staff function limits their authority as technical specialists, requiring, as it does, that they channel much of their advice and activities through their bureaucratic superiors. Only when their activities can be insulated from the main line activities – as they are, for example, in Computergraph's R & D department – can British engineers achieve high levels of technical involvement and autonomy without achieving a managerial position.

Not all engineers are managers, and some, especially those with high levels of technical involvement, express a lack of interest in becoming so. None the less engineers and technical managers belong to the same labour market. All managers are recruited 'through the ranks', there is no direct entry into technical management, and most engineers, certainly those who become engineers before they are 35, have an opportunity of becoming a manager, however lowly, at some point during their careers.

At Metalco most engineers did want to become managers, and this was actively encouraged by the company, which structured both job involvement and monetary rewards to develop such an orientation, even when this led engineers out of the technical function altogether. At Computergraph, where most engineers had a technical orientation, the company encouraged this because it fitted its needs. It is because the labour market for engineers contains both 'expert' and 'management' positions that companies are able to channel orientations this way. It is also this which makes career trajectories, rather than jobs or occupations, the most relevant unit of analysis.

The Organisation of Technical Work in France[4]

French engineers are products of a very different system for producing responsible employees. Most are graduates of élite engineering schools, including such *grandes écoles* as the *Ecole centrale des arts et manufactures* and the *Ecole d'arts et métiers*, or the 170 other *petites écoles d'ingénieur*. These engineering schools are separate from the university system, and in many ways more prestigious.

Despite this very different recruitment source, when French employers extol the virtues of recruiting from these schools, they emphasise the same personality characteristics extolled by British employers in their HNC engineers: hard work, commitment to business values and loyalty to the firm; values they do not find in the typical university graduate. There is a significant difference, however. The British engineer, particularly the industrially trained one, is likely to surround his knowledge in a rhetoric of practicality, even when this clearly underestimates the role of formal knowledge in his job. The French engineer is likely to develop a rhetoric of theory, of mathematics and of engineering science, even though there is no evidence that he makes any more use of such science than his British counterpart. When Poulantzas and Gorz write about the role played by the ideological division between mental and manual labour in defining the new middle class, it is this ready appeal to theory that they are referring to. The strength of these appeals, however, is strictly French, and is rooted in the high prestige of logic and theoretical discourse in French culture, a prestige which predates French industrialism, if not French capitalism, and which the *grandes écoles* defend as their own.

Graduates of these élite engineering schools enter the company as *cadres*, and as *cadres* they are marked off from technicians by as many social distinctions as those marking the works/staff boundary in most British companies. At the traditional French company studied by Crawford (1984), *cadres* had their own housing areas, dining-rooms, and distinctive headgear, as well as the separate recruitment procedures, pay schedules, contractual arrangements and career ladders which all *cadres* possess. From the beginning of the engineer's career as a *cadre*, he is on a pay scale and promotion ladder that begins where that of the less qualified *technicien* ends, and already superior in rank and authority to them.

These engineers function not as technical specialists but as polyvalent managers. French engineers expect to have a technician personally assigned to them to carry out detailed or routine tasks almost as soon as they join the firm. Their prime identification is as managers rather than specialised technical staff, and the ability to assign the work of technicians is part of their self-image. Even at the earliest stage of their career, French engineers do much less detail work than the typical British engineer, and they also experience much less supervision.

Only in high-tech R & D units do engineers work as technical staff in any numbers without having supporting technicians assigned to them, and they experience it as a loss of status. Unlike the British engineers, for whom R & D project work delivered a high level of technical involvement and organisation autonomy, French engineers find the absence of technicians a threat to their managerial image and a potential source of proletarianisation. It is partly this development which drew Mallet to high-tech companies as a source of potentially rebellious engineers.

French engineers not only begin higher up the ladder than their British counterparts, but have better long-term prospects. Fully half of all graduates of such schools will reach at least the rank of factory manager during their career. Fine distinctions between different institutions continue to affect the engineer's career long after graduation, and not simply in an informal way. Companies often use details of education to plot out salary curves and promotion prospects.

Technicians, on the other hand, many of whom perform similar technical tasks to British engineers, often have no training, although a growing number of *techniciens diplômés* have two years of post secondary (or high school) education. A few technicians do cross the *cadre* barrier – up to one-third of French engineers, the so-called *ingénieurs maison*, have not graduated from engineering school – but such a passage typically occurs in mid-career or later, and is perceived as an individual act of social mobility, not part of a normal career ladder. In contrast to non-credentialled British engineers who experience this kind of promotion, it is not transferable outside of the company in which it occurs. It is a direct reward for company loyalty, not a recognition of the general relevance of experience. The sense of blocked mobility, which is strong for these French technicians because it is institutionally recognised, is partly responsible for their greater militancy. They are aware that French employers do not consider them to be trusted workers of the same kind as engineers.

The Organisation of American Technical Work[5]

In the United States, too, engineers and other 'trusted workers' are largely the product of the higher education system; this time of the vocational engineering schools located in the university. Here, too, they learn not only the necessary techniques of their trade but are socialised into the norms of business (Berg, 1971; Collins, 1971).

In contrast to the French engineer's role as a technically trained manager, American engineers play prime roles as technical specialists. They are accepted as 'experts' in their own right, even in traditional industry, and have considerable autonomy. Most of the engineers in the traditional industry studied by Zussman (1985) worked out of their own office, and had considerable freedom to schedule their own work. Many had technicians working for them as assistants, though they did not conceptualise this as management *per se*. A relatively trivial but revealing feature of their jobs is their informal capacity to schedule their own working hours despite the absence of any formal flexitime system.

Though they function as technical specialists, American engineers also have strong managerial ambitions, only relinquishing them when signs of their failure are too visible to ignore.

Although about half of Zussman's sample of engineers had not begun their work careers with degrees, many of these acquired them by part-time education while working as technicians, and this practice is extensive. Though many engineers had passed through technicians' positions, the line between engineers' jobs, as 'exempt' professionals, and those of technicians is clearly marked, though not with the same strength of symbolism as in France. Unlike in the United Kingdom, engineers with appropriate qualifications join the firm directly as engineers, as superior to technicians.

As a consequence of this system the division of labour becomes structured into a series of bounded occupations in which transition from one position to another is via the obtaining of an additional qualification. For a technician to become an engineer, the surest way is to go to school part-time to obtain a degree. For an engineer to become a manager, the surest route is via the acquisition of an MBA. Thus general management, where most of the career rewards of management lie, is increasingly seen as a separate occupation from engineering *per se*, and opportunities for positions in top management are probably in decline for engineers unwilling or unable to obtain an MBA.

Although lacking the strength to control entry and to insist on peer group evaluation, this American model of technical work is the only one that approaches the professional model. Although accreditation of engineering education is actually in the hands of bodies which have traditionally had very strong employer influence (Noble, 1977), the formal autonomy of the universities helps weaken any impression of close employer control, and firms' use of qualifications to segment occupations also helps to cement the ideological role of the professional model (Larson, 1977). But while it once helped engineers in their collective mobility project by clearly demarcating them from technicians and manual workers below, the emergence of management itself as its own 'profession' threatens to exclude engineers from the senior management positions which were theirs for most of the American period of industrialism.

PRODUCTION AND REPRODUCTION

These differences are the outcomes of each nation's particular historical experiences, and the particular form taken by the developing interaction of the supply and demand for labour. One of the major gaps in our knowledge of the developing structures of industrial capitalist societies is caused by the rarity of explicitly comparative and historical studies of the structuring of work (Littler, 1982). Here I want only to stress one strand in these historical experiences, the effects of the particular patterns of recruitment of trusted labour on the overall structuring of technical work.

As I argued in Chapter 3, the unwillingness of the English middle class to participate in technical activities after the mid-nineteenth century – which in turn partly resulted from the early dominance of apprentice-trained working-class mechanics in such positions – reinforced British employers' reliance on apprenticeships, on-the-job training and promotion from within to secure their trusted labour supply. In the absence of a potential labour force already socialised to accept capitalist domination by family upbringing, and in the absence of universities willing to produce engineers of the 'right type', British employers were forced to rely on producing their own engineers. The maintenance of the apprenticeship model – modelled closely on that of craft apprenticeships – served to reinforce the general feeling that engineers were not suited for the higher ranks of management, and were significantly inferior to members of more respectable professions such as accountancy. Only recently and reluctantly have most employers, particularly those in traditional industry, been willing to rely on the education system for prior socialisation and selection.

In France engineering has fewer links with the artisan tradition. Early state sponsorship of élite technical schools, modelled after the élite military engineering schools of the eighteenth century, provided a source of middle-class recruits willing to learn engineering science to find jobs as chief assistants to entrepreneurs looking for help in their expanding companies. This was combined with a shortage of highly skilled artisans, largely brought on by the destruction of traditional guild apprenticeships in the Revolution. Nineteenth-century French engineers were already polyvalent technical managers, with high social pretensions (Weiss, 1982).

Even though many of the early industrial engineers began their careers as skilled workmen and came from modest origins, the privileged access to senior management positions for graduates of élite engineering schools provided the model for collective mobility. Thus the technical lycées, which initially trained many company-promoted engineers, fought for, and eventually won, the right to award engineering diplomas. Lacking skilled mechanics but having broadly trained engineers with pretensions to manage strongly affected the structure of modern French engineering.

The United States occupies an intermediate position between these two extremes. Although the American occupation, like the British, traces its origins back to the skilled mechanics of the nineteenth century, there was no status barrier preventing the children of the entrepreneurial middle class from seeking their fortunes as engineers and managers in the new corporate bureaucracies of the late nineteenth century. American engineers of the nineteenth century were often drawn from middle and upper class backgrounds. Noble (1977, p. 39) argues that the autonomy and managerial careers that American engineers were able to carve out for themselves were as a much a consequence of their own class background as of their technical skills.

Despite this high status background, nineteenth century American engineering had a strong 'shop culture', where the rhetoric of practicality and the distrust of the products of 'theoretical' academic training was as strong as that found in the traditional parts of British industry today (Calvert, 1967). As Noble puts it: 'Engineers of the "rule of thumb", "cut-and-try" method resented the pretensions of the younger scientifically-oriented, "hypothetical" engineers, who invariably worked under them before rising into managerial positions' (Noble, p. 27).

The history of American engineering education in the nineteenth and early twentieth century is the history of the tension between the rejection of the 'academicism' of university training by the 'shop culture' engineers, and the desire by corporations to externalise their training costs. Noble's discussion of this struggle mirrors, in almost the same words, British employers' rejection of the attempts by the professional associations and engineering educators to put engineering education in the hands of British universities. The common complaints against the universities were that they did not develop a strong enough commitment to business values, that their products were too 'theoretical', and even that college graduates did not get on so well with the shop-floor.

However, American industrialists, containing among them a large number of engineers, were not isolated from the dominant élite culture as they were in England, and the decentralised nature of the American university system made it more susceptible to local pressure. By the early 1930s the Engineers Council for Professional Development, dominated by employers, achieved control of educational accreditation, and the companies could control the curricula to their own liking. This was also the period of the depression and companies were looking to find ways to externalise as many costs as possible. Just as the thirties saw the end of the experiments in corporate welfare as responsibilities were transferred to the state, so they also saw the beginning of the end of the great company training schools, although General Motors continued to operate the General Motors Institute to educate its own automotive engineers until very recently.

The setting of 'professional' schools within the American educational establishment ensured that employers could both externalise their training costs and be sure of a supply of engineers socialised into business values and not contaminated by the inclination to pursue the pure research found in academic institutions. Although they have been largely successful in these aims, the pressures on engineering departments within universities to conform to more acceptable academic values of science education have led to continued pressure to raise the scientific and theoretical components of engineering education, though there is no real evidence that they are ever used on the job. Perhaps in consequence employers have been encouraging the growth of Bachelor of Technology graduates, supposedly more practical and supportive of the professional engineer, but in practice employed to do much the same work. The academic rhetoric of engineering science, although not employed by American engineers themselves, seems to have misled some writers to take the scientific base of 'professionalism' too seriously.

The general implication of these illustrations is that the structure of work itself and, in particular, the nature of crucial boundaries such as that between the service class and lesser workers are shaped not only by factors operating on the terrain of production, as much recent Marxist writing would have it, but are the outcome of processes which shape the production of labour as well as its consumption.

ENGINEERS AS TRUSTED WORKERS

What are the main advantages of conceiving of engineers as trusted workers, members of a service class? There are two. The first is that it accounts more directly than most other conceptual frameworks for the salient features of the social relations in which engineers find themselves embedded. The second is that it accounts more parsimoniously than competing views for the distinctive features of engineers' ideologies that we have been exploring. Since both these sets of issues have been the main topic of the book, I will only briefly summarise them here.

There are three structural issues that need to be stressed. First, seeing engineers as trusted workers allows us to account for the reluctance of employers to proletarianise engineers despite long and repeated predictions. Engineers, and other members of the service class, are not the partly incorporated remains of some pre-capitalist petty bourgeoisie waiting to be brought under 'real control'. Instead they are employed to perform tasks which it would be inefficient to deskill. Furthermore, even when efficiency criteria might suggest deskilling, because engineers are 'trusted workers' employers are reluctant to deskill them unless cost savings are great. Engineers are part of the salaried work force whose value to the company tends to be assessed over longer periods of time than are hourly-wage workers: they are treated as an overhead rather than a variable cost. It is also not in the employers' interest to deskill and routinise the jobs of employees who are part of the pool from which future high-level managers are to be selected. This is not to say that particular tasks may not be transferred across the class boundary, but this normally occurs only when they come to be performed by a different group of workers. Deskilling, as we argued in Chapter 4, requires the redrawing of labour market boundaries as well as the routinisation of tasks.

Second, this model avoids the common mistake of placing managerial and expert employees into different classes. Engineering and managerial positions are routinely part of the same career line. In Britain they offer alternative routes for securing job satisfaction, whereas in France they are both an integral part of the engineer's role. In either case the similarity of interests that engineers share with managers as trusted workers is far more critical in defining their joint class interests than is any issue of diverse training or functional specialisation separating them.

Third, it puts engineers' 'knowledge' in perspective. Those writers who are most likely to see technical workers as creating problems for integration into the firm are those who also stress the autonomy of knowledge and engineers' orientation to science. But an engineer's 'knowledge' only becomes 'expertise' – becomes embodied in labour power – if employers are willing to accept it. Craftsmen and other production workers continue to know many things about the production process, but their knowledge is not sanctioned by the employer. Engineers' knowledge is sanctioned just because it comes wrapped in a package also containing 'trustworthiness' and 'responsibility'. To this extent Habermas, Gouldner, and others who have emphasised the essential *subservience* of technical knowledge are correct. However, this subordination does not stem from the nature of the knowledge itself, but derives from the way it becomes sanctioned in the process of embodiment as labour power.

In addition to providing an account of engineers' structural position, it is equally important to be able to comprehend their ideological responses. Again, there are three points that are worth repeating here in summary form.

First, as Burawoy (1978) has pointed out, the essential problem for the capitalist employer is how to extract surplus value without being seen to do so, or, to put it another way, how to ensure during the day-to-day operations of the firm that the employer's interests and the employees' interests are seen to be the same. This is particularly critical for employees in discretionary positions. If an employer has extensive use for creative technical ability, as Computergraph did, engineers can be given interesting technical problems to solve within fairly wide parameters. They can be insulated from the commercial side of the business so that they do not face any conflict between their technical interests and the interests of the firm.

On the other hand, as at Metalco where there was a potential conflict, the company can direct engineers' interests towards managerial involvement and ensure that any constraints on engineers' work are seen to derive from the 'factual' constraints of the market place, rather than from the whim of management or the search for capital accumulation. Profit centres, cost centres, and other instruments of decentralisation to 'internalise the market' can all serve this purpose. By 'exposing' their engineers to the exigencies of a poor product market rather than – as would have been equally possible in a company the size of Metalco – funding technical development out of corporate funds, any decision not to invest in new development work appears to flow directly from the state of the market.

Second, if engineers make any demands for participation, they are likely to be self-interested. When they are interested in the matter at all, engineers seek managerial-style involvement, a collective assertion where individual participation might be limited. In general, they reject manual workers' participation in the running of the firm on meritocratic grounds, and when they do agree that such workers should have more participation they argue that this would encourage the same kind of responsible behaviour that engineers themselves display.

Third, seeing engineers as trusted workers helps reveal the dilemmas involved in engineering unionism, particularly in Britain where employers have not supported a strong lower boundary to their occupation. Engineers may be trusted workers, but they are workers none the less, and may therefore need a union. To be successful engineers' unions have to be willing to organise everyone the employer calls an engineer, since the failure to control entry into the labour market means that occupational-based unions such as UKAPE are as unsuccessful as the professional associations. If unions cannot control entry, the only other source of bargaining power available is numbers. Hence engineers are caught in a potential dilemma. Joining a union with strength in numbers – TASS, for example, which is willing to organise any and all white-collar staff in the industry – risks the loss of differential privileges, and even the engineers' distinctive position as trusted workers. The solution has been to push for differentiated bargaining units for the various grades of employees, rather than to emphasise collective solidarity.

THE FUTURE OF BRITISH ENGINEERING

The structuring of technical work is not static, and there are developments other than those stemming from the rise of science-based industry which continue to shape the fate of British engineering. There is the continuing effort to upgrade the status of engineers by the professional associations and the training establishments. Attempts to open up the higher ranks of British management to engineers is seen as one solution to the British economic malaise. A number of academic programmes have been developed with government support to develop 'super engineers', engineers who are expected to be high-flyers in management soon after their graduation. If this kind of programme is extended then it is possible that British companies might develop the French practice of recruiting most technical managers direct from the university, with its corollary of closing off technicians' access to engineering positions, and having engineers begin their careers by supervising groups of subordinate technicians. Though promotion from technician positions will never reach zero, it could diminish to the point of becoming an example of individual mobility rather than routine career development. The oft-heralded proletarianisation of technicians might then become a reality.

Although British employers have a history of resisting such changes, if the supply of industrially trained engineers is cut off by further changes in the education system, and if companies are faced with hostile collective bargaining by unions such as TASS but can resist the unionisation of managerial staff, then they might be willing to accept this segmentation of the technical workforce more willingly than at present. Engineers will become supervisors on the French model, and the occupation of technician will become fully institutionalised. Since such an organisation of the workforce prompted the militancy of technicians in Italy and France, such a change may have broader social consequences.

In contrast, the expansion of university and polytechnic education may simply channel the same percentage of schoolchildren into degree programmes as previously trained by the part-time route. If this occurs the major impact will be on the class base of recruitment since working-class students have had greater proportional representation in part-time studies. This might have its own consequences, however, in further driving a cultural wedge between management and the shop-floor.

Unionisation will continue but there is no reason to assume increased militancy except perhaps as a consequence of massive lay-offs in nationalised industry. There is little likelihood of grass-roots pressure for an alliance with manual workers, even though TASS might encourage such moves at both union and national levels. Engineers, by and large, are reasonably happy organisational employees and unless their pay becomes seriously affected by inflation there will be little increased activism. Employers have strong incentives to continue to maintain engineers' allegiance.

There are distinctive national configurations in the structure of technical work and the class location of technical workers. Much of the French and American writings about engineers and technical workers in advanced industrial society seem somewhat parochial when applied to the British case. The stress on professionalism seems especially American, while that on the potential radicalisation of technicians seems very French. The explanation for such differences, however, cannot be sought solely in different cultural traditions, which assume that engineers in similar structural positions will act differently because of different political and ideological factors. Although they undoubtedly play some role, neither a French tradition of radical white-collar unionism nor an American tradition of status-striving professionalism is enough to explain present differences. Rather, explanations need to be sought at the structural level, in the structuring of the service class itself. This in turn is a consequence of historical variations in the 'production', 'consumption' and 'exchange' of technical labour power.

Appendix The Interview Schedule

SECTION A

Section A was normally completed in writing by the engineer before the interview began. Occasionally it was completed at the beginning of the actual interview.

1. Could you please provide the name, location, type of school and dates of attendance for all secondary schools attended from age 13.
2. Please give information about any external qualifications earned while at school; e.g. number of 'O' and/or 'A' level passes, Higher or Ordinary School Certificates etc.
3. Please give your highest post-school qualification.
4. Please provide the following information about all places of education that you have attended (or still attend) for more than one month since leaving school. Name, location, dates attended, course(s) followed, whether full-time or part-time (if part-time, indicate whether day release, block release, evenings etc.). If sandwich course please give details of scheduling, name of company sponsoring course (if any). List all qualifications received.
5. Further Training. Please give details of any apprenticeship scheme (craft, technical or graduate etc.) which you have participated in. Include type, dates, name of company, and any other details you may think relevant.
6. Please provide name, dates, company sponsorship and location of any course you have attended for more than one week in the last five years.
7. Please indicate any other training you have received in the last two years, stating its length, type, location etc.
8. Job History. Please provide the following information for each job you have held since leaving school. This should include information on different positions in the same company. Job title, Company, Location, Type of industry, Dates of employment, Department, Nature of tasks performed and responsibilities held.

SECTION B

1. At what age did you first decide to become an engineer?
2. What made you decide?

200

3. (*Asked for all company changes, and changes in type of department.*) I see you moved from ——— to ———. What did your new job or position offer you that you were not getting in the old one?
4. Was the experience you gained at ——— something you could sell to ———?
5. What made you join ——— (*Give first department*)?
6. *If has made a major function change during career*: Are you glad you made the department change you did? Why?
7. In the past, what sorts of things have been most valuable to you in getting the kinds of jobs you wanted, or in getting promotion?
8. Have you ever been unemployed? *If yes*: When was that? How did it happen?
9. How secure would you say your job is now? Why is that?
   9.1. *If no mention of possible insecurity*: Can you imagine any conditions or situations where it might not be so secure?
10. Have you ever thought of working for yourself?
    10.1. *If yes*: In what area?
11. What would be the advantages? And the disadvantages?
12. Is there anything that you've been especially pleased with or disappointed with in the way your career has turned out so far?
13. Have you ever thought of leaving (*Metalco* or *Computergraph*)?
    If yes:
    13.1. Why is that?
    13.2. What sort of job would you be looking for?
    13.3. Do you think one would be difficult to get? Why do you say that?
    13.4. Would your experience here be something you could sell to another company?
14. What do you hope to be doing five or ten years from now? (*Probe for managerial versus technical or sales or production management.*)
15. Would your answer be the same if you could receive equal pay for doing technical work without going into management?
16. What do you think will be the highest position you will ever hold?
17. Is that likely to be with this company, or not?
18. How good do you think your chances are of achieving your ambitions?
19. What sort of things does it take to get on in this company?
20. Ideally, what should it depend on?
21. Do you think you would improve your chances by moving?
22. How important is it for you to be promoted?
    22.1. *If negative*: What is it, if anything, that you wouldn't like about the higher positions?
23. If things turn out the way you'd like, do you think there will be any disadvantages?
24. Do you think your technical skills are fully utilised in this job?
    If no: Do you mind this particularly? Why not?
25. Do you think a degree is useful (would be useful) for the job you do at present?
26. What about for career purposes? Would (Is) a degree be useful for that?
27. Are there any parts of the job that could be done by someone with less technical education than yourself?

27.1 *If yes*: Do you think it would be a good idea if it were? Why? Why not?

28. In the job you have now, do you find that you can pretty much do it in the way you think best?

29. Do you get as much chance as you would like to try out new ideas or new ways of doing things?

30. Is there as much variety as you would like in the job, or do you find that you deal with the same problems over and over?

31. Do you always know why a particular job has to be done? Or why it has to be done in a particular way?

32. Do you ever get told to do things that you disagree with?

33. Do you think it would be a good idea to increase your responsibility so that you could make more decisions on your own?

34. Do you think it would be possible to increase the scope of your work so you could be more involved in more parts of what is going on? For example, to follow the same product through from start to finish?

34.1. *If yes*: How? Would you like that? Why? Why not?

34.2. *If no*: Why not?

35. Do you think there are any jobs around here that have become so specialised and routinised that there isn't any interest or challenge left in them?

35.1. *If yes*: Why do you think this has occurred?

35.2. *If no*: Have you ever worked at a company where that has happened to jobs at your level?

36. Are there any constraints on you doing the best technical job you could?

36.1. *If yes*: Does this bother you? Why? Why not?

37. Thinking about all the sorts of things you do here, what are the parts of the job that you get the most satisfaction out of?

38. And what are the parts of the job you find the least satisfying?

39. *If respondent does not currently have managerial position*: Have you ever had any supervisory responsibilities?

39.1. *If yes*: Who did that involve? How many? What type? What did it involve?

40. *For both past and present supervisors*: Is (Was) that a part of your job you enjoy(ed)?

40.1. What would you say it was that gives (gave) you the right to supervise others?

41. *If manager does not directly supervise manual workers ask*: Have you ever had any line or production management responsibilities?

41.1. *If yes*: Was it very different from your responsibilities now? How? Which do you prefer? Why?

41.2. *If no*: Have you ever thought of going in for that side of the company? Do you think it would be very different? How? Which do you think you would prefer? Why?

42. If you make a mistake, do poor work, or don't do the job satisfactorily, who is likely to notice it first?

43. How will they notice this?

44. Do you know how the company assesses its engineers? (*If answers in terms of a formal system, probe*: Is that how it really works?)
45. Of all the persons above you in the company, who has the most control over what you actually do on the job?
46. Who has the most control over your future prospects?
47. If your boss doesn't think you are doing such a good job, what sorts of things are likely to happen?
48. Do you think your boss really is in a position where it's fair for him to evaluate you? Why? Why not?
49. What gives him the right to supervise you?
50. In situations like yours, what do you think your boss is for?
51. Is he really necessary at all? Why?
52. Do you know much about the overall financial situation of the company?
53. Do you think it's part of an engineer's job to be concerned with these things?
54. Would you like to know more? Why? What sorts of things?
55. Are there any decisions at this company that you think you and other engineers should have more say in? Can you give me an example?
56. What about the production workers, are there decisions that they should be involved in?
57. There has recently been published a government report – the Bullock Report – which recommends that employees should have the power to vote worker representatives on to the board of directors of the company they work for, and that they should have equal voting rights with directors representing shareholders and a number of outside directors. What do you think about this proposal?
58. The report specifically recommends that the employee directors should be sponsored by unions, what do you think of this provision?
59. Do you feel part of management?
60. Do you think of yourself as a professional? What do you mean by that?
61. Are you a member of a professional institution? If so, which?
    61.1. *If yes*: How often do you attend meetings? Why did you join? Do you think it's important for engineers to belong to a professional association? Why? Why not?
    61.2. *If no*: Why haven't you joined?
62. What do you think is the purpose of the professional institutes? What do you think they should do for their members?
63. Do you think they fulfil that purpose now? (*Probe*.)
64. What do you think of the attempt to restrict professional membership to graduates?
65. Have you published any technical articles, papers, or books? How many?
66. Have you given any technical lectures or delivered any technical papers to an outside audience? How many?
67. Have you made any innovations that have been patented? How many?
68. Do you belong to a trade union?
    If yes:

68.1. Which one?

68.2. How long have you been a member?

68.3. Do you hold (or have you ever held) any union office? if so, which? When?

68.4. How often do you go to office or company union meetings? When did you last go to one?

68.5. How often do you go to union area branch meetings? When did you last go to one?

If a non-member:

68.6. Have you ever belonged to one in the past? Which? When? Why did you leave?

If a union member ask:

69. Why did you join a union?

70. Why did you join that particular union?

71. Is there anything you dislike about your union?

72. Do you pay the political levy?

73. Do you vote in union elections? *If not*: Why not?

74. Have you ever stood, or thought of standing for union office?

74.1. *If yes*: Have you ever done anything about it? What?

If not a union member ask:

75. Have you ever belonged to a union in the past?

If yes:

75.1. Which one?

75.2. Why did you leave?

75.3. Did you pay Labour Party dues?

75.4. Why don't you belong to a union now?

75.5. Are there any circumstances under which you would consider joining a union? What are they? What kind would you want to join?

All:

76. Do you think unions are a good idea for people like yourself? Why?

77. What do you think accounts for the recent increase in unionisation amongst engineers and other technical staff?

78. Do you think belonging to a union is a good idea for all employees? *If yes*: Including management?

79. What kinds of things do you think a union for engineers should do?

80. Would you support a strike? (*Probe for conditions*)

81. What about a closed shop?

82. What is the relationship between the staff and the shop-floor unions here? Do you think they should give each other mutual support – including joint action?

83. Do you think being active in a union could hamper your promotion chances?

84. Do you think a company owes an employee anything more than the minimum laid down by law?

85. Do you think this company provides more than this?

86. Does an employee owe his company anything more than the contract requires?

87. Do you think all employees in your kind of job think the same?

88. What about other groups, production workers, technicians, and so on?
89. Are you satisfied with your salary? *Probe*: Is this because you think the work you do is worth more? Or because you need the money?
90. Do you sometimes compare your salary with that of other occupations or groups?
    90.1. *If yes*: With whom? How do you feel about it?
    90.2. *If only mentions people within the company*: And outside of the company, do you make any comparisons between your own standard of living and others? How do you feel about it?
91. What is there about the difference in job between an engineer and a production worker that means an engineer should earn more?
92. What is there (if anything) about the difference in job between an engineer and a manager that means a manager should earn more?
93. What about the range of pay between different grades of engineer, is it too wider, or too narrow?
94. What sorts of things do you think should be taken into consideration in deciding what an engineer gets paid?
95. Some firms pay individuals strictly according to the particular job grade they occupy, while others pay on a more individualised system. Which way do you prefer? Why?
96. Do you think there really are 'fair' ways to determine what different groups and occupations in the country should earn?
97. How would you feel if everyone received the same income whatever their jobs?
98. When you think of all the things you do in life, what are the things that really give you the most satisfaction?
99. And what are the things that really get you to feel the most dissatisfied?
100. What was your father's usual occupation while you were growing up?
101. What was your father's final occupation?
102. What was your mother's usual occupation?
103. Paternal grandfather's usual occupation?
104. Maternal grandfather's usual occupation?
105. Father-in-law's usual occupation?
106. Father-in-law's final occupation?
107. Mother-in-law's usual occupation?
108. Brother(s)' occupation(s)?
109. Sister(s)' occupation(s)?
110. Sister(s)' husband(s)' occupation(s)?
111. Wife's brother(s)' occupation(s)?
112. Wife's brother-in-law(s)' occupation(s)?
113. Occupations of four nearest neighbours?
114. Date of birth?
115. Place of birth?
116. Family's total income last year?
117. Respondent's total income last year?
118. Approximate value of house (if owned)?
119. Approximate value of total savings?

Notes

1 ENGINEERS IN ADVANCED INDUSTRIAL SOCIETY

1. But see Nichols and Beynon's description of 'Chemco' in *Living with Capitalism*, which shows the extent to which even highly automated plants rely on the heaviest and dirtiest forms of unskilled labour (Nichols and Beynon, 1977).
2. Exact figures are hard to produce because of difficulties of settling on appropriate criteria. There were 604 500 scientists and engineers with a degree or a Higher National Certificate or Diploma in 1971 (Finniston, 1980) but counts based on credentials ignore the large number of engineers who have not been formally trained. Counts based on job definitions, on the other hand, run into problems of comparability across companies, even departments. For a general critique of occupational data as normally collected and and used by sociologists, see Udy (1981) and Baron and Bielby (1980).
3. The leap from the politics of the workplace to the politics of society is embedded deeply in the conceptual structure of both Marxism and its 'industrial society' critics. We do not directly investigate this connection here. Without an adequate conceptualisation of the social arrangements of work, however, attempts to assess the relationship between work and society are bound to be inadequate.
4. Engineers are, of course, not the only occupational group to whom such arguments could apply, but in many ways they are the most salient. They are by far the largest of the industrial 'professions' and they are involved in industrial production more closely than any other group of 'experts'.
5. See also Brody's description (1960) of the organisation of steel production in the nineteenth century, where craft workers could also be said to 'hire' capital.
6. Poulantzas uses two sets of criteria to distinguish non-manual employees from the working class. The first is the performance of productive or non-productive labour in the Marxist sense, i.e. whether or not the employee produces surplus value, or is simply a charge against revenue as in the case, for example, of bank clerks. Only productive workers can be considered part of the working class, since all non-productive workers owe their jobs to the maintenance of capitalism and hence their interests are inevitably tied to it. Since engineers are productive workers, and by

that criterion, working class, this particular debate does not immediately concern us. It is by Poulantzas' second set of criteria, their performance of 'mental labour', that engineers belong to the petty bourgeoisie.
7. Most of this literature has been American-inspired (Perrucci and Gerstl, 1969a, 1969b), including the only study of this kind to be done on British engineers (Gerstl and Hutton, 1966).

2 INDUSTRY: OLD AND NEW

1. See Sabel (1982) for discussion of the impact of flexible manufacturing techniques on the Italian fashion industry.
2. I focused on technological variations because these seem to be the most direct indicators of what is meant by post-industrial society. But one other source of variation has been given attention by some of the theorists we have discussed, and that is the market situation of the firm in which the technical workers are employed: in particular the extent to which the market position of the firm is dominated by the state (Mallet, 1975). This is an interesting argument and deserves research, though to my knowledge it has received none, but it is not one that has direct ties with the dominant thrust of the high-technology thesis, though some such as Mallet have attempted to make it so. Some science-based firms operate in severely competitive civilian markets, others in defence-oriented, state-controlled ones, others are nationalised. The same is also true of low technology industries. Defence-oriented industries and nationalised industries do raise interesting, related questions and deserve study, but they could not be incorporated into this research.
3. There was also an additional interview sample of twenty accountants at Computergraph and its parent company. Though these interviews have not been fully analysed for this report, material from them will occasionally be drawn upon to make appropriate points of comparison.
4. All but five of the interviews used for this book I carried out myself. Pressure of time, however, required that five of the interviews at Metalco's Pressco division be done by a sociology graduate student from a local university. Reviews of the tapes suggest that this made no significant difference and in each case I had extensive informal conversations with these engineers while conducting the field research. Most of these engineers were also interviewed, by myself or others, about their political and social ideologies. The results from this latter research will be reported elsewhere.
5. The names of all of the companies, their divisions and subdivisions, as well as those of all individuals have been altered to preserve anonymity. Similarly descriptions of products and places have been left vague where it was felt that more exact descriptions would have been revealing. Where data is provided for the company these have been approximated, but relative proportions have been maintained. This data is meant to be illustrative while maintaining confidentiality.
6. Various attempts to explain decentralisation/centralisation as functions of technology, stability and so on, underestimate the importance of

managerial strategies especially in large corporations. British Leyland, for example, since its formation out of a diverse group of companies has gone through a complete cycle of centralisation under the Lords Stokes and Ryder and now decentralisation under Edwardes. The two electronics giants, Philips and GEC, have very different models of organisation with a centralised corporate personnel and R & D functions at Philips and a highly decentralised structure at GEC. The arguments given for centralisation are based on rationalisation and planning, those for decentralisation on flexibility and adaptation. Pfeffer (1979) has an interesting discussion of the managerial strategies involved.

7. For a more extensive discussion of these unions, see Chapter 7.
8. In 1978 this latter company had sales of about £110 million and employed about 9000 people.
9. It is perhaps symptomatic of the low prestige given to 'making things' in academic culture that while we all learn enough about numbers to be awed by the complexity of book-keeping and accountancy, and are literate enough to appreciate the complexity of written reports, learning to read (let alone to produce) an engineering drawing is unlikely to be part of the curriculum for any university-oriented schoolchild.

3   KNOWLEDGE, TRUST AND LABOUR MARKETS

1. There are 16 major professional associations in Britain which are members of the Council of Engineering Institutions, each representing a different specialisation. They primarily function as learned societies but have combined to develop single qualifying standards. A fuller discussion of the role of the institutions will be found in Chapter 7. On the possibility of the institutions further restricting members see the Institution of Electrical Engineers' submission to the Finniston Committee (Institution of Electrical Engineers, 1978).
2. The numbers of engineering graduates increased from 7700 in 1969 to 10 800 in 1978, while the number of new engineers with HNC/Ds declined from 10 500 in 1969 to 7700 in 1980 (Finniston, 1980, pp. 48–9).
3. A system of training grants and levies is designed to even out the costs of industrial training between companies who do the training and those that recruit ready-trained labour. The Engineering Industry Training Board (EITB) had jurisdiction over both Metalco and Computergraph.
4. For an extended discussion of the political vicissitudes of manpower planning in the British political context see McCormick (1977) and the references cited therein.
5. These technician engineers are encouraged to join 'junior' institutions, such as the Institution of Electrical and Electronics Technician Engineers, set up expressly to cater for the new grade. Outside the public sector, however, where membership is formally encouraged, such institutions have never been very popular, and their total membership was only 45 978 in 1977, compared to a total CEI chartered membership of 211 000 (CEI, 1977, p. 13). There are 45 institutional members of the

Technician Engineer Section of the CEI, 10 of which are also full members. The rest are either specially constituted for Technician Engineers – often as offshoots of the senior institutions – or are institutions which do not have such high educational criteria for membership, or are highly specialised.

6. B. C. Roberts *et al.*'s *Reluctant Militants* (1972) details the various attempts to foster a 'technician's' identity in the 1960s (pp. 38–55), and while they accept for themselves the idea that an explicit technician's occupation does exist, much of the rest of the book can be more profitably read as an attempt to understand the diversity of behaviours of a group of technical workers with very different work and market positions.

7. Certain qualifications, for example, have supposedly changed their technical and social meaning over time. There has, for example, been a much discussed but undocumented decline in the standards of the HNC since the early 1970s. The large-scale expansion of British higher education in the 1960s inevitably produced a larger number of graduates – many recruited, no doubt, from the same ability pool as the old HNC. Such discussions merge into and indeed become inseparable from arguments about the change in the intellectual standards of the recruits from the various programmes. An HNC meant as much in the past as a degree does now, it is argued, because of the quality of the recruits it once drew but no longer does.

8. It was certainly prevalent in most of the companies with whom I came into contact during the research, and its prevalence is confirmed in a study done by Mace and his associates which documents extensive willingness to substitute different categories of labour, occupations if you will, for each other (Mace and Taylor, 1975; Mace and Wilkinson, 1977). The lack of relationship between education and position is also reported for a larger sample by Sorge and Warner (1980). They compare their British sample with the situation in Germany, where there is a strong correlation. The British chemical industry, especially ICI, is the most notable exception to this.

9. Neither Computergraph nor Metalco possessed anything like complete records of the qualifications of their technical staff. Those for Metalco's staff shown in Table 3.2 were pieced together from company training records and from the memories of the personnel managers. At Computergraph, where most of the engineers were trained elsewhere, no such records were available even from the personnel files.

10. A 'sandwich degree' refers to the arrangement where students alternate time spent at university with time spent at the factory. These might be alternative periods of six months at each, or arrangements where longer periods at work are 'sandwiched' with university study. Part-time study on the American pattern, where work and study are pursued simultaneously, is rare at university level in England.

11. Indeed a number of ex-technical apprentices with HNCs had chosen to work in the toolroom as craftsmen because of the pay advantages available there during the first five or ten years of work life.

12. See Chapter 5 for a more extensive discussion of engineers' orientation towards management careers.

13. The system had been introduced unilaterally by the company, although management claimed to have spent a good deal of time propagandising the new arrangement and discussing it with the staff.
14. The grade structure in R & D ran:

electronic engineer II	grade 4
electronic engineer I	grade 6
senior electronic engineer	grade 7
principal engineer	grade 9
project manager	grade 9
chief engineer	grade 11

In the drawing office the grade structure ran:

detailer	grade 4
design draughtsman	grade 5
project design draughtsman	grade 6
section manager	grade 7
design services manager	grade 10

In production engineering it ran:

production engineer II	grade 4
production engineer I	grade 5
senior production engineer	grade 6
production engineering manager	grade 7

15. Indeed the whole production department had recently been regraded to redress a perceived undergrading which had created morale problems.
16. Blackburn and Mann (1979) report that most manual workers use far more skill driving to work than they do on the job. For engineers, see Chapter 5.
17. For discussions of the relationship between industry and education in Britain see Cotgrove (1958), Hinton (1970), Musgrove (1967), Ashby (1958), and the Finniston Report (Finniston, 1980).
18. Much effort was spent by personnel staff at Computergraph trying to attract new staff to meet expansion needs; this meant expensive newspaper advertisements, and engineers being used to interview prospective candidates at work and at outside locations.
19. There have been numerous discussions as to whether or not engineers have been in short supply in Britain in the last two decades (see Wilkinson and Mace, 1973), and the argument has been made that this 'substitution of labour' via internal promotions has been a response to such shortages. The question is unresolved and is probably unresolvable as it immediately becomes tangled in a web of definitions. One thing is clear: if there has been such a shortage employers have not attempted to meet it by bidding up wages. This in itself implies that even if employers would have preferred to recruit more 'engineers', say graduates, they have none the less decided that any costs in inefficiency generated by imperfect substitutions are not worth removing by bidding up wages. Since they have not been shy to bid up the wages of other groups in short

supply – say, those of computer programmers – this would seem to indicate that employers do not find such inefficiency very burdensome.

20. The United Kingdom Association of Professional Engineers; a trade union organised to recruit only members of the professional institutions or their educational equivalents. For further discussion see Chapter 8.

21. These are similar to figures given by Gerstl and Hutton (1966) for their sample of professional mechanical engineers.

22. See also Littler's (1982) account of the resistance of British workers to various prewar attempts at scientific management which were more successful than their US counterparts.

23. Dilution is the term used to describe employers' use of non-apprenticed labour to do craft, or draughtsmen's jobs.

24. For this image of career trajectories I am indebted to conversations with Sandy Stewart and to Stewart, Prandy and Blackburn (1980).

25. This has similarities to Giddens' (1975) notion of social closure as a mediate class structuring factor, but excludes the aspect of mobility between generations.

4   THE ORGANISATION OF WORK

1. On internal contracting see: Clawson (1980), Hobsbawm (1964), Pollard (1968), Littler (1982). This craft control was not the only form of controlling labour. In many industries, food and drink for example, direct control of labour by employers or their representatives was the norm (Littler, 1982, p. 71).

2. The relentless supersession of craft control by authoritarian centralised planning, the portrayal of which Harry Braverman draws from the writings of Frederick Taylor, nowhere took place with the rapidity, inevitability, and lack of resistance he implies. Taylor's theories of scientific management are best seen as an ideological justification of engineers' position in the new order (Stark, 1980) and had comparatively little direct impact in Britain (Littler, 1982). They certainly should not be seen as the only, or even the most, typical mode of labour control under capitalism.

3. Since we are dealing with organisational work, and with organisations in which engineers are subordinate employees, the concepts of autonomy and constraint are severely restricted in meaning. They refer only to the freedom to carry out tasks, not to decide what those jobs should be or the parameters within which work should be carried out. Though there may be some input into these things ultimate decisions lie outside of the engineers' sphere of decision making. Edwards (1979) prefers to call this limited freedom 'self direction' rather than autonomy, while Friedman (1977) calls it 'responsible autonomy'. In this chapter we will simply assume these parameters. The relationship of engineers to the setting of them will be dealt with in Chapter 6.

4. Because we are measuring engineers' perception of constraint it is

possible that those with low expectations of what a job should be will experience little constraint in a job others would find constraining. Low-Beer (1978) in his study of Italian technicians argues that technicians in less involving jobs had low expectations and therefore were not dissatisfied with them. He used his own classification of the jobs to develop this finding. For this sample the engineers' characterisations of their jobs were similar to those I would have produced myself from observation, and were widely shared in the company as a whole.

5. These two dimensions were indicated by a factor analysis of all work-related variables. The two dimensions, however, could not be orthogonally derived and are correlated with each other. It was decided for conceptual clarity to use a simple additive version of the scale rather than a weighted one. See also Low-Beer (1978) for a related discussion.

6. A similar argument can be advanced against the tendency to use size as an independent variable in explaining the structure of work. Size of the immediate organisational structure is, in part, an outcome of the various calculations involved in organisational design.

7. The relationship between the two phenomena is in any case a chicken and egg question. Were the drawing offices permitted less technical freedom because they had no graduates? Or did they have no graduates because they were seen as being places where there is little autonomy? A case could be made for either position, but the answer is probably that both are true.

8. It operates, therefore, in a similar way to the education system (Sennett and Cobb, 1972).

9. Though it was initially assumed that this might be a significant problem for engineers, none of them actually found it so. In the first place, technologies continue to have applications long after they have been replaced as 'the latest thing'; electronics engineers trained in analogue systems often found themselves in demand for their special skills just because the younger engineers had all specialised in digitals, since there were special applications in which analogue technology remained superior. Secondly, the pace of development was rarely so fast that engineers could not keep up through special courses. And third, in those industries where the technology was rapidly changing so too was the demand for employment, and engineers could readily find positions, often in management, where knowledge of the latest technology was not crucial. In all, technological obsolescence did not seem the problem it has sometimes been portrayed; at least not in Metalco or Computergraph, nor in any of the other companies that I had contact with during this research.

5 EXPERTS AND MANAGERS

1. In this case, as in others, data drawn from members of the professional institutions is misleading. Most chartered engineers do have a managerial role, but this is because they are as a group both older than the general population of engineers, and self-selected. Membership in institutions seemed to increase in importance as engineers climbed the

managerial ladder. There is no doubt that the most senior engineers in all the companies I talked to – engineers whose managerial positions generally took them out of the sample population because they were too senior – were the most vociferous in their identity as 'engineers' and the most concerned with the professional institutions. This may well be a case of certification *confirming* position, rather than creating it (Stewart *et al.*, 1980). As we shall see in Chapter 7, most staff engineers regarded membership as irrelevant.

2. It is necessary to distinguish between two conceptions of 'management', conceptions which are inadequately caught by the terminology of 'line' and 'staff'. When writers who focus on problems of 'professionals' working in organisations write about 'management', they usually distinguish between 'line' adminstration and 'staff' professionals. In the latter group they include both specialists with supervisory and administrative functions – 'professionals' whom the company might well recognise as 'management' – as well as those who have neither. Though the distinction is often not clear, they are making a functional distinction not a hierarchical one. All experts are assumed to have an occupational identity which transcends hierarchical differences, uniting them against 'line' adminstrators who do not share the occupational expertise. This, however, is to ignore the central control function of management, its position in the social relations of production as well as the technical.

3. At both Pressco and Massfas, indeed in Metalco as a whole, there was an ongoing debate, often led by the few engineers who had achieved high positions, about the wisdom of such low technology, mass production strategies. Any decisions that either company made to move into a higher value-added business, which would inevitably have led to increased emphasis on product development, would have been consequential for the position of engineers in the company.

4. See Prandy (1965) for one example of a general tendency to treat scientists and engineers together as 'technologists'. The fallacy in this has been pointed out by Mike Fores of the Department of Industry (Fores, 1978) and has now become part of the official view (Finniston, 1980, p. 90; and see Glover, 1978).

5. Draughtsmen have one other career alternative, contracting; draughtsmen employed as temporary labour of the kind more familiar in secretarial work. The attractions of this kind of employment were certainly not technical involvement – though it was sometimes claimed that the variety of work made up for its lack of difficulty – but cash. The daily fees paid to the contractors were far greater than those paid to the regular salaried staff, supposedly compensated by job security and fringe benefits, including vacation pay. But above and beyond the increased income were the considerable, though legally dubious, benefits of exemption from direct taxation at source, in favour of the legendary 'fiddles' available to the self-employed. A number of draughtsmen considered contracting a practical alternative to management, at least in the short term. Tim Speirs (Computergraph, Design office):

> In 10 years' time I hope to have the mortgage paid, and to be working contract in the winter and having the summers off. Unless you're fully

absorbed in your work, then climbing ladders leads to worry and it's not that important. For someone 'on the board' the highest position is chief draughtsman and it's boring and you don't get overtime pay. I earn more than the section leader. I want to have time with my family. If you can earn enough money as a contractor to be off work for six months then you're as secure in contracting as you are in a regular job.

The existence of contracting tempted even those who were not quite so enamoured of its virtues. Alf Green (Computergraph, Design Office):

I would prefer to work on the promotion bit but I can't see it happening here. It's difficult to get into production engineering or management without experience. Finance is very important for home and family so now I'm looking for contract work. Contracting really goes against the grain though. I'd work better with responsibility, work harder and be happier but I need the money.

Contracting is still restricted largely to draughtsmen – at least in Britain – though it shows signs of increasing in computer software programming. If it continues to expand, it could transform the organisation of work for many engineers.

6. In fact one-third of Computergraph's engineers rejected the idea that managers *should* be paid more than technical staff, whereas at Metalco there was little opposition to the normal hierarchy of pay (chi.sq. sig. at .05 level).
7. Education had no impact on orientation to management, either for the overall sample, or for each company and function taken separately.
8. See Crompton (1976, 1979), Crompton and Gubbay (1978), Carchedi (1977), and the discussion of the issue in Stewart *et al.* (1980).
9. Sandy Stewart and his colleagues (1980) have argued strongly that much of the argument about the proletarianisation of clerical labour is misconceived because it fails to take the time element in careers seriously enough.
10. Twenty-seven per cent of the staff engineers at Pressco mentioned nepotism as an important source of future advancement at the company.
11. In contrast to the formal 'career' development which Sofer (1970) discusses, Metalco (and Computergraph) did not have a structured system. There was no formal internal job structure to manipulate, nor a clear sense of appropriate stages (though there had been in the past at Massfas). But neither Metalco nor Computergraph were unusual in this. A heavy investment in staff career development is restricted to a few companies in the United Kingdom, those either influenced by American practice or where there is a tradition of 'progressive' personnel management such as at ICI.
12. Education made no significant difference to perceived future equities, though graduates were more likely to mention qualifications as having helped them in the past.
13. Fifty per cent of the engineers were born locally and 70 per cent within a fifty-mile radius. Seventy-seven per cent had been locally educated and

80 per cent of the graduates had been hired through the company sponsorship scheme.

14. Twenty-six per cent of the Massfas sample thought that their company experience would be of low value outside because of lack of competing firms in the United Kingdom. Only 6 per cent of Pressco and Computergraph's engineers thought their experience at the company would be of little value.

15. Which is significantly more than the 39 per cent at Computergraph.

16. Only 18 per cent said they felt their jobs were insecure, and six out of the ten of those were in Massfas methods units which had had a history of redundancies. Only two engineers had ever experienced a lay-off.

17. All of the production managers claimed to be very or fairly ambitious compared to 53 per cent of the rest of the Metalco sample. Some of this undoubtedly had to do with age – three-quarters were between 25 and 35 and all between 25 and 45, the age of the most ambitious.

18. Sofer (1970) has pointed out that the industrial scientists he studied were more tied to their company by its product specialisation than were the much less specialised automobile engineers with fewer qualifications.

19. This does not mean that current organisational affiliations change orientations, simply that the availability of certain types of jobs in a variety of organisations permits the particular orientations to develop.

6   AUTHORITY, PROFIT AND PARTICIPATION

1. In Carchedi's terminology, the problem is to distinguish between the manager's role in the global function of capital and his functioning in the performance of collective labour (1977, pp. 43–126). The difficulties involved in making such a distinction are enormous, involving as they do the need to distinguish criteria of 'capitalist efficiency' from those of 'socialist efficiency', or of distinguishing a 'forced division of labour' from a 'normal' one (Durkheim, 1933). It also raises questions about the relation of function to structure, as in the differences between Wright's attempt to distinguish contradictory *positions* derived from the performance of two activities – accumulating capital, and labour – which are *functionally* different (Wright, 1976, 1978).

2. Only when they may be held personally responsible do they concern themselves with professional goals defined in such a way as to be potentially at odds with commercial values. Product safety had the potential of becoming one such area.

> Yes at certain times business constraints can be a problem. Design is always a compromise. Sometimes more than others. One is always cost limited. It bothers me sometimes but you have to be realistic. There might be a problem now that designers are to be held legally responsible for designs. It's not clear how far it will apply yet. It worries me that I may have compromised on something to keep costs down, and that it might fail and I'll be test case. You have to be careful of letting financial considerations rule all the time. (Alf Wood, Massfas methods engineer)

But such situations were rare for company employees.

3. I am not arguing that Metalco introduced these changes purely with their technical staff in mind. It was primarily introduced as a financial control mechanism and is directed as much at divisional managements and manual trade unions as at engineers. The company was, however, very self-conscious of the impact of such changes on the attitudes and orientations of its staff.

4. Managerial ambition was correlated with both perception that financial information was central to technical work (r = .29, sig. = .02), and the desire for more such information (r = .40, sig. = .001) for the sample of staff engineers.

5. Nearly all engineers felt they owed their company some kind of diffuse responsibility, either in moral terms (58 per cent, and particularly likely at Metalco), or more pragmatically (29 per cent, but stronger at Computer-graph). However, they saw manual workers as less company oriented than themselves. When asked if they thought all employees felt the same as they did about the company, nearly half argued that manual workers did not share their attitude.

7 COLLECTIVE ORGANISATION

1. Unfortunately the study of such factors has come to be divorced from the study of changes in class structure, and instead become the centrepiece of an opposing approach, the so-called 'industrial relations' model (Bain *et al.*, 1973; Crompton, 1976). The opposition between the two approaches is misconceived, since one cannot be understood without taking into account the other.

2. The full members of the CEI in 1977 were:
   Royal Aeronautical Society
   Institution of Chemical Engineers
   Institution of Civil Engineers
   Institution of Electrical Engineers
   Institution of Electronic and Radio Engineers
   Institute of Fuel
   Institution of Gas Engineers
   Institute of Marine Engineers
   Institution of Mechanical Engineers
   Institution of Metallurgists
   Institution of Mining Engineers
   Institution of Mining and Metallurgy
   Institution of Municipal Engineers
   Royal Institution of Naval Architects
   Institution of Production Engineers
   Institution of Structural Engineers

3. The major institutions are those institutions which are full members of the Council of Engineering Institutions. 'Minor institutions' are those

institutions which are associate members of the CEI. There are also purely managerial institutions such as the British Institute of Management.

4. TASS had approximately 183 000 white-collar members in 1977. It claims to be the fastest growing union outside the public sector, having doubled its membership in the previous decade. Of its members, 120 000 are 'technicians' (draughtsmen and similar status) and 30 000 and 'professional engineers', though these categories are products of a similar kind of arbitrary calculation to those used by the professional associations. They represent categories for collective bargaining units rather than positions in the division of labour. TASS claimed between 10 000 and 15 000 graduate or professionally qualified engineers, largely in the aerospace and electrical industry, and also claims that this is its fastest growing sector of membership.

5. UKAPE was founded in 1969 to act as a collective bargaining agent for members of the professional institutions. It was a successor to the Engineers' Guild, which had been set up as a limited liability company in 1929 to offer salary information, appointment services and other facilities for engineers, but which was legally unable to serve as a union (Prandy, 1965). The leading members of the guild set up UKAPE when they recognised that the strategy of being the British Medical Association of engineers had failed. Unlike the BMA they could not control the supply of labour, nor, like lawyers, control their own fees.

6. ASTMS had over 400 000 members at the time of the research, and claimed to have doubled its membership in the previous decade. In the engineering industry it is particularly strong among supervisory personnel.

7. Until the mid-1970s EMA had been the Electrical and Power Engineers' Association and had been restricted to the state-run electrical-generating industry. After its expansion it became involved in a series of bitter jurisdictional disputes with TASS and ASTMS. Though EMA claims to be a union for professionals (in the senior expert, rather than qualification sense), TASS claims that its profile in the power-generating industry is similar to that of TASS in the engineering industry. TASS, in particular, is opposed to any union that tries to recruit only managers, partly because they think this will ultimately encroach on their turf, but also because they think it will be attractive to other grades of career-minded staff.

8. The differences are exaggerated by the fact that Computergraph salaries were collected nine months later than Metalco's, and London wages are generally higher than those in the regions. This does not alter the general argument however.

9. They do not adequately differentiate between groups of 'technicians' who were at the beginning of careers likely to lead them to management – those with HNCs for example – and those who were likely to end their careers as technicians – those who had been promoted off the shop-floor at middle age.

10. There are two factors that we have not considered in the text but which have received mention in the discussion of white-collar unionism;

credentials and social background. It has been suggested that the decline in mobility opportunities may be restricted for certain educational categories of engineers and that these are more likely to unionise as a consequence, regardless of individuals' perceptions of their own chances. There were certainly clear differences in unionisation rates amongst the different educational groups, with those with the highest qualifications – graduates and other chartered engineers – having the lowest rates. There was, however, no difference amongst the Metalco engineers. The biggest difference was at Computergraph, where the membership is concentrated in the less formally educated drawing office and production engineering units. Only one out of nine of the union members at Computergraph was a graduate. However, once again the pattern holds only for membership, not for attitudes. Although class of origin is not normally considered part of the blocked mobility thesis – which relates to intra-generational mobility – the possible effects of it were also examined. There was no relationship between class of origin and attitudes towards unions, except for some indication that those from upper white-collar backgrounds – largely professional and managerial – had a less favourable attitude than other groups. But the effect was small. There was a stronger effect on membership patterns, with those from skilled manual backgrounds being the most likely, and those from professional and managerial groups the least likely to belong to a union. Although a formal analysis could not be completed because of small cell sizes, there was some indication that these differences were largely mediated through education and functional choices.

11. At Metalco the union did not insist on a closed shop though it could probably have done so, but there was strong pressure on new employees to become members. Engineers who had worked in the company prior to unionisation, and those with strong religious or moral objections, were given a free choice, though all were included in the bargaining unit. At Computergraph the weakness of the union meant that the question was not a practical issue.

12. The Act imposes an obligation on employers to notify employees up to ninety days in advance of any lay-offs and to consult with them: but only where members of recognised unions are concerned. If the employee is not in a union, or the organisation is not recognised as an independent union – as might be the case for some company-based staff associations – then these statutory notice-periods do not apply.

13. See also Kuhn (1971), who reports a similar phenomenon occurring with US engineers in the 1940s.

8   THE SOCIAL PRODUCTION OF TECHNICAL WORK

1. For a comparison of British engineers' salaries with those of other members of this group, which shows their relative underprivilege, see Glover (1977).

2. It is necessary to add this qualifier since there are workers such as janitors,

who have 'jobs' in Westergaard's sense, who also have discretion because they cannot easily be supervised, but who are not 'responsible' for decisions which can potentially be very costly to the employer.

3. At this level of abstraction one could say all class-divided societies, but the specific social relations in which such workers are embedded are likely to be so different in 'presently existing socialist societies', that it is preferable to limit the level of generality in the absence of further research.

4. I am greatly indebted to Stephen Crawford for sharing with me his great knowledge of the organisation of French engineering. However, I take full responsibility for the way the material is used in this book. For a fine, in-depth analysis of French engineering, see Crawford (1984).

5. I owe much of the information in this section to the work of Bob Zussman. For a study of American engineers which raises many of these issues in more depth and also examines the politics and community life of American engineers, see Zussman (1985).

Bibliography

Althauser, Robert P. and Arne L. Kalleberg (1981) 'Firms, Occupations and the Structure of Labor Markets: a conceptual analysis', pp. 119–49 in Ivar Berg (ed.), *Sociological Perspectives on Labor Markets* (New York: Academic Press).

Armytage, W. H. G. (1961) *A Social History of Engineering* (London: Faber & Faber).

Aronowitz, Stanley (1971) *False Promises* (New York: McGraw-Hill).

Ashby, Sir Eric (1958) *Technology and the Academics* (New York: St Martins Press).

Bain, George S. (1970) *The Growth of White Collar Unionism* (Oxford: Oxford University Press).

Bain, George S., D. Coates and V. Ellis (1973) *Social Stratification and Trade Unionism* (London: Heinemann Educational Books).

Bain, George S. and R. Price (1972) 'Who Is a White Collar Employee?', *British Journal of Industrial Relations* 10:325–39.

Baron, James N. and William T. Bielby (1980) 'Bringing the Firm Back in', *American Sociological Review* 45:737–65.

Becker, Gary S. (1964) *Human Capital* (New York: Columbia University Press).

Bell, Daniel (1973) *The Coming of Post-Industrial Society* (New York: Basic Books).

Bennis, Warren (1973) *Beyond Bureaucracy* (New York: McGraw-Hill).

Bensman, Joseph and Arthur Vidich (1973) *Craft and Consciousness: occupational techniques and the development of world images* (New York: Wiley Interscience).

Berg, Ivar (1970) *Education and Jobs: the great training robbery* (New York: Praeger).

Blackburn, Robert M. (1967) *Union Character and Social Class* (London: Batsford).

Blackburn, Robert M. and Michael Mann (1979) *The Working Class in the Labour Market* (London: Macmillan).

Blackburn, Robert M. and Kenneth Prandy (1965) 'White Collar Unionisation: a conceptual framework', *British Journal of Sociology* 16:111–22.

Blau, Peter, and R. Schoenherr (1971) *The Structure of Organizations* (New York: Basic Books).

Blau, Peter, Cecilia McHugh Falbe, William McKinley and Phelps K. Tracy (1976) 'Technology and Organization in Manufacturing', *Administrative Science Quarterly* 21:20–46.

Blauner, Robert (1964) *Alienation and Freedom* (Chicago: University of Chicago Press).

Blum, Albert A. (1971) *White Collar Workers* (New York: Random House).

Box, Steven and Stephen Cotgrove (1966) 'Scientific Identity, Occupational Selection and Role Strain', *British Journal of Sociology* 17:20–28.

Braverman, Harry (1974) *Labor and Monopoly Capital* (New York: Monthly Review Press).

Brody, David (1960) *Steel Workers in America: the non-union era* (Cambridge, Mass.: Harvard University Press).

Burawoy, Michael (1978) 'Towards a Marxist Theory of the Labor Process: Braverman and beyond', *Politics and Society* 8:247–312.

Burawoy, Michael (1979) *Manufacturing Consent* (Chicago: University of Chicago Press).

Burnham, J. (1941) *The Managerial Revolution* (Harmondsworth: Penguin Books).

Burns, Tom and G. M. Stalker (1961) *The Management of Innovation* (London: Tavistock).

Burris, Val (1980) 'Capital Accumulation and the Rise of the New Middle Class', *The Review of Radical Political Economics* 12:17–34.

Calhoun, Daniel H. (1960) *The American Civil Engineer* (Cambridge, Mass.: Harvard University Press).

Calvert, Monte A. (1967) *The Mechanical Engineer in America, 1830–1910* (Baltimore: Johns Hopkins Press).

Carchedi, Guglielmo (1977) *On the Economic Identification of Social Classes* (London: Routledge & Kegan Paul).

Carr-Saunders, A. M. and P. A. Wilson (1933) *The Professions* (Oxford: The Clarendon Press).

Carter, R. (1979) 'Class Militancy and Union Character: a study of the Association of Scientific, Technical and Managerial Staffs', *Sociological Review* 27:297–316.

Caves, Richard E. & Associates (1968) *Britain's Economic Prospects* (London: Allen & Unwin).

Chandler, Alfred D. J. (1962) *Strategy and Structure* (Cambridge, Mass.: MIT Press).

Child, John, Michael Fores, Ian Glover and Peter Lawrence (1983) 'A Price to Pay? Professionalism and Work Organisation in Britain and West Germany', *Sociology* 17:63–78.

Clark, D. G. (1966) *The Industrial Manager: his background and career pattern* (London: Business Publications).

Clawson, D. (1980) *Bureaucracy and the Labor Process* (New York: Monthly Review Press).

Clements, R. V. (1958) *Managers: a study of their careers in industry* (London: Allen & Unwin).

Cole, Robert E. (1979) *Work, Mobility and Participation* (Berkeley: University of California Press).

Collins, Randall (1971) 'Functional and Conflict Theories of Educational Stratification', *American Sociological Review* 36:1002–19.

Cooley, Mike (1976) 'Contradictions of Science and Technology in the Production Process', in Hilary and Steven Rose (eds) *The Political Economy of Science* (London: Macmillan).

Cooley, Mike (1980) *Architect or Bee? The Human/Technology Relationship* (Boston: South End Press).

Cotgrove, Stephen (1958) *Technical Education and Social Change* (London: Allen & Unwin).

Council of Engineering Institutions (CEI) (1975a) 'The General Requirement for the Training and Experience of Engineers for Chartered Status', *Education and Training Statement No. 11* (London: CEI).

Council of Engineering Institutions (CEI) (1975b) *Professional Engineers and Trade Unions* (London: CEI).

Council of Engineering Institutions (CEI) (1977) *Annual Report* (London: CEI).

Council of Engineering Institutions (CEI) (1978) *Submission to the Committee of Inquiry into the Engineering Profession* (London: CEI).

Crawford, Stephen (1984) 'The Work and Values of French Engineers in Traditional and Advanced Industry', unpublished PhD diss., Columbia University, New York.

Crompton, Rosemary (1976) 'Approaches to the Study of White-Collar Unionism', *Sociology* 10:407–26.

Crompton, Rosemary (1979) 'Trade Unionism and the Insurance Clerk', *Sociology* 13:403–26.

Crompton, Rosemary and John Gubbay (1978) *Economy and Class Structure* (New York: St Martins Press).

Dahrendorf, Ralph (1959) *Class and Conflict in Industrial Society* (London: Routledge & Kegan Paul).

Dickens, Linda (1972) 'UKAPE: Study of a Professional Union', *Industrial Relations Journal* 3, No.3:2–16.

Doeringer, Peter B. and Michael Piore (1971) *Internal Labor Markets and Manpower Analysis* (Lexington, Mass.: Heath).

Dore, Ronald (1973) *British Factory, Japanese Factory* (Berkeley: University of California Press).

Durkheim, Emile (1933) *The Division of Labour in Society*, trans. G. Simpson (London: Collier Macmillan).

Edwards, Richard (1979) *Contested Terrain* (New York: Basic Books).

Ehrenreich, Barbara and John Ehrenreich (1977) 'The Professional-Managerial Class', *Radical America* 11 (nos. 2–3).

Engineering Industry Training Board (EITB) (1970) 'The Technician in Engineering', *EITB Research Report* no. 1 (London: EITB).

Engineering Industry Training Board (1975) *Professional Engineers, Scientists and Technologists in the Engineering Industry* (Watford: EITB).

Engineers' Registration Board (ERB) 'General Requirements for the Training and Experience of Technician Engineers and Technicians', *ERB Statement* no. 1. (London: ERB).

Finniston, Sir Montague (1980) *Engineering Our Future*, Report of the Committee of Inquiry into the Engineering Profession (Sir Montague Finniston, Chairman) (London: HMSO).

Flanders, Allan (1964) *The Fawley Productivity Agreements* (London: Faber & Faber).

Florman, Samuel C. (1976) *The Existential Pleasures of Engineering* (New York: St Martins Press).

Fores, Michael (1978) 'Whatever Happened to Home Faber?', paper presented to the British Association Annual Meetings, Bath.

Fores, Michael (n.d.) 'On Engineers in Western Europe', unpublished paper, Department of Industry.

Fox, Alan (1974) *Beyond Contract: Work, Power and Trust Relations* (London: Faber & Faber).

Freidson, Eliot (1973) 'Professionalization and the Organization of Middle Class Labour in Postindustrial Society', in P. Halmos (ed.), *Professionalization and Social Change, Sociological Review*, monograph no. 20 (Keele, England: Keele University Press).

Friedman, Andrew (1977) *Industry and Labour* (London: Macmillan).

Galbraith, John Kenneth (1967) *The New Industrial State* (Boston: Houghton Mifflin).

Gallie, Duncan (1978) *In Search of the New Working Class* (Cambridge: Cambridge University Press).

Garnsey, Elizabeth (1978) 'Women's Work and Theories of Class Stratification', *Sociology* 12:223–43.

Gerstl, Joel and S. P. Hutton (1966) *Engineers: the anatomy of a profession.* (London: Tavistock).

Giddens, Anthony (1975) *The Class Structure of Advanced Societies* (New York: Harper & Row).

Giddens, Anthony and Gavin MacKenzie (eds) (1982) *Social Class and the Division of Labour* (Cambridge: Cambridge University Press).

Glover, Ian (1973) *The Sociological and Industrial Relations Literature on British Professional Engineers and Engineering* (London: The City University).

Glover, Ian (1977) 'The Economic Standing of the Engineering Profession', unpublished paper.

Glover, Ian (1978) 'Social Science, Engineering and Society', paper presented to the British Association meetings, Bath.

Goldner, Fred H. and R. Ritti (1967) 'Professionalization as Career Immobility', *American Journal of Sociology* 72:489–502.

Goldthorpe, John, D. Lockwood, F. Bechofer and J. Platt (1969) *The Affluent Worker in the Class Structure* (Cambridge: Cambridge University Press).

Goldthorpe, John (1982) 'On the Service Class, Its Formation and Future', in A. Giddens and G. Mackenzie (eds), *Social Class and the Division of Labour* (Cambridge: Cambridge University Press).

Gordon, David M. (ed.) (1973) *Labor Market Segmentation* (Lexington: Heath).

Gorz, André (1967) *Strategy for Labor* (Boston: Beacon Press).

Gorz, André (1972) 'Technical Intelligence and the Capitalist Division of Labor', *Telos* 12:27–41.

Gorz, André (1976a) 'Technology, Technicians and Class Struggle', pp. 158–89 in André Gorz (ed.), *The Division of Labor: The Labor Process and Class Struggle in Modern Capitalism* (Atlantic Highlands, N.J.: Humanities Press).

Gorz, André (1976b) 'On the Class Character of Science and Scientists', in Hilary and Steven Rose (eds), *The Political Economy of Science* (London: Macmillan).

Gouldner, Alvin W. (1957) 'Cosmopolitans and Locals: towards an analysis of latent social roles', *Administrative Science Quarterly* 2:281–306.

Gouldner, Alvin W. (1976) *The Dialectic of Ideology and Technology* (Boston: Seabury Press).

Gramsci, Antonio (1971) *Prison Notebooks: Selections*, Quinton Hoare and Geoffrey Nowell-Smith (trs) (New York: International Publishers).

Great Britain, Department of Trade (1977) *Report of the Committee of Inquiry on Industrial Democracy* Cmnd 6706 (Bullock Report) (London: HMSO)

Greenbaum, Joan (1979) *In the Name of Efficiency* (Philadelphia: Temple University Press).

Habermas, Jürgen (1970) 'Technology and Science as Ideology', in Jürgen Habermas, *Toward a Rational Society* (Boston: Beacon Press).

Hage, Jerald and M. Aiken (1972) 'Routine Technology, Social Structure and Organizational Goals', in Richard Hall (ed.), *The Formal Organization* (New York: Basic Books).

Hall, Richard H. (1972) *Organizations: Structure and Process* (Englewood Cliffs, N.J.: Prentice-Hall).

Hickson, David H., O. S. Pugh and Diana C. Pheysey (1969) 'Operations Technology and Organizational Structure', *Administrative Science Quarterly* 14:378–97.

Hinton, Lord (1970) *Engineers and Engineering* (New York: Oxford University Press).

Hobsbawm, Eric (1962) *The Age of Revolution: 1789–1848* (New York: World Publications).

Hobsbawm, Eric (1964) *Labouring Men* (London: Weidenfeld & Nicolson).

Hobsbawm, Eric (1969) *Industry and Empire: from 1950 to the present day* (Baltimore: Penguin Books).

Humphries, Jane (1977) 'Class Struggle and the Persistence of the Working Class Family', *Cambridge Journal of Economics* 1:241–58.

Ingham, Geoffrey K. (1970) *Size of Industrial Organisation and Worker Behaviour* (Cambridge: Cambridge University Press).

Institution of Electrical Engineers (1978) 'Submission to the Committee of Inquiry into the Engineering Profession' (London: IEE).

Jackson, John A. (ed.) (1970) *Professions and Professionalisation* (Cambridge: University Press).

Jamous, Haroun and B. Peloille (1970) 'Changes in the French University–Hospital System', in J. A. Jackson (ed.), *Professions and Professionalisation* (Cambridge: Cambridge University Press).

Jenkins, Clive and Barrie Sherman (1979) *White Collar Unionism: the Rebellious Salariat* (London: Routledge & Kegan Paul).

Johnson, Terence J. (1972) *Professions and Power* (London: Macmillan).

Johnson, Terence J. (1977) 'The Professions in the Class Structure', in Richard Scase (ed.), *Industrial Society: class cleavage and control* (London: Allen & Unwin).

Kalleberg, Arne and Aage B. Sorensen (1979) 'The Sociology of Labor Markets', *Annual Review of Sociology* 5:351–79.

Kanter, Rosabeth M. (1977) *Men and Women of the Corporation* (New York: Basic Books).

Kornhauser, William (1962) *Scientists in Industry: conflict and accommoda-*

tion (Berkeley: University of California Press).

Kraft, Philip (1977) *Programmers and Managers: the routinization of computer programmers in the U.S.* (New York: Springer Verlag).

Kuhn, James (1971) 'Engineers' Unions', in A. Blum (ed.), *White Collar Workers* (New York: Random House).

Kumar, Krishan (1978) *Prophecy and Progress: the sociology of industrial and post-industrial society* (Harmondsworth: Penguin).

Lansbury, Russell (1974) 'Careers, Work and Leisure among the New Professionals', *Sociological Review* 22: 385–400.

Larson, Magali Sarfatti (1977) *The Rise of Professionalism: a sociological analysis* (Los Angeles: University of California Press).

Lawrence, P. R. and Jay W. Lorsch (1967) *Organization and Environment: managing differentiation and integration* (Homewood, Ill.: Irwin).

Layton, Edwin T., Jr (1971) *The Revolt of the Engineers: social responsibility and the American engineering profession* (Cleveland: Case Western Reserve University Press).

Lederer, Emil (1937) 'The Problem of the Modern Salaried Employee', 1912 mimeo, trans. as part of WPA project no. 459–97–3–81 (New York: Columbia University, Department of Social Science).

Lewis, Roy and Angus Maude (1952) *Professional People* (London: Phoenix).

Littler, Craig (1982) *The Development of the Labour Process in Capitalist Societies* (London: Heinemann).

Lockwood, David (1958) *The Blackcoated Worker: a study in class consciousness* (London: Routledge & Kegan Paul).

Loveridge, Ray (1983) 'Sources of Diversity in Internal Labour Markets', *Sociology* 17:44–62.

Low-Beer, John (1978) *Protest and Participation: the new working class in Italy* (New York: Cambridge University Press).

Lumley, Roger (1973) *White Collar Unionism in Britain* (London: Methuen).

McCormick, Kevin (1977) 'The Political Context of Manpower Forecasting in Britain', *British Journal of Industrial Relations* 15:403–13.

Mace, J. D. (1979) 'Internal Labour Markets for Engineers in British Industry', *British Journal of Industrial Relations* 17:50–63.

Mace, J. D. and S. Taylor (1975) 'The Demand for Engineers in British Industry: some implications for manpower forecasting', *British Journal of Industrial Relations* 13:175–93.

Mace, J. D. and G. C. G. Wilkinson (1977) 'Are Labour Markets Competitive? A Case Study of Engineers', *British Journal of Industrial Relations* 15:1–17.

McLoughlin, Ian (1981) 'Professional Engineers and Theories of the New Middle Class'; paper presented at annual meeting of British Sociological Association, Aberystwyth.

Mallet, Serge (1975) *The New Working Class* (Nottingham: Spokesman).

Mann, Michael (1973) *Consciousness and Action among the Western Working Class* (London: Macmillan).

Marcuse, Herbert (1964) *One Dimensional Man: studies in the ideology of industrial society* (Boston: Beacon Press).

Marglin, Steve (1974) 'What Do Bosses Do?', *Review of Radical Political*

Economics 6:60–112.

Marsh, Catherine (1979) 'Problems with Surveys: method or epistemology?', *Sociology* 13:293–305.

Maurice, Marc (1977) 'Theoretical and Ideological Aspects of Universalism in the Study of Work Organizations', in *Sage Studies in International Sociology* (New York: Sage).

Miller, George A. (1967) 'Professionals in Bureaucracy: alienation among industrial scientists and engineers', *American Sociological Review* 32:755–68.

Millerson, Geoffrey (1964) *The Qualifying Associations: a study in professionalization* (London: Routledge & Kegan Paul).

Mills, Charles Wright (1956) *White Collar: the American middle classes* (New York: Oxford University Press).

Musgrove, Peter W. (1967) *Technical Change, the Labour Force and Education* (Oxford: Pergamon Press).

Nichols, Theo and Huw Beynon (1977) *Living with Capitalism* (London: Routledge & Kegan Paul).

Noble, David (1977) *America by Design: science, technology and the rise of corporate capitalism* (New York: Alfred Knopf).

Oakeshott, Michael (1962) *Rationalism in Politics* (London: Methuen).

Oppenheimer, Martin (1970) 'White Collar Revisited: the making of a new working class', *Social Policy* 1:27–32.

Oppenheimer, Martin (1973) 'The Proletarianization of the Professional', in P. Halmos (ed.) *Professionalization and Social Change*, *Sociological Review* monograph no. 20 (Keele, England: Keele University Press).

Parkin, Frank (1979) *Marxism and Class Theory: a bourgeois critique* (New York: Columbia University Press).

Perrow, Charles (1979) *Complex Organizations*, 2nd ed. (New York: Random House).

Perrucci, Robert (1973) 'Engineers: professional servants of power', in Elliot Freidson (ed.), *The Professions and their Prospects* (Beverly Hills, Calif.: Sage).

Perrucci, Robert and Joel Gerstl (1969a) *Profession without Community: engineers in American society* (New York: Random House).

Perrucci, Robert and Joel Gerstl (1969b) *The Engineers and the Social System* (New York: Wiley).

Pfeffer, Jeffrey (1979) *Organizational Design* (Arlington Heights, Ill.: AHM Press).

Pignon, Dominique and Jean Querzola (1976) 'Dictatorship and Democracy in Production', in André Gorz (ed.), *The Division of Labor* (Atlantic Highlands, N.J.: Humanities Press).

Pollard, S. (1968) *The Genesis of Modern Management* (Harmondsworth: Penguin).

Poulantzas, Nicos (1975) *Classes in Contemporary Capitalism* (London: New Left Books).

Prandy, Kenneth (1965) *Professional Employees: a study of scientists and engineers* (London: Faber & Faber).

Prandy, K., A. Stewart and R. M. Blackburn (1983) *White-Collar Unionism* (London: Macmillan).

Pugh, D. S., D. J. Hickson, C. R. Hinings and C. Turkner (1968) 'The Context of Organizational Structures' *Administrative Science Quarterly* 14:91–114.

Reader, W. J. (1966) *Professional Men: the rise of the professional classes in nineteenth century England* (London: Weidenfeld & Nicolson).

Ritti, Richard R. (1971) *The Engineer in the Industrial Corporation* (New York: Columbia University Press).

Roberts, B. C., Ray Loveridge *et al.* (1972) *Reluctant Militants: a study of industrial technicians* (London: Heinemann Educational Books).

Rosenbaum, James E. (1979) 'Organizational Career Mobility: promotion chances in a corporation during periods of growth and contraction', *American Journal of Sociology* 85:21–48.

Roslender, R. (1981) 'Misunderstanding Proletarianization: a comment on recent research', *Sociology* 15:428–30.

Routh, Guy (1980) *Occupation and Pay in Great Britain, 1906–1979* (Cambridge: Cambridge University Press).

Sabel, Charles (1982) *Work and Politics: the division of labour in industry* (Cambridge: Cambridge University Press).

Saint-Simon, Henri, Comte de (1952) *Selected Writings*, trans. F. M. H. Markham, first published 1859 (New York: Macmillan).

Sanderson, Michael (1972) *The Universities and British Industry* (London: Routledge & Kegan Paul).

Scott, W. Richard (1966) 'Professionals in Bureaucracy', pp. 265–75 in H. M. Wollmer and D. L. Mills (eds), *Professionalization* (Englewood Cliffs, N. J.: Prentice-Hall).

Scott, W. Richard (1981) *Organizationas: Rational, Natural and Open Systems* (Englewood Cliffs, N. J.: Prentice-Hall).

Sennett, Richard and Jonathan Cobb (1972) *The Hidden Injuries of Class* (New York: Alfred Knopf).

Sieber, Sam D. (1973) 'The Integration of Fieldwork and Survey Methods' *American Journal of Sociology* 78:1335–59.

Sklair, Leslie (1973) *Organised Knowledge: a sociological view of science and technology* (London: Hart-Davis, MacGibbon).

Sofer, Cyril (1970) *Men in Mid Career: a study of British managers and technical specialists* (Cambridge: Cambridge University Press).

Sorge, Arndt and Malcolm Warner (1980) 'Manpower Training, Manufacturing Organization and Workplace Relations in Great Britain and West Germany', *British Journal of Industrial Relations* 18:318–33.

Speir, Hans (1969) 'The Salaried Employee in Modern Society', in Hans Speir, *Social Order and the Risks of War* (Cambridge, Mass.: MIT Press).

Spilerman, Seymour (1977) 'Careers, Labor Market Structures and Socioeconomic Achievement', *American Journal of Sociology* 83:551–93.

Stark, David (1980) 'Class Struggle and the Transformation of the Labor Process'. *Theory and Society* 9:89–130.

Stewart, A., K. Prandy and R. M. Blackburn (1980) *Social Stratification and Occupations* (London: Macmillan).

Stinchcombe, Arthur L. (1959) 'Bureaucratic and Craft Administration of Production', *Administrative Science Quarterly* 4:168–87.

Stinchcombe, Arthur L. (1965) 'Social Structures and Organizations', in

James March (ed.), *Handbook of Organizations* (Chicago: Rand McNally).

Stone, Katherine (1974) 'The Origins of Job Structures in the Steel Industry', *Review of Radical Political Economics* 6:113–73.

Sturmthal, Adolph (1960) *White Collar Unions* (Urbana: University of Illinois Press).

Touraine, Alain (1971) *The Post-Industrial Society* (New York: Random House).

Udy, Stanley H. (1981) 'The Configuration of Occupational Structure', in Hubert Blalock, Jr (ed.), *Sociological Theory and Research* (Glencoe, Ill.: Free Press).

United Kingdom Association of Professional Engineers (UKAPE) (1978) 'Submission to the Government Committee into the Engineering Profession' (Leatherhead, Surrey: UKAPE).

Veblen, Thorstein B. (1963) *The Engineers and the Price System* (New York: B.W. Huebsch).

Walker, Pat (ed.) (1979) *Between Labor and Capital* (Boston: South End Press).

Weiss, John H. (1982) *The Making of Technological Man: the social origins of French engineering education* (Cambridge: MIT Press).

Westergaard, John (1984) 'Class of 84', *New Socialist* (Jan/Feb) no. 15:30–6.

Whyte, William H. Jr (1956) *The Organization Man* (New York: Simon & Schuster).

Wiener, Martin J. (1981) *English Culture and the Decline of the Industrial Spirit, 1850–1980* (Cambridge: Cambridge University Press).

Wilensky, Harold L. (1960) 'Work, Careers and Social Integration', *International Social Science Journal* 12:543–74.

Wilensky, Harold L. (1964) 'The Professionalization of Everyone?', *American Journal of Sociology* 70:137–58.

Wilkinson, G. C. G. and J. D. Mace (1973) 'Shortage or Surplus of Engineers: a review of recent U.K. evidence', *British Journal of Industrial Relations* 11:105–23.

Willis, Paul (1977) *Learning to Labour* (Westmead: Saxon House).

Wood, Adrian (1978) *A Theory of Pay* (Cambridge: Cambridge University Press).

Wood, Stephen (1982) *The Degradation of Work? Skill, Deskilling and the Labour Process* (London: Hutchinson).

Woodward, Joan (1958) *Management and Technology* (London: HMSO).

Woodward, Joan (1965) *Industrial Organisation: theory and practice* (Oxford: Oxford University Press).

Woodward, Joan (1970) *Industrial Organisation: Behaviour and Control* (Oxford: Oxford University Press).

Wright, Erik Olin (1976) 'Class Boundaries in Advanced Capitalist Societies', *New Left Review*, July: 3–41.

Wright, Erik Olin (1978) *Class Crisis and the State* (London: New Left Books).

Wright, Erik Olin (1980) 'Varieties of Marxist Conceptions of Class Structure', *Politics and Society* 9:299–322.

Zeitlin, M. (1974) 'Corporate Ownership and Control: the large corporation and the capitalist class', *American Journal of Sociology* 79:5.

Zussman, Robert (1985) *Mechanics of the Middle Class: work and politics among American engineers* (Berkeley: University of California Press).

Index

accountants, 92, 156, 187 207n3
AESD, 89, 159–60, 167
American engineers, *see* United
    States
apprenticeships, 40, 42, 47–8, 63,
    192
    see also education
Armytage, W. H. G., 66
Aronowitz, Stanley, 11
Ashby, Sir Eric, 210n17
ASTMS, 24, 64, 89, 160–1, 167,
    181–2, 217n6, 217n7
AUEW, 26, 173, 177
authority, 3, 7, 124–31 *passim*, 142,
    148–50, 185–6
autonomy, 4, 6, 8, 10, 38, 59–60,
    70–83 *passim*, 125–39, 185, 187,
    190, 193, 211n3, 211n4
    loss of, and unionism, 170–1
    see also division of labour,
        deskilling

Bain, George, S. 94, 216n1
Baron, James N., 206n2
Becker, Gary S., 95
Bell, Daniel, 2, 3, 5, 17, 39
Bennis, Warren, 6
Berg, Ivar, 61, 190
Beynon, Huw, 206n1
Bielby, William T., 206n2
Blackburn, Robert M., 94, 151,
    158, 159, 168, 210n16,
    211n24, 213n1, 214n8, 214n9
Blau, Peter, 60
Blauner, Robert, 16
Braverman, Harry, 9, 11, 60, 66,
    71, 211n2
Brody, David, 66, 206n5
Bullock Commission, 143
Burawoy, Michael, 8, 196

Burnham, J., 5
Burns, Tom, 6, 70
Burris, Val, 8
business values, conflict between
    technical rationality and, 3,
    4, 7, 13, 124, 131–43 *passim*,
    148–59, 195–6

Calvert, Monte A., 193
Carchedi, Gugielmo, 10–11,
    92–4, 109, 125, 214n8, 215n1
careers, 13, 33, 38, 44, 47–9,
    51–3, 59, 64–5, 92–123
    passim, 185–9
    and deskilling, 85–8, 90–1
    and engineers' equities, 95–6,
        113–16
    and external labour markets,
        87, 117–23
    and qualifications, 53, 63, 89,
        109–16
    and trusted workers, 59, 61–4
    and unionism, 169–71
Carter, R., 151, 158–9
chartered engineers, 41–2
Child, John, 7
class consciousness, 3, 7, 9–10,
    13, 38, 151, 158, 172, 180–3,
    198
class structure
    engineers' position in, 3, 6–11,
        93–6, 123, 184–6, 194–7
    see also proletarianisation
Clawson, D., 211n1
closed shop, 175, 218n11
Cobb, Jonathon, 212n8
Cole, Robert E., 84
Collins, Randall, 61, 190
computer-aided design (CAD),
    83

Computergraph, 1, 18–21, 24–6,
    29–34, 36–7, 42–5, 49–59, 63,
    67–9, 71–83, 90–2, 96–7,
    103–8, 110–12, 115–16, 121–2,
    126, 128–9, 131–4, 138–9, 140,
    145, 152, 154, 161, 165–7, 171–2,
    177–8, 188, 209n9, 214n11,
    218n10, 218n11
contracting, as a career
    alternative, 213n5
control
  by market, 133–43, 146–50,
    195–6
  over the labour process, 4, 6,
    9–11, 60, 66, 70, 87, 90,
    211n1, 211n2
  see also trusted workers
Cooley, Mike, 11, 88
Cotgrove, Stephen, 210n17
Council of Engineering
    Institutions (CEI), 41, 156,
    182, 208n1, 208n5, 216n2,
    216n3
Crawford, Stephen, 61, 68, 189,
    219n4
credentials, *see* educational
    qualifications
crisis of legitimacy, 3–8, 142, 150,
    184
Crompton, Rosemary, 3, 11, 71,
    88, 94, 109, 159, 169, 214n8,
    216n1

Dahrendorf, Ralph, 5
design engineers, 21, 23, 25,
    36–7, 50–2, 54, 69, 82–3,
    88–9, 105–6, 115–16, 121,
    127, 138–9, 161
  see also draughtsmen
deskilling, 11, 13, 70–91 *passim*,
    195, 211n2
  see also proletarianisation
dequalification of labour, 109
Dickens, Linda, 160
division of labour, 12–13, 20, 45,
    66–91 *passim*, 187–88
  and careers, 85–8
  and hierarchy, 31, 64, 59–60,
    81–2

and unionism, 13, 88–9, 171–2
  effect of labour supply on,
    84–5, 191–4
  effect of product cycle on, 31,
    74
  effect of socio-technical
    environment on, 81–3
  impact of qualifications on,
    42–3, 57, 64, 82, 89–90,
    209n8
  occupational, 41–2, 50, 70, 90
  separation of conception from
    execution, 28, 33, 66–8,
    206n6
  see also grade structure,
    manual/non-manual
    boundary, design
    engineers, planning
    engineers, production
    managers, methods
    engineers, research and
    development engineers,
    service engineers, test
    engineers
Doeringer, Peter B., 62
draughtsmen, 36, 88–9, 159–60,
    210n4, 211n23, 213n5
  see also design engineers
Durkheim, Emile, 215n1

education
  and careers, 109–16, 121–2
  and class background, 63, 198
  and professionalism, 152–8
  and science, 2, 6, 39
  and the division of labour, 84,
    89–90, 209n8
  and unionism, 118, 174
  of engineers in Britain, 19, 40,
    44, 47–8, 52, 57–8, 60–3,
    66, 110, 122, 187, 192, 197,
    206n2, 209n7
  of engineers in the United
    States, 109–4
  of engineers in France, 188–9,
    192
  see also educational
    qualificatons

educational qualifications
and professional institutions,
40–1, 152
and position in the division of
labour, 42–53 *passim*, 84,
89–90
effect on career success, 109–12
passim
effect on unionism, 218n10
see also Higher National
Certificate, graduate
engineers
Edwards, Richard, 60, 84, 142,
211n3
electronics industry, 1, 17–18
see also Computergraph
EMA, 160, 173, 217n7
employment conditions, 35, 45–6,
49, 185–6, 189
distinctions between those of
engineers and
management,
28, 35, 47, 97–8
distinctions between those of
engineers and manual
workers, 28, 45, 49
flexitime, 30, 33
see also environment, salaries
Employment Protection Act, 84,
182, 218n12
Engineering Industry Training
Board, 208n3
Engineering Registration Board,
41
engineers
as corporate staff, 3, 8–10
as 'experts', 3–8, 10, 92, 94–6,
103–9
defining, 19–20, 53, 187
growth in number of, 2, 206n2,
208n2
reasons for becoming, 99,
108–9
supply of, 210n9
see also class structure,
education, management,
manual/non-manual
boundary,
professionalism, trusted

workers, unionism,
France, United States,
design engineers, planning
engineers, production
managers, methods
engineers, research and
development engineers,
service engineers, test
engineers
environment, work, 22–5, 27–9,
30, 32, 34, 36
equities, engineers' investment
in, 95–6, 112–16
estimating engineers, *see*
planning engineers

field work, 18–19
Finniston Committee, 15, 40, 54,
62, 206n2, 208n2, 210n17,
213n4
Florman, Samuel C., 68
Fores, Michael, 57, 213n4
Fox, Alan, 59
France, engineers in, 13, 45, 61,
68, 93–4, 150, 185–90, 195,
197–8
fragmentation of job, *see*
deskilling
Freidson, Eliot, 3, 5, 6, 39, 95, 96
French engineers, *see* France,
engineers in
Friedman, Andrew, 211n3

Galbraith, John Kenneth, 3, 4,
96, 124, 132
Gallie, Duncan, 16
General Motors Institute, 194
Gerstl, Joel, 15, 95, 108, 207n7,
211n21
Giddens, Anthony, 64, 211n25
Glover, Ian, 213n4, 218n1
Goldner, Fred H., 95
Goldthorpe, John, 16, 186
Gorz, André, 3, 7, 9, 93–4, 124,
135, 188
Gouldner, Alvin W., 8, 95, 124,
196
grade structure, 44–53 *passim*,
61–4, 210n13–16

see also careers
graduate engineers, 34, 47–8, 53,
    55–61, 63, 84, 89–90, 94–5,
    109–12, 115, 120–1, 128, 154,
    187–8, 190–4, 198
Gramsci, Antonio, 8
Greenbaum, Joan, 82
Gubbay, J., 11, 71, 109, 214n8

Habermas, Jürgen, 196
hegemony, 8–10
high-tech industry, 1, 2, 4–5, 7,
    10, 15–17, 24, 39–40, 70, 82,
    197
    see also Computergraph,
        post-industrial society
Higher National Certificate
    (HNC), 19, 40, 42–4, 47–9,
    52, 57–8, 63, 84–5, 109–12,
    128, 152, 206n2, 208n2,
    209n7, 209n11
Hinton, Lord, 210n17
Hobsbawm, Eric, 211n1
Hutton, S., 15, 108, 207n7,
    211n21

incomes policy, 45, 167
    and union growth, 181
Institution of Electrical
    Engineers, 152, 216n2
    see also professional
        institutions
Institution of Mechanical
    Engineers, 108, 152, 216n2
    see also professional
        institutions
Institution of Production
    Engineers, 152, 216n2
    see also professional
        institutions
internal labour market, *see* labour
    markets
internalising the market, *see*
    markets
interviews
    defining population and
        sample, 19–21, 207n4
    schedule, 21, 200–5
    involvement in technical work,

71–91

Jamous, Haroun, 40
job evaluation, 46, 50, 63,
    210n13, 210n15
Johnson, Terence J., 95, 151

Kanter, Rosabeth M., 59–60, 96,
    112, 185
knowledge
    and hierarchy, 76, 81
    and labour market position, 53,
        65, 115–16
    and legitimation of position,
        12, 54–8, 61, 188–92
    and trusted workers, 58–65
    application to production, 1, 2,
        17, 39
    experientially-based, 53–8,
        187, 192–3
    ideological nature of, 8–9,
        195–6
    obsolescence of, 87, 212n9
    see also education, science
knowledge technology, 17–18, 32,
    70
knowledge workers, 2, 184
Kornhauser, William, 95
Kuhn, James, 218n13

labour markets, 43–4, 49
    and deskilling, 84–8, 90–1, 123,
        195
    and knowledge, 12, 53, 59, 61,
        63
    internal, 47–53, 61–2, 84–5,
        95–6, 116–22
    external, 51, 87, 95–6, 116–122,
        184
    and unionisation, 167–8
    occupationally controlled, 5–6,
        39–40, 53–4, 64–5
    segmentation of, 59–60, 63–5,
        88, 187–8, 190–1
    see also careers, equities
labour supply
    effect of on division of labour,
        191–4
    nature of supply of engineers,

210n19
see also labour markets,
   deskilling
Larson, Magali Sarfatti, 5–6, 40,
   95, 191
Lawrence, P. R., 6
legitimation
   of capitalist firm, 3–9, 131–43
      passim, 148–50
   of engineers' position, 12,
      54–6, 58, 61, 65, 157,
      187–8, 193
   of managerial authority, 13,
      130–1, 148–50
line superintendents, *see*
   production managers
Littler, Craig, 66, 191, 211n22,
   211n1–2
Lockwood, David, 3
logic
   of capitalist accumulation, 12,
      186
   of industrialism 12, 186
Lorsch, Jay, 6
Loveridge, Ray, 7, 61
Low-Beer, John, 16, 212n4,
   212n5

Mace, J. D., 53, 56, 62, 209n8
McCormick, Kevin, 208n4
McLoughlin, Ian, 15, 151
Mallet, Serge, 3, 7–9, 16, 94, 96,
   124, 132, 184, 189, 207n2
management
   as a career option for
      engineers, 13, 48, 50–2,
      60, 84–7, 90, 92–112
      passim, 122–3, 187–8, 196
   as an occupation, 60, 99, 107–8
   as different from technical
      experts, 5–6, 13, 94
   boundary with staff engineers,
      47, 168–9
   employment privileges of, 28,
      35, 47
   legitimation of, 13, 130–1,
      148–50
   relationship with engineers, 47,
      75–7, 81, 83, 93, 142

managers
   and importance of financial
      information, 138–9, 150
   and participation, 140, 143, 150
   and professionalism, 152, 154,
      156
   and unionism, 24, 161–3,
      168–70, 173–7, 183
   attitudes towards strikes, 175,
      177
   perceived functions of by
      engineers, 125–31
manpower planning, 40, 208n4
Mann, Michael, 210n16
manual workers
   employment conditions, 45, 49
   relations with engineers, 27–8,
      34–5, 62–3, 143–8, 177–9,
      216n5
manual/non-manual boundary, 7,
   8, 28, 33, 35–6, 45, 49, 62–3,
   66–8, 206n6
   see also division of labour,
      trusted workers
Marglin, Steve, 125
markets
   internalising, 135–39, 148–50,
      195–6
   as a control mechanism,
      133–43, 146, 150, 196
   see also labour markets
Massfas, *see* Metalco
metal-working industry, 18
   see also Metalco
Metalco, 1, 18, 22–4, 26–9,'31–2,
   34, 42, 45–9, 53–8, 62–4, 71–2,
   75–90, 97–103, 108, 110,
   112–15, 116–20, 122–3, 127–41,
   143–50, 152–7, 161–78, 188,
   196, 207n4, 209n9, 213n3,
   214n11, 215n17, 216n3, 218n11
   Pressco division, 22–3, 26–9,
      45, 76, 118, 135, 207n4
   Massfas division, 22–3, 34–6,
      69, 76, 118, 135–7, 215n14
methods engineers, 21, 23, 31–2,
   80–1, 100–1, 135–8
Miller, George A., 95
Millerson, Geoffrey, 151–2

Mills, C. Wright, 3
Musgrave, Peter W., 210n17

nationalised industry, engineers'
  attitudes towards, 149
National Economic Development
  Council, 182
new working class, 7, 9, 12, 184
Nichols, Theo, 206n1
Noble, Daivd, 8–9, 60–2, 125,
  191, 193
Oakeshott, Michael, 58
Oppenheimer, Martin, 11, 71
Ordinary National Certificate, 47,
  52
Ordinary National Diploma, 47,
  52
organisational constraint, 71–83,
  127
  see also division of labour.
organisational structure, 37,
  68–91, 128, 135–39, 207n6
  at Computergraph, 26
  at Metalco, 22–3
  effect of age of industry on, 17,
    18, 32
  effect of knowledge technology
    on, 17, 32, 70
  effect of product market on,
    17, 32, 207n2
  effect of production technology
    on, 2, 16–17, 80–3, 207n1
  impact on orientations, 93–123
  see also division of labour
orientations
  effect of organisational
    structure on, 193–23
  to labour market, 116–22
  to managerial careers, 50–1,
    92–4, 97–103, 105–8,
    122–3, 188–91, 196
  to technical expertise, 6–8, 10,
    92–94, 97, 100–1, 103–9,
    122–3

Parkin, Frank, 159
participation, 9, 13, 130–50

passim, 196
  of manual workers, 143–5, 196
  and unionism, 182
pay policy, *see* incomes policy
Peloille, B., 40
Perrow, Charles, 127, 142
Perrucci, Robert, 95, 207n7
petty bourgeoisie, engineers as,
  10, 11
  see also class structure
Pfeffer, Jeffrey, 60, 82, 208n6
Pignon, Dominique, 142
Piore, M., 62
planning engineers, 21, 23, 26–9,
  69, 75–6, 81, 86, 127
Pollard, S., 211n1
post-industrial society, 1, 2, 6, 11,
  12, 17, 39, 70
Poulantzas, Nicos, 8–9, 93–4,
  188, 206n6
Prandy, Kenneth, 1, 94, 151, 156,
  158, 159, 168, 211n24, 213n1,
  213n4, 214n8, 214n9, 217n5
Pressco, *see* Metalco
Price, R., 94
production engineers, 21, 23,
  35–6, 51, 54, 69, 80, 106
production managers, 21, 23,
  34–5, 51, 55, 58, 80, 86, 98,
  112, 120, 129, 215n17
production technology, 16–17,
  80–3, 207n1
professionalism
  and class consciousness, 151–8,
    180–3
  and engineers, 5, 13, 50, 94–5,
    152–8, 184
  and post-industrial society, 5,
    13, 39, 70, 80–1, 83, 95
  ideology of, 6, 157–8
  weakness of for British
    engineers, 5, 39–65
    passim, 152
professional institutions
  and collective bargaining,
    156–7
  and the status of engineers,
    152, 154–8
  and technician engineers, 152

engineers' attitudes towards,
152–8, 180–3
engineers' membership in, 13,
40, 152–7
certification role of, 152
see also Council of Engineering
Institutions
profit centres, 22, 135, 196
proletarianisation
and unionism, 168–71
of engineers, 3, 11–12, 93–4,
109
of technicians, 197
see also deskilling

qualifications, *see* educational
qualifications, HNC, graduate
engineers
Querzola, Jean, 142

Ritti, Richard, R., 95
Roberts, B. C. *et al.*, 94, 109, 151,
169, 209n6
Rosenbaum, James E., 112
Roslender R., 15
research and development, 17,
22, 24–5, 29–32, 39, 57, 67,
132, 208n6
research and development
engineers, 21, 26, 29–33,
37–8, 50–4, 56–9, 63, 67–8,
73–5, 103–7, 112, 115, 121,
126–9, 138–9, 154, 161, 166,
187, 189, 210n14
routinisation of work, *see*
deskilling
Routh, Guy, 2

Sabel, Charles, 66, 207n1
Saint-Simon, Henri, Comte de, 4
salaries, 27–8, 38, 45, 84, 101,
167, 213n5, 214n6
sandwich degrees, 47, 209n10
science
application to production, 1–3,
17, 39, 92
basis of engineers' knowledge,
5–7, 12, 39–41, 53, 57–8,
61, 70, 92, 95, 125, 184,

188, 191, 194–4
subservience to capital, 9,
195–6
see also knowledge
Scott, W. Richard, 6, 70, 130
Schoenherr, R., 60
self-management, *see*
participation
Sennett, Richard, 212n.8
service class, 186, 194–5, 199
service engineers, 21, 25, 33,
50–1, 73–5, 86, 103, 126
skill, 12, 33; 57–9, 87, 115–16, 157
see also knowledge, deskilling
Sofer, Cyril, 214n11, 215n18
Sorge, Arndt, 68, 209n8
specialisation, 68–70
see also deskilling, division of
labour
Spilerman, Seymour, 94
Stalker G. M., 6, 70
Stark, David, 71, 211n2
status consciousness, 5, 151–2,
154–8
Stewart, A., 94,168, 211n24,
213n1, 214n8, 214n9
Stinchcombe, Arthur L., 17
strikes, engineers' attitudes
towards, 175–7

task structure, *see* division of
labour
TASS, 24, 26, 45, 63–5, 89–90,
159–61, 165, 167, 173–5,
177–83, 197–8, 217n4, 217n7
Taylor S., 53, 56, 209n8
technical involvement, 71–91
see also division of labour
technical rationality, conflict with
profit motive, 3, 7–8, 124,
132–9, 148–50, 195–6
technician engineers, 20, 41, 64,
152, 208n5
technicians, 11, 20, 30, 41–3, 50,
53, 59, 64, 67–8, 71, 84–5, 89,
94, 187, 197, 209n6
in France, 189–90
in the United States, 190–1
technocrats, 4
technological determinism, 8

technology, *see* high-tech industry, knowledge, knowledge technology, production technology,
technostructure, 4
test engineers, 21, 25, 32–3, 38, 49–51, 67, 69, 73–5, 86
Touraine, Alain, 3
trade unions, *see* unions
Trades Union Congress (TUC), 160
training boards, 40, 208n3
trusted workers, 13, 58–65, 70, 186, 192, 194–7
 and career hierarchies, 59, 61–4
 and deskilling, 60, 87, 90
 and education, 60–62
 and skill, 65
 and unionism, 171–2, 178–9
 in France, 188–90
 in the United States, 190–1

Udy, Stanley H., 206n2
union leadership, engineers' attitudes towards, 179–181
unioniateness, 158–9
unionism, 88–9, 151, 158–83 *passim*, 197–8
 and attitudes to strikes, 175–7
 and career mobility, 169–71
 and class consciousness, 13, 151, 158, 180–3
 and credentials, 181
 and education, 174, 218n10
 and incomes policy, 181
 and loss of job autonomy, 170–2
 and participation, 182
 and political involvement, 173–4
 and proletarianisation, 158, 168–172
 and relations with manual workers, 177–9
 and social background, 218 n10
 and the closed shop, 175, 218n11
 and the division of labour, 13, 88, 168–72

 and the labour market, 167
 and trusted workers, 171–2, 178–9, 197
unions
 and the Employment Protection Act, 182
 attitudes towards, 161, 163–5, 179–81
 membership in, 13, 24, 26, 88–9, 160–2, 164, 198
 strategies of, 159–60, 172, 181
 typology of, 159–60
 see also ASTMS, AESD, AUEW, EMA, TASS, TUC, UKAPE
United Kingdom Association of Professional Engineers (UKAPE), 41, 62–3, 159–61, 166, 173–4, 181–2, 197, 211n20, 217n5
United States, engineers in, 60–2, 68, 94–5, 157, 185, 190–4,198
universities, relationship with industry, 61, 193, 198, 210n17
 see also education, graduate engineers, sandwich degrees

Veblen, Thorstein B., 4, 124, 132

Warner, Malcolm, 68, 209n8
Weiss, John H., 192
Westergaard, John, 185–6
Whyte, William, H. Jr, 96
Wiener, Martin J., 61
Wilkinson, G. C. G., 53, 62, 209n8, 210n19
Willis, Paul, 58
Woodward, Joan, 16
work, structure of, *see* division of labour
worker directors, 143–8
Wright, Erik Olin, 10–11, 94, 215n1

Zeitlin, M., 5
Zussman, Robert, 190, 219n5